THE ITALIAN PSYCHOANALYTIC ANNUAL

2008

SELECTED TEXTS FROM THE LAST VOLUME OF

RIVISTA DI PSICOANALISI

JOURNAL OF THE ITALIAN PSYCHOANALYTIC SOCIETY

Theory and observation: redefining the field

BORLA

RIVISTA DI PSICOANALISI
JOURNAL OF THE ITALIAN PSYCHOANALYTIC SOCIETY

EDITOR
Patrizio Campanile

EDITOR IN CHIEF
Alberto Luchetti

ANNUAL PUBLISHING SUPERVISOR
Anna Meregnani

EDITORIAL BOARD
Andrea Braun, Paola Camassa, Alessandra De Marchi, Ronny Jaffè,
Enrico Mangini, Anna Meregnani, Marina Parisi, Diomira Petrelli

ENGLISH TRANSLATIONS BY
Carol Carmody, Tina Cawthra, Romano C. Cerrone
Isabella Negri, Janice Parker, Jeremy Scott, Philip Slotkin

ENGLISH TRANSLATIONS REVISED BY
Giuseppina Antinucci, Anna Meregnani, Leonardo Resele

EDITORIAL ASSISTANT
Giulia Vicentini
tel./fax +39055290377

EDITORIAL OFFICE
Via Panama, 48 – 00198 Roma – Italy
tel. +39068546716 – fax +390685865336 – e-mail: riv.psa@mclink.it
www.rivistapsicoanalisi.it

Marketing and distribution:

In Italy - Borla Edizioni s.r.l.
00165 Roma (Italy) - Via delle Fornaci, 50
Tel.+390639376728
Fax +390639376620
www. edizioni-borla.it
borla@edizioni-borla.it

Outside Italy - Karnac Books
118 Finchley Road., London NW3 5HT
(United Kingdom)
Tel: +44(0)20 7431 1075
Fax: +44(0)20 435 9076
www.karnacbooks.com
shop@karnacbooks.com
Payment methods: Visa/Mastercard/Switch

2007 © **THE ITALIAN PSYCHOANALYTIC ANNUAL**
ISBN   978-88-263-1704-5
Borla Edizioni s.r.l.
00165 Roma (Italy) - Via delle Fornaci, 50

TABLE OF CONTENTS

As illustrated by the 2007 volume, the first in the series, The Italian Psychoanalytic Annual *presents a selection in English of the papers published during the previous year in the* Rivista di Psicoanalisi, *the journal of the Italian Psychoanalytic Society.*

Theory and observation: redefining the field. *That is standard procedure in science, and the contributions in this volume of the* Annual *likewise identify some of the cornerstones of psychoanalysis that must be present if it is to thrive in the contemporary situation.*

In a journal such as ours that does not have issues devoted to specific subjects but accepts contributions spontaneously submitted by authors, a title is used for indicative purposes only, and it is in this spirit that we present the papers featuring in the 2008 Annual, *many of which are devoted to the institution of psychoanalysis, training processes and the ethics of psychoanalysis. The same approach can be applied when reading the other contributions, which examine specific examples of clinical experience as a basis for the possible redefinition of our theoretical and observational field.*

Hence this volume can be seen at one and the same time as continuous and discontinuous with its predecessor, Freud after all.

Theory and observation: redefining the field. That is Freud's legacy, or indeed his challenge, to future generations, as stated at the end of the article which opens this volume, and which therefore connects it with last year's Annual – *namely, discovering how to «re-specify our theoretical and observational field so as to extend it to non-symbolic processes and the laws governing their transformation into symbolic processes». This approach should in our view be applied across the board, and the matters to be observed and reflected upon should include the discipline of psychoanalysis itself and its institutions – the processes of transformation necessary for our «science», those that seem feasible and the resistances to putting them into practice.*

These resistances are admittedly defensive manifestations, but they also represent forms of protection that are to some extent beneficial, as defences sometimes are. After all, continuity and discontinuity characterize the horizon of symbolization.

Perspicuous examples *drawn from clinical practice is a section of the* Rivista di Psicoanalisi *of which this volume presents two examples, preceded by the original introductory note. The section not only offers a space for discussion of clinical matters but also helps to stimulate reflection on the large number of possible approaches to clinical work and on how clinical work can become an object of study in its own right.*

«*The cases of illness which come under a psycho-analyst's observation are of course of unequal value in adding to his knowledge. There are some on which he has to bring to bear all that he knows and from which he learns nothing; and there are others which show him what he already knows in a particularly clearly marked manner and in exceptionally revealing isolation, so that he is indebted to them not only for a confirmation but for an extension of his knowledge*» *(Freud, 1913, 193). With these words Freud introduced a new section of the* Internationale Zeitschrift für Psychoanalyse, *and the editors of the relevant section of the* Annual *have based their own introduction on the same conception.*

The need to give more space to clinical aspects in the psychoanalytic literature has been voiced in various quarters; some, indeed, place their trust in the comparison and extended presentation of examples of clinical experience for the purpose of developing new perspectives on both the clinical and theoretical levels and of helping to consolidate an area of common ground whose absence has long been regretted. Perspicuous examples *is an approach specifically intended as a way of encouraging the close interweaving of clinical practice and theory – and we are thoroughly convinced that this interweaving is not only desirable but also absolutely essential.*

(p.c.)

(Translated by Philip Slotkin MA Cantab. MITI)

Remembering, repeating and working-through: Freud's legacy to the psychoanalysis of the future

FERNANDO RIOLO

> [Memory] usually chronicles the things that
> have never happened, and couldn't possibly have
> happened.
> OSCAR WILDE, *The Importance of Being Earnest*

O f the three terms considered by Freud in his well-known paper, it is the first that seemingly possesses the most clearly defined conceptual status: the classical theory of memory, repression, remembering and working through. As we know, this is not actually so, since the theory in each case has – even in the thought of Freud himself – undergone significant and sometimes radical revision. Furthermore, the investigation of mnemic processes has been substantially enriched by the recent contributions of the neurosciences, whose research remains an ongoing source of important confirmation, as well as offering new stimuli and posing new questions.

I should like to emphasize that many of the present-day findings of the neurosciences, based on empirical evidence, coincide with what we ourselves have long known – namely, that the processes of reception, selection and storage of stimuli from the external and internal worlds are largely dynamic and unconscious, as are also the processes whereby memories are recalled. Memory is not an archive of immutable data that can be faithfully recovered in consciousness, but a «system of transformation». Both the encoding (the consolidation of traces) and the retrieval of memories are the outcome of a complex process of selection and mixing of elementary fragments that is subject to constant restructuring. In other words, memories are always *a posteriori* (*nachträglich*) «constructions» – revisions, distortions and sometimes even actual «falsifications». For this reason, Freud himself concluded

Introduction to the Fifth Meeting of the Italian Psychoanalytic Society (SPI) and the Argentine Psychoanalytic Association (APA) held in Bologna on 4-5 February 2006 that analysis did not by any means consist in the tracing of historical truths or in a simple operation of remembering.[1]

Already in the *Studies on Hysteria* Freud writes that cases in which pathogenic memories are recoverable are not only extremely rare but, in the case of one kind of representations that «are unconscious, not because of their relatively small degree of liveliness, but in spite of their great intensity», are actually impossible to recall. These representations are *bewusstseinsunfähig* – «incapable of consciousness» – «thoughts which never came about, which merely had a possibility of existing, so that the treatment would lie in the accomplishment of a psychical act which did not take place at the time [...] something that is absolutely not recognized as a memory» (Freud, 1895, 300).

When Freud returned to this concept in 1914, he made the important distinction that there are some processes that are unconscious because they are repressed and others that are unconscious for other reasons: «phantasies, processes of reference, emotional impulses, thought-connections, which, as purely internal acts [...] could never have been "forgotten" because [they were] never at any time noticed – [were] never conscious» (Freud, 1914, 148f.). These are purely internal experiences, which have never been «thought» and which sometimes become representable in dreams – but which, Freud adds, are repeated in the form of action during the course of the treatment.

We today are in a better position to appreciate the vast implications of this idea. They include the widening of the field of analysis from investigation of the contents of thought to that of its formation, and from the work of deciphering symbols or the unveiling of already existing unconscious meanings to the work of symbol production – that is, the psychic work needed to transform into thought the level of experience that is not yet, or is no longer, thought. The analytic method, too, in its specific operational sense, now takes on the function of a system of transformation, whereby unconscious somato-psychic processes (whether repressed or non-repressed) become representable. What was initially a drive-related or affective quantity – a sensation, emotion or action subject to the circuit of repetition – can be converted into a dream-like image, the representation of a wish or of anxiety, a word, a memo-

---

[1] For this reason it is hard to understand how some can instead portray these confirmations as invalidating Freud's hypotheses. Peter Fonagy (1999), for instance, states that Freud's model of the elimination of repression and the recovery of infantile memories coincides with only a part of the treatment and cannot by itself explain the therapeutic action of psychoanalysis. We should all agree with him if it were not for the fact that this is precisely what Freud himself thought, for he used almost the same words to express the same concept – that remembering constitutes *Vorarbeit* (preliminary work), which is not always possible and in any case does not suffice to bring about therapeutic change. To maintain that Freud conceived the analytic process in terms of the mere recovery of memories is tantamount to ignoring the entire conception of memory and of the treatment as it unfolds throughout his oeuvre, from the *Studies on Hysteria*, via *Screen memories*, to *Remembering, repeating and working-through* (*Durcharbeitung*) and the major revisions of *Analysis terminable and interminable* and *Constructions in analysis*.

ry, an association and ultimately a meaning, and can thereby be released from its fate of repetition.

The distinction between symbolic unconscious processes connected with semantic contents or word presentations, on the one hand, and non-symbolic processes that conform to the need for repetition and are expressed in action, on the other, brings us to the second of the three terms with which we are here concerned – namely, repetition (*Wiederholung*). This is a concept of paramount importance for understanding the psychopathologies that confront us today. Its status, however, is uncertain, ranging between an excessively narrow sense in which it coincides with acting out and an excessively broad sense whereby it is even seen as a manifestation of the death instinct.

I therefore agree that the various forms of repetition must be differentiated from each other. We should distinguish between repetitions that are transference replications in the present of repressed conflictual nuclei; repetitions that are expressions of narcissistic nuclei antagonistic to the transference relationship; and repetitions as manifestations of defensive nuclei and mechanisms which are antagonistic not only to the transference but also to the processes of symbolization. This is not just a theoretical requirement, but is also dictated by clinical considerations.

Let me begin by distinguishing between «repetition» and the «compulsion to repeat». The two terms are generally treated as synonymous, and that is how Freud uses them in 1914, but they form the background to an extremely diverse range of theories and phenomena. As we know, Freud originally assigned the function of repetition to dreams and connected it with repression: what was represented in dreams were «presentations» (*Vorstellungen*) through which contents excluded from consciousness exerted pressure on the psychical apparatus and obtained access to it in distorted form (*Entstellungen*).

However, already in the case of Little Hans the concept was extended to forms of expression other than representation. The repressed attempts to return in the present in the form of fantasies, symptoms and enactments: «a thing which has not been understood inevitably reappears; like an unlaid ghost, it cannot rest until the mystery has been solved and the spell broken» (Freud, 1909, 122). Repetitions – images, symptoms or actions – are here still seen as instances of the return of the repressed; they are *phantasmata* or *fueros*.

The conceptual framework that gave birth to the second theory of the compulsion to repeat, or *Wiederholungszwang*, is quite different. As Lagache points out, it is now a matter not of repetition of the need but of the *need for repetition*, as an expression of the conservative economy of the drive and of the form of psychic functioning subject to the drive – namely, the primary process. The death drive is not yet involved; for Freud, it is the sexual drive that conforms to this principle, the *Lustprinzip*, which by its nature seeks discharge so as to re-establish the undisturbed state.

Moreover, this idea recurs throughout Freud's oeuvre, even in his later writings, alternating with that other notion, the death drive; indeed, he sometimes appears unsure which of the two to espouse. From time to time he considers possible exceptions to the «pleasure principle» – traumatic dreams, fate neuroses, the negative therapeutic reaction, or masochism – and on each occasion he also suggests an explanation. The compulsive character of these experiences is attributed to a number of factors and involves all psychic systems. Freud invokes the attraction exerted by unconscious prototypes on the repressed drive process – which he was later to call «id resistance» – to which he ascribed the need for working through (*Durcharbeitung*); the ego's attempts at retrospective mastery of the traumatic experience;[2] the need for punishment stemming from the superego;[3] or, again, the irreducible conflict between primary narcissism and object cathexis.

These explanations of the compulsion to repeat might seem to us to be sufficient as they are; they do not necessarily involve recourse to the death drive. Not so, however, for Freud. Each time, in his view, there remains an unresolved residue that points towards his postulate. While it would be interesting to enquire in depth into the reasons for this requirement, such a consideration would be beyond the scope of this contribution.

Another important question is whether the concept of the «compulsion to repeat» finds clinical expression in a manner that requires it to be distinguished from other forms of «repetition». My answer is yes. After all, the phenomena discussed by Freud cannot be attributed to repression alone.

As stated, the theoretical and clinical horizon of Freud's ideas has now changed profoundly and he is investigating the phenomenon of the analytic impasse and the processes that concern the relationship between psychic and external reality. Alongside the compulsion to repeat, we have splitting of the ego and the various defences: not just *Verdrängung* (repression) and *Verneinung* (negation), but also *Verleugnung*, the disavowal of perceptual reality, and its counterpart, *Verwerfung*, the repudiation of both perceptual and psychic reality. Here the subject not only disavows external reality, but even eliminates its internal traces that could have led back to it: «not only is the acceptance of new perceptions refused, but the internal world, too, which, as a copy of the external world, has up till now represented it, loses its significance (its cathexis)» (Freud, 1924a, 150f.).

So the repudiation involves the «expulsion from the ego» (*Ausstoßung aus dem Ich*) of the complexes of affects, mnemic representations and meanings that have inherited and preserved the ego's relations with reality.[4]

---

[2] In this case the source of the compulsion to repeat is seen as the ego and no longer the id; it is a «restitutive» compulsion in the service of the ego (E. Bibring).

[3] Here too, the unpleasure «does not contradict the pleasure principle: unpleasure for one system and simultaneously satisfaction for the other» (Freud, 1920, 20).

[4] As the brief passage just quoted shows, for Freud the removal of cathexis (*Besetzung*) from representations coincides with the removal of their meaning (*Bedeutung*).

Psychosis, however, is not content merely to suppress reality, but seeks to create a new reality devoid of the impediments inherent in that which has been abandoned. For this reason, the «ego creates, autocratically, a new external and internal world [...] constructed in accordance with the id's wishful impulses» (*ibid.*, 151). This opens the way to hallucination: «Thus the psychosis is also faced with the task of procuring for itself perceptions of a kind which shall correspond to the new reality; and this is most radically effected by means of hallucination» (Freud, 1924b, 186).

Hence the expulsion of the internal world and its meanings is followed by the «hallucinatory fulfilment» of an external world whose objects are produced by the subject, in so far as they are the result of the subject's «evacuations». These too are repetitions, since, in them, «what was abolished internally returns from without» (Freud, 1911, 71).

Freud stresses that the task of analysis must remain unchanged even where the compulsion to repeat takes the form of hallucination and action, and that it does not in turn call for a recourse to action: the analyst's aim, to which he must adhere, is still «reproduction in the psychical field» (Freud, 1914, 153). This concept is reaffirmed by Bion: the fundamental rule of analysis is to lead the patient towards representation.

What will then be the status of action? There are some forms of action that are tantamount to representation, constituting dramatizations or externalizations – for instance, acting out in the transference. Other forms, however, have remained below the level of meaning, or lie beyond meaning, either because they have never been conscious and never been «thought», or because they have been decathected, denied and expelled. Such actions, Bion says, do not express meanings, but are merely somatic and sensory facts. However, even dreams, words and theories (including psychoanalytic theories) can be used not to convey meanings but as modes of action.

Is there a place for these too in our work? I think there should be. Unlike religion, Bion points out, psychoanalysis does not have the aim of keeping thought and action in a mutually exclusive state, because in «this condition thought and action do not modify each other but persist commensally in the same personality. Actions that appear to be compulsive are in reality beta-elements confined to the domain of action and thus insulated against thoughts, which are confined to the domain of thought – which includes psycho-analysis. Similarly, thoughts are within the domain of thought and cannot be influenced by beta-elements confined within the domain of action» (Bion, 1970, 121). Analysis, by contrast, demands that the conflict between thought and action be shared and kept active, so that the two can influence each other and both can be transformed.

Yet there is more. Consideration of action as the expression of experiences and impulses that lack a psychic meaning not only has the consequence that there is more to the sphere of treatment than the forms of language, but also involves its unconscious somato-psychic *referent* – namely, whatever, in the guise of the id, the body, the drive, or emotion, lies outside and beyond the symbolic but nevertheless constitutes the origin of the symbolic. Precisely for this reason, analysis proves to be a method suitable for revealing the non-symbolic and transforming it by way of its derivatives – its «repetitions».

In other words, precisely because it is neither representation nor word, action is the theatre of what is *pressing* on the psychical apparatus to be received and to have meaning assigned to it, while at the same time *resisting* the psychic work of signification. The domain of action calls for a reference to a meta-phenomenal reality, an «O», which, not being language, dream, transference or relationship, requires analysis to enable it to evolve into language, dream, transference and relationship.

In conclusion, the analytic field cannot dispense with the combined presence of two elements: representation, as the starting point for the process of signification; and the drive, as the origin of the process of repetition.

It is now no longer sufficient for the level of words and language to be assigned to that of affective relational experience, for, as Freud points out, the operational instrument of the treatment – the instrument that performs the psychic work (*Durcharbeitung*) – entails constant conflict with the patient in order to keep within the psychic field all the impulses to which the patient would like to give motor expression. Among these, «new and deeper-lying instinctual impulses, which had not hitherto made themselves felt [so he is here referring to non-repressed impulses], may come to be "repeated"» (Freud, 1914, 153). This makes repetition our best ally, for, as the well known quotation reminds us, it is impossible to destroy anyone *in absentia* or *in effigie*.

Perhaps the most important legacy of Freud's 1914 essay to the psychoanalysis of the future is in fact a challenge: that of re-specifying our theoretical and observational field so as to extend it to non-symbolic processes and the laws governing their transformation into symbolic processes. A theory of the *effigia* – a purely hermeneutic theory – does not suffice for investigating the dramatic phenomena that confront analysis today, which constantly exceed its capabilities and hold sway over it.

SUMMARY

On the basis of Freud's ideas on the limitations of the work of remembering, the author considers the different forms of repetition and the need to distinguish between, on the one hand, repetitions that are expressions of repression and, on the other, those that express the denial of both external and internal reality, such as splitting of the ego, disavowal, repudiation, hallucination and action. The author therefore considers it essential to broaden our theoretical and observational field to include non-symbolic processes and the laws that govern their symbolic transformations.

KEYWORDS: Memory; compulsion to repeat; repetition; repression; disavowal; rejection; hallucination; representation; action; transformation.

REFERENCES

BION W.R. (1970). *Attention and Interpretation*. London, Tavistock.
FONAGY P. (1999). Memory and therapeutic action. *Int. J. Psycho-Anal.*, 80, 215-223.
FREUD S. (1895). *Studies on Hysteria*. S.E. 2.
FREUD S. (1909). *Analysis of a phobia in a five-year-old boy*. S.E. 10.
FREUD S. (1911). *Psycho-analytic notes on an autobiographical account of a case of paranoia*. S.E. 12.
FREUD S. (1914). *Remembering, repeating and working-through*. S.E. 12.
FREUD S. (1920). *Beyond the pleasure principle*. S.E. 18.
FREUD S. (1924a). *Neurosis and psychosis*. S.E. 19.
FREUD S. (1924b). *The loss of reality in neurosis and psychosis*. S.E. 19.

Original italian version:
Riv. Psicoanal., 2007, 2, 439-446

Fernando Riolo

Via Notarbartolo, 4

90141 Palermo

(Translated by Philip Slotkin MA Cantab. MITI)

Plato was the eldest

LAURA AMBROSIANO

Psychoanalytical Societies originated out of a need to build a space, a setting, in which clinical experience and theoretical ideas that develop out of them, can be gathered together and compared. Institutions established on these grounds have a holding function for their members, and together, a function of working through a *shared purpose*.

Psychoanalytical Institutions, similarly to Associations of Psychotherapists, are involved in transmitting knowledge to their new members who guarantee the continuity and fertility of their discipline and the Institutions themselves. In Italy, in this regard, we experienced major change when the transmission of knowledge became organized in schools regulated by state law. This has generally been seen as an opportunity and has led to the birth of numerous schools of various lines of study: even those elements of psychoanalytical societies assigned to carry out training have merged into *postgraduate schools*.

Over the years, bodies assigned to the transmission of knowledge have acquired an increasingly central position within organizations to the extent that they have moved beyond their training function, to become the supporting structure of the whole Institution. As a matter of fact, in Psychoanalytical Societies (as in Associations of psychotherapists) those elements involved in teaching have ended up regulating relations between members and constructing an extremely rigid internal hierarchy.

The Italian Psychoanalytical Society in particular also had to deal with changes brought about by its very size: if in the 1950s it was more or less as big as a private, traditional, elitist club that was culturally refined, today it is nationwide, with ten psychoanalytical Centres and approximately one thousand members. This has brought with it quite difficult changes for individual members and for the Institution, which have involved statutory reviews and the establishment of planning, coordinating and management bodies.

All of this demands broad and shared reflection upon the company-like structure that the Psychoanalytical Institutions have given themselves.

Since the 1990s, as far as the SPI (the Italian Psychoanalytical Society) and other IPA societies are concerned, attention towards organizational aspects seems to have grown. Whereas the traditional running of the society was, for psychoanalysts, the *unthought*, everyone tending towards clinical work and research, this organizational aspect has begun to be noticed, observed, and perhaps criticized in several aspects as being antidemocratic, rigid, obsolete, etc.

My analysis of these phenomena shall be in reference to the Italian Psychoanalytical Society, even though many IPA Societies and many schools of psychodynamic psychotherapy in Italy have gone through similar experiences and debates.

Lombardi's commendable contribution, which recently appeared in the *Rivista di Psicoanalisi* (2006), offers a view of the positions that are emerging in European and American psychoanalytical societies. I shall use it widely as a model for my discussion, since, even though I do not know Lombardi personally, in that I cannot put a face to his name, I feel, through his writing, as if he were a living part of the same group of which I am also part.

THE INSTITUTION-ORGANIZATION

The Institution is the new *thing* that is founded by members when there is what is *considered* to be a common goal in sight. In the name of this goal, Institutions organize themselves accordingly, that is, with rules, regulations and procedures, and lay down tasks, roles and a hierarchy which stand guarantors for the common purpose. These rules and regulations aim at safeguarding the emerging Institution, which is surrounded by uncertainties that arise out of numerous internal variables as well as external pressures (political and legislative power, competition, patients etc.).

The *organization* is a kit that is established in order to guarantee the safeguarding of the Institution and the internal and external recognition of its members with regard to common accomplishments. For this reason, each organizational change rouses panic in that there is a fear of the whole organization crumbling and its members being displaced.

Until the 1970s, sociology considered the organization as a ground of *rationality*: it was only thereafter that it came to be understood as a *political arena* that is not governed by a greater logic but which corresponds to *many* kinds of logic – contingent, empirical, fleeting (Manoukian, 1990, 21). As opposed to being the result of a greater kind of rationality, organizational decisions are an expression of the fantasies, expectations, implicit models and idealizations of the members of the Institution itself. In this conception, the history of the Institution, its tradition and the myth of its origins, are considered as elements which *silently direct* towards a set of rules and procedures that have developed over time.

The organization is the product of an overall *political* view that brings to the fore and integrates the various points of view, writings, and aspirations and ambitions of the many actors of the institution. In this sense, the norm that excludes Associate members from voting on matters relative to training seems incongrous and ahistorical today. Indeed, it is important that the Institution should support the ideas and hypotheses relative to the running of the society that are expressed by *all its members*. This is not in response to a demand for equality, but because *we need to do so* in order to release our Institutions from the current *impasse*.

It often happens within institutions that rules, regulations and procedures gradually become *things in themselves*, disconnected from the meaning that had generated them: there is the tendency to forget that they are fleeting organizational measures, of a *lay nature*, the meaning of which lies in the connection with the purpose that had led to their generation.

Paradoxically, the proliferation of rules and regulations, at a national and international level, bears witness to the sense of inadequacy that psychoanalysts feel when faced with tasks at an organizational level. This inadequacy is connected, in my opinion, to a traditional *split between clinical and organizational* aspects, one which seems to make us all not terribly interested in understanding how our ways of seeing, using and feeling the Institution can influence our mental framework with patients and candidates alike (Ambrosiano, 1999). The consulting room and the meeting room seem to have no link or connection between them, to the extent that we tend to treat the clinical and the organizational aspects of the institution as areas that are isolated from one another.

I think this split can be dangerous as it promotes the idea of a clinical encounter as being a *niche that is isolated* from the rest of the world, as well as the idea of the organization as a place of impersonal rules, regulations and *bureaucratic practice*.

By treating the organization as something *external*, extra-analytical and extra-therapeutic, means, paradoxically, that we risk falling into a *fideistic* attitude towards rules and procedures. It is as if we can entrust (deposit) our way of working to these procedures once and for all: we invoke them as a panacea, we imagine them in the abstract as good in themselves: this route makes them become the space where we *act*.

PLATO, THE ELDEST

The psychoanalytical Institution originated out of Freud's ambivalent wish to let *the partition between his consulting room and waiting room* (the place of the first scientific meetings) *be permeable*: but at the same time it also originated out of Freud's trouble with this permeability. I have in mind the interesting comment by Napolitano (1999) on the meetings of the Viennese group in 1910. At the beginning of psychoanalysis there were transference relations, identification and idealization activity, and complex, unmentioned drives towards the disidentification of members in relation to the founding father. The negative side of the co-transference, which Freud included in group dynamics, became routed in conflicts and rivalries among members.

In the early days those conflictual goings on in the background which permeated the group and could not be disentangled, were being transferred onto the Institution. The *transmission* of conflicts in the new Institution did not allow them to be worked through and hence transformed, which means that they are perpetuated in the form of an implicit mandate from one generation to the next. In this way, denial pervades the group and the Institution, and unresolved transgenerational problems get in the way of creative conflict, mourning and emancipation (Gaburri and Ambrosiano, 2003).

The risk is that we *implicitly* invite candidates to identify with senior members through idealization of psychoanalysis and the institution. This results in a form of learning in which *heads are bowed* and differentiation is discouraged. It leads to candidates taking on an archaic Super-ego which Ferenczi on several occasions (1909; 1924; 1932) had described as a tyrant that requests only obedience.

Lombardi highlights, quoting Reeder (2004), that envy, rivalry and conflicts of power, and the emergence of small groups which generate disagreement, are a standard part of psychoanalytical and psychotherapeutic Institutions. Relations between colleagues are often characterized by destructiveness and pervaded by hatred, but Lombardi adds that hatred is not to be understood «on the basis of the activity of certain individuals or groups, but rather as the consequence of constituent conditions set down for the running of the organization» (2006, 193).

The running of the organization is hostage to aspects of our history that as yet have not been much worked through.

«Plato was the eldest», quotes Napolitano (1999, 89) from the Wednesday seminars. It is Freud who says this when taking part in the discussion on Tausk's work (27-10-1909): all those present actively took part without pointing out that in the paper Aristotle was defined as Plato's master! This phrase of Freud's, «Plato was the eldest», seems to be the organizing principle that we favour inwardly by idealizing an obsolete hierarchy, and also outwardly in the form of an antidote to competition arising from the proliferation of new, and extremely new, schools of analytically oriented psychotherapy. If it is the «the eldest» one who is identified as being the keeper of authentic analytical skills, then this leads to an understanding of the doorway into the psychoanalytical community as being supported by a Super-ego that has been prescribed by tradition: in exchange it offers each individual member a strong and unassailable professional identity.

This induces all mechanisms of masochistic submission to the Institution ... that which Lombardi (2006, 197) describes as a risk of a filiation, which is deadly through and through, of silent but annihilating paranoid anxieties.The role of the Institution is to support the growth of both the individual and the group as a whole, as well as to support the enthusiasm for clinical work and for the elaboration of such in theory building, which is the spirit of exchange among colleagues. But within a situation of a repressed filiation, it is as if the Institution provides a *family and family-like bonds.*

Beyond the seemingly Oedipal scenario, in this situation, institutions seem to favour *primary identification, pre-Oedipal and undifferentiated* bonds. So protests against the older generations, when they emerge, are imbued with equal rights, as described by Macciò and Vallino (1996) which allude to the nostalgic fantasy of building a non-conflictual, idyllic and magmatic group, that is, a basic assumption group.

Speziale Bagliacca (2002) speaks of the euphoric climate of the first group of psychoanalysts and links it to a hypomanic tendency of Freud himself, brought about by an avoidance of the conflictual side of the relationship with his mother. Freud would have kept «inside himself an idealized mother and an idealized relationship through splitting and denial» (*ibid.*, 176).

Within this (narratological) hypothesis, if the bond with the mother and related expectations had allowed Freud to begin those unprecedented explorations on which psychoanalysis was founded, then the denial of his hostile feelings towards the mother had influenced his most intimate relationships, often characterized by abrupt changes from idealization to disillusioned resentment. Fliess, Breuer, Ferenczi, Jung… seem like personifications of the idealized mother who, once the idealization crumbles, become the advocates not only of internal conflicts but of interpersonal and institutional conflicts as well.

As we know, Freud himself was and is idealized by patients and followers (Speziale Bagliacca, 2002, 255): the denial of hostile sentiments, which are the bearers of the disidentification in development, is passed from one generation to another under the appearance of strict orthodoxy or, alternatively, of its fanatical rejection. Even today we still seem to carry around with us a little of that hypomanic climate, perhaps as an antidote to paranoid concerns over the future. On the other hand, when our patients unexpectedly take a step forward, or withdraw out of fear after having made that step, do we not feel each time as if we ourselves are explorers faced with the vast territory of mental pain?

I made a reference to the work of Speziale Bagliacca because it brings on to the scene Freud's relationship with his mother which is of interest to me at this point in order to develop Bion's (1961) thought, according to which the relationship with the group is just as formidable as a newborn's encounter with the breast: a group encounter opens up again for each of us primitive patterns and problems.

LEARNING IN AN OEDIPAL AND PRE-OEDIPAL REGISTER

The mind, equipped from the start with a potential endowment, develops by introjecting a historical and intersubjective heritage, a cultural world inside which the individual seeks recognition for the self and for his/her own uniqueness. The lability and permeability of boundaries between the subject and the other, between the inside and outside world, portrays development as being dialectical, and at times conflictual, moving between attunement and distance, and between participation and individuation.

The transmission of psychoanalytical knowledge refers to two different experiences and abilities: one is being able to carry out a caring activity; the other is being able to describe and communicate this activity to the group of colleagues and to the scientific community.

From the 1950s onwards, when psychoanalysis gave full recognition to the emotional attitude of the analyst during the session (Bordi, 1995), the task of training candidates became more complex and reflections on the matter more refined. If the analyst's presence is fundamental to the session, then the candidate must receive support in order to develop as well as possible the ability to listen to preconscious products of his/her unconscious mental world, so that *his/her* affective and ideational responses may be captured and worked through in the context of the encounter with the patient.

This is not all. The candidate must be helped to tolerate losing himself/herself at times, without saturating the clinical encounter with that which he/she *already knows*.

In order to deal with these dimensions of the clinical encounter, personal analysis needs to make the candidate's ability for self-analysis develop to its full potential: allowing oneself to become involved, finding the distance to be able to pull oneself, along with the patient, out of the (relatively) shared undifferentiated and painful condition, to then organize the live experience into theoretical hypotheses that can be communicated.

Learning psychoanalytical theories is an unavoidable need the analyst has: they come to his or her rescue in dark, difficult passages, and offer a point of reference. They also represent a connection to a group with which the analyst shares the tension related to treating and to searching for meaning. This connection is the *third* player of the analytic encounter and it guarantees the pair at work a parameter against which to gauge shared knowledge that borders on the ever-present risk of *drifting* (Ambrosiano, 1998).

The learning space of the Institution takes the form of a complex environment which includes the ensemble of the candidates' relationships with each other, with their teachers, with the wider group and with the other interlocutors of the world of the Institution.

The pathway to learning, because of the particular condition of dependence it holds, opens the mind towards taking in transformational introjections. Identifications and introjections do not refer exclusively to objects (teachers and the teachings they transmit), but to rhythms, styles, ways of thinking and searching, and attitudes and expectations towards psychoanalysis that are communicated to the students by the Institution and which go to make up a kind of un-conscious memory that will imbue subsequent evolution.

During training, even if the individual candidate has the impression that he/she is moving in time with regard to becoming a psychoanalyst, the path to learning brings into play a *spatial dimension* in which acquisitions, introjections and identifications come in and modify the self. During training, the boundaries of the self, so to speak, open up to receive what is new, and to refine one's clinical skills via the relationship with teachers. This opening up process of identification leads the individual towards experimenting exposure towards the other which is so intense that at times it creates a sense of unbearable fragility, of *excessive permeability* in relation to the environment, which can be compared to that which the newborn experiences in relation to the primary environment.

The sensation of being exposed, at times dangerously, to the influence of the other means that *the conflict between being ourselves and remaining connected to the others is kept active.*

The Oedipal conflict is where this conflict is worked through: it is the space of transit from the undifferentiated to individuation. The Oedipal conflict is where elements of primary identification are worked through, so as to allow the potential uniqueness of the individual to come through. Oedipal pain, alongside new identifications, promotes disidentifications, too, thanks to the subject's deeply felt drive to put himself/herself in the place of the adult, to become better than him, to create a more integral humanism, and a more sensitive and efficient psychoanalysis. This Oedipal pain sets the *mourning process* in motion, one which concerns a spatial dimension of the self (Gaburri, 1997): it refers to the separation of objects and the transformation of the primary bond.

It is necessary to bear Oedipal pain in order to realize one's diversity, that is, one must reach the point of experiencing the Oedipal constellation, in order to work through the ideals and idealizations that the road to becoming psychoanalysts was opened up by, otherwise the desire *to become the pupil that the teachers have in mind* will be reinforced.

All of this means that the paths to learning open up a wide Oedipal[1] scene that includes not only the intrapsychic events of each pupil, but also the *attitude of the teachers* towards the diversity that each young pupil brings. The teachers themselves, in their teachings, bring traces of those who are *not* present: colleagues, groups and theories are references which, in the teacher's mind, precede the encounter with the pupils and guide his/her way of teaching.

But if the encounter with the group is an event that is just as formidable as the encounter with the breast for a newborn, as Bion says (1961), this implies that

---

[1] Oedipus as a representation that includes object behaviour is in the work of many Authors such as H.W. Loewald (1980), H. Faimberg (1993), Gaburri and Ambrosiano (2003).

learning is an area that is stimulated not only by Oedipal but also by archaic, pre-Oedipal values. In an undifferentiated pre-Oedipal mental state, the group is understood as a mentality, that is, as a series of values and beliefs, of implicit workings and defences, that are not quite that of anyone, but which emerge out of the basic assumptions of the Institution as a whole.

Freud described a «natural connection» (1921, 12) which promotes a mental state that is based on sharing and being in harmony with others, rather than grappling with conflicts. For this reason, he maintained that individual psychology all along is also social psychology (*ibid*, 11). The individual is brought towards an undifferentiated mental state by the fear that individual feelings and thoughts are «too weak to be of any value on their own» (*ibid*., 66). The mass, the group in its basic sense, gives the individual the impression of it being an endless power, and so «[…] it is clearly perilous for him to put himself in opposition to it, and it will be safer to follow the example of those around him and perhaps even hunt with the pack» (*ibid*., 29).

The individual, in the name of a need to connect, favours bonds of identification with regard to object investments, and in so doing, gives up his/her own way of being a separate person.

As we know, Freud indicates the road along which the individual can leave this *collective* mental state, and lift himself/herself towards a minimum degree of independence and originality: he does so via the metaphor of the poet who is able to dream the *dream* of placing himself in the role of the father after having killed him within himself. «The poet creates the myth of the hero who wants to substitute the father, who takes responsibility for the killing, and who frees himself from collective psychology» (*ibid*., 86). The poet who has taken this step «knows, however, the way that leads back to the mass, which in fact he takes, to then tell the mass of the hero's actions which he himself invented» (*ibid*., 87). In this way, the other parts of the mass can *share* the same desire towards emancipation.

The two mental states described by Freud, collective and individual, are in an oscillating relationship with one another: shifts of transformation and of returning (regression) from one mental state to another are always possible. It can happen at any moment that circumstances such as the emotional group climate, individual needs, or those of the organization, may stimulate individuals towards either a conformist and undifferentiated adhesion, or towards participation characterized by differentiation. Both values are actually always available and ready to be activated in the scene of the intrapsychic, the social and the institution.

Both mental states are involved in pathways to learning.

At a primary level we can imagine an Institution which implicitly promotes a mass identification amongst its members and the individual members as being obscurely imbued with the *attraction* towards this kind of bond. We can imagine both an institutional group that discourages differentiation, and individuals who are attracted by the idealization of undifferentiated harmony.

So we can sense how the poet's metaphor becomes charged with an unsettling level of catastrophic change (Bion, 1959) which spreads panic: there is fear that the bond will break and the Institution will split.

The institutional environment may represent itself as a mentality (a basic assumption group) whose unconscious purpose is to transmit to candidates a set of established meanings, seemingly self-evident and obvious, which makes it possible to avoid dismay and anxiety when faced with what is different or unknown. Specularly, the individual can develop primary identifications that are static and impermeable to experience, and whose transformation may be felt as dangerous for the group and the Institution.

Every group has a conflictual tendency between these two states, that is, between the need for spaces in which to work and the drive to organize itself into a mentality that groups together, sheltering individuals from the fear of isolation and the group from the fear of not surviving.

The role of the group is to discover and recommend the psychic means with which differences, deviations, limits and fear of the future may be dealt. But at times the group organizes itself so as to avoid these dimensions. Situated between working through and avoidance, is the changeable and oscillating line between working group and basic assumption group.

It then becomes even more important that the *teachers* themselves are willing to observe the vicissitudes of teaching and, in turn, are interested in working through the ideal they began *their* own professional journey with. Even the teacher, to the same extent and more than the pupil, needs to actively maintain focused attention towards his/her own professional vicissitudes: the nature of his/her bond with groups of reference; memberships and identifications that punctuate such; the degree of undifferentiated bond that lies at the bottom of his/her participation; the amount of reactive shaping and counter-identification in which his/her differences are at times consumed etc. (Ambrosiano, 2001).

I defined (Ambrosiano, 2005) «professional romance» the continual and changing narrative that emerges from an analyst's re-examination of his/her own professional biography: emotional and affective vicissitudes that have punctuated his/her identity and professional journey. This narrative is interweaved with the evolution of cultural, theoretical and clinical tendencies of both the analyst and the Institution. The psychoanalyst *needs* to share his/her professional journey with a community of colleagues. This implies that theoretical options are not simply conscious and rational. They develop out of the work with patients, but also out of the vicissitudes with colleagues and with the Institution's groups of reference.

Theories carry traces of groups (and subgroups) that each analyst is connected to.

We can therefore suppose that our theories carry *into the consulting room the group* of colleagues and our bond with the Institution itself.

The working through of these vicissitudes does concern pupils, but it firstly concerns the masters, teachers, supervisors and the group.

THE DOUBLE REGISTER OF KNOWLEDGE TRANSMISSION

Ideally, psychoanalytical training looks to promote clinical competence and skills of exchange among colleagues with regard to formulated theories inspired by clinical experience.

Napolitano (1999) highlighted the hardened incompatibility there is between the aims of personal analysis and those of Institutional training.

Napolitano believes that the experience of personal analysis represents an *oral dimension* (not written) of learning which promotes introjection and identification with the interlocutor within the richness of a relationship. The memory of what has been learnt from one's own personal analytical experience is there to be drawn forth in clinical work, and is reinforced by the collective memory that is transmitted across generations.

Unlike personal analysis, the transmission of knowledge is regulated by *writing*, by published theories: it regards knowledge other than that of the self and promotes *distance and disidentification*. Both methods of learning, one through identification and the other through disidentification, do not occur one after the other but «co-evolve together» (Napolitano, 1999, 30)

The identification-disidentification dynamics pointed out by Napolitano, defines learning as a conflictual journey in which «each pupil is the teacher who has been incorporated during the meal and has therefore been destroyed as such», and each lesson, he adds citing Jonesco, «is the defensive and preventive killing of the pupil by the teacher» (*ibid.*, 34). Acquiring knowledge demands «the deconstruction of the other's building inside us and its re-assembling according to the ways of the individual pupil» (*ibid.*, 28), which should lead to becoming ourselves in that we are *different* from the teacher.

During the learning process each of us needs to continually re-examine the memory that was formed out of personal analysis as well as the knowledge that was acquired during theoretical seminars, if we want to place a hold on the internal drive to adapt, which may go as far as a sort of «sleepwalking» (*ibid.*, 47). Fortunately, this drive to adapt is upset by «the quite disturbing impression that part of my inclinations and theoretical choices do not really arise out of what I consciously thought they did, but they go back to oral sources that are further back along the river's course» (*ibid.*, 130), an impression that each of us has experienced many times.

Noticing differences and also *inconsistencies* between learning that has taken place during personal analysis and that which has occurred during theoretical seminars opens the painful and creative road of mourning. There, in the middle, between analysis and training there is always and inevitably if analysis has gone well, an *as yet unexplored territory, a hiatus.*

When we turn our attention towards this hiatus we feel estrangement and fear, and it is there that we experience our need of the group, a work group which holds its «position», as Di Chiara would say, on the edge of the unknown. It is a group which makes this hiatus the object of its research and makes the need to theorize its future.

This position is where the pupil needs to *meet* the teachers, as representatives of the psychoanalytical Institution. The teacher's *primary* task is to pass on to the pupils tolerance of the cracks and fragility of our theories, and aspects of them which make them seem approximate and not yet sufficient. The incompleteness of our models should be pointed out to the pupil, as it is from such models that new pathways are opened up for exploration.

If this does not occur, it would be difficult for the pupils to think their own thoughts about theories, or generate theoretical hypotheses. Pupils and younger members may fear detaching themselves *too much* from the theoretical body of teachers, which becomes idealized as compact and coherent, *carved to perfection.* These idealizations can promote either mimetic learning, or specularly, the crumbling of idealizations may lead to an opaqueness of the candidates in the society's debates, making them seem (apparently) as if they are *passive receivers* of the teachings of the masters, «the eldest».

Pointing out to pupils that metapsychology is a *witch beyond reach* may be difficult, due to it being felt as a threat to the Institution: the euphoric climate of the foundation provides support for new projects. But gradually, this climate will fade as it will be necessary to face up to the regret concerning the limits of our knowledge and a solid Institution, which is disappointing and never the same as the imagined Eden.

Reeder (2004) stresses that change may be brought about by motivating the young generations, starting from candidates at the very beginning of their training, to participate more actively in scientific debate and in matters concerning the running of the organization. But in order for this to occur it must be thought that psychoanalysis is capable of encouraging their awareness of the road they are taking: a road along which they will encounter emotions, ambivalence towards training, and hatred as well as attraction towards the teachers and supervisors, and towards the group.

TRAINING

Emphasis on the survival of the Institution is no doubt a priority for our future, but it presents a problem which I think ought to be carefully considered: there is a *creeping risk* that training, teaching, and the transmission of knowledge *will saturate the purpose and the function of the whole Institution* and will be adopted as the privileged aim of the organization. We can feel this risk in psychoanalytical Societies, in the low participation, for instance, of training analyst in the everyday life of the Centres and in scientific meetings. Training analyst are absent, of course not all of them and not all the time, but often and in significant numbers, since they are taken up precisely by problems related to training. It is a very visible absence.

Such *visible absence* implicitly spreads several general assumptions among us, which are independent of individuals' thoughts. Some of these implicit assumptions could be expressed as follows: once knowledge of the psychoanalytical tradition has been acquired, there is no need to do anything else; once the older members have reached maturity, so to speak, interest in listening to the creative research of the younger members fades; once each analyst has coherently arrived at his/her own ideas, there is no personal need to question them again; teaching and theoretical reflection are two distinct and separate areas, etc.

With specific regard to the SPI, the increasingly central role of the training Institute in relation to the main body of the society strongly *marks* relations among members: one thinks of the rule that *discriminates associate members* by not recognizing the opportunity for them to vote on statutory changes which have to do with training. In fact, this rule seems to sanction that training is not the product of common goals and interests, but that it is a *dimension which determines the organizational models* of the whole Society.

In this way, the running of the society is *hostage* to a lack of confidence towards the future, which is not worked through but simply turned about by sheltering in and around the structures assigned to teaching.

This is what Kernberg, Andrade de Azevedo, Reeder and many other colleagues, quoted and referred to by Lombardi (2006), have been stressing for some time. It is not solely an Italian phenomenon, but one which seems to concern other psychoanalytical Societies. In fact, Tuckett and Faimberg, two colleagues who, thanks to their transnational and key positions, have sensed this unease which permeates our groups, have inaugurated a new style of working and exchange among colleagues at the EPF congressional meetings which strengthens the link between clinical and theoretical areas, and among theories.

This institutional unease concerns us all, and it cannot be *simplified* as *fear of exams* with regard to candidates, or as a *shelter* for the *status quo* with regard to senior members. Both dimensions are connected by fear of the future: fear of being isolated from the context, and anxiety related to an inability to bridge the gaps in our knowledge.

Between these two paths, both of which Lombardi indicated as partial (*ibid.*) – that of noting the oversights *of* individual candidates and analysts, and that of noting the misrepresentation *of* the institutional organization – it is necessary to find a way to express the unease that involves us all. Demonizing the Institution, or assigning a pathology to those individuals who dare to protest is neither useful nor beneficial to broadening our knowledge: they are just different ways of *projectively displacing* fear and uncertainty.

Each group needs to change in order to survive and often change is brought about by those members who create some disturbance, since frequently they personify the widespread pain. Common experience tells us that schisms have never resolved such unease, and actually tend to reproduce the same problems in the «new» institution they have created.

As Reeder (2004) notes, some problems recur over time according to a peculiar *ahistorical* connotation. Any consideration of changes to our organizational working must take into account the group and the institution as the third player in our work during sessions, with candidates and patients alike (Rocchi, 2003).

In order to bring the training institute back into the wider working of the society, at least two aspects, which I believe are correlated, must be reconsidered: recognition of the right of all participating members of the institution to *vote*; and recognition that the permanent training *of teachers* has its natural and privileged place in scientific debate within the Centres. Bringing teachers back into the Centres welds the training institute to the society as a whole and to the Institutional goals of exchange and research. It also acts as a reminder that taking up teaching tasks is not a hierarchical passageway, but a response to a motivation to teach which some develop during their professional experience.

THE GROUP OF COLLEAGUES

Once Luciana Nissim Momigliano said, as a bitter joke, that our best qualities are kept for the patients, and our *worst for our colleagues*. It took me several years to realize that these words, perhaps unconsciously, had sensed the help the group provides for each one of us. I think it is important to realize that each of us makes the daily effort to *prevent* one's ambitions and desires to be recognized, conflicts, dislikes, and intense hates and loves from *falling upon* patients. Perhaps each of us *lays down in the group* and in the Institution their own emotional vicissitudes that are too violent to be easily contained (we can think of Bleger). The holding capacity offered by the group of colleagues does, I must admit, seem quite far from being transforming; it might seem more like a *dumping ground* with a certain parasitic quality; but it is an initial level of help that we receive from the group when practicing a profession such as ours. Perhaps we need to *think* about and *recognize* this help a little more, and feel it more even in the place where traditionally we would not expect to be able to bring it out: in the consulting room.

Freud «the eldest» is much loved because he was always attentive to the provisional and imprecise nature of his theoretical formulations, and he told us so! Looking to «the eldest» represents a fertile necessity to «recognize the need for constant returns to the founding work of the discipline. Here, the geometrical image that comes to mind is not that of the line but of the circle, contact with the original sources of psychoanalytical thought fructifying in noticeably new ways at each turn of the spiral» (Petrella, 2006).

The «eldest» knew how to tolerate incoherence and incompleteness, and in a certain sense he loved it, which is why we continue to think of him as a master.

This is to say that if we *need* the concurrence of all members, their vote and their ideas in order to rethink our way of working, I do not believe that what we need is a society of *equals*. The equality idea frightens because it risks flattening the *differences* between us which are the substance of our group.

Let us remember with Lombardi, who quotes him, that Bion said, «I do not believe that what separates scientists is their theories [...] the fracture must be measured in an area different from that of theories» (quoted in Lombardi, 2006, 201). The sources of unease are elsewhere. It is for this reason I believe that what Lombardi (*ibid.*) stated must be stressed: the road that considers mistakes as belonging to single candidates and analysts does not work, nor does that which sees the distortions of the institutional organization as responsible tout court for the oversights. Rather, it is a case of getting hold of the vicissitudes that all of us are experiencing with regard to the future of our discipline.

SUMMARY

The author discusses some aspects of the way the Italian Psychoanalytical Society functions, presenting the organisation as a complex political arena that is answerable to a contingent, transient, and empirical logic. She focuses on the way each member experiences and makes use of the institution, which becomes an element we take with us into the consulting room and forms part of our relationship with the patient. She emphasizes the role of colleagues and the analytic community in maintaining the mental organisation that makes our clinical work possible. She sees a danger in the National Training Institute's breaking away from the main body of the Institution, and for this reason believes that it is essential that all members should be involved equally in the running of the society, in order to face these changes.

KEY WORDS: Institution, to learn, training, group.

REFERENCES

AMBROSIANO L. (1998). Il complesso intreccio tra teoria ed esperienza clinica. *Riv. Psicoanal.*, 44, 1, 41-66.

AMBROSIANO L. (1999). Tra clinico e istituzionale: nessi possibili. *Riv. Psicoanal.*, 45, 3, 475-492.

AMBROSIANO L. (2001). Ululare con i lupi. Note su narcisismo e socialismo. *Riv. Psicoanal.*, 47, 2,283-302.

AMBROSIANO L. (2002). La trasmissione del sapere in psicoanalisi. *Costruzioni Psicoanal.*, 2, 17-34.

AMBROSIANO L. (2005). The analyst: his professional novel. *Int. J. Psycho-Anal.*, 86, 1611-1626.

BION W.R. (1992). *Cogitations*. London, Karnac Books.

BION W.R. (1961). *Experiences in groups*. London, Tavistock.

BION W.R. (1962). *Learning from experience*. London, Heinemann.

BION W.R. (1970). *Attention and interpretation*. London, Tavistock.

BLEGER J. (1967). Psicoanalisis del encuadre psicoanalitico. *Rev. de Psychoan.*, 24, 2, 241-258.

BLEGER J. (1971). Temas de psicologìa (Entrevista y grupos). *Buenos Aires Nueva Vision*, 89-104.

BORDI S. (1995). *I seminari milanesi di Bordi*. A cura del Centro Milanese di Psicoanalisi C. Musatti.

DI CHIARA G. (1999). L'inconscio e la formazione psicoanalitica. *Riv. Psicoanal.*, 45, 445-463.

FAIMBERG H. (2005). *The telescoping of generations*. London, New Library of psychoanalysis.

FERENCZI S. (1909). Introjection and transference. In *First contributions to Psycho-analysis*. London, The Hogarth Press, 1952.

FREUD S. (1909). *Family romances*. SE, 9, 235-244.

FREUD S. (1921). *Group psychology and the analysis of the Ego*. SE, 18, 67-143.

GABURRI E. (Ed.) (1997). Introduzione a *Emozione e Interpretazione*. Torino, Boringhieri.

GABURRI E. (2002). Pensiero associativo e lutto: l'attenzione fluttuante e il senso comune. *Riv. Psicoanal.*, 2.

GABURRI E., AMBROSIANO L. (2003). *Ululare con i lupi. Conformismo e rêverie*. Torino, Boringhieri.

LOEWALD H.W. (1980). *Papers on Psychoanalysis*. Yale Univ.

LOMBARDI R. (2006). Passione e conflittualità nelle istituzioni psicoanalitiche. *Riv. Psicoanal.*, 1, 191-212.

MANOUKIAN F. OLIVETTI (1990). La conoscenza dell'organizzazione. In Manoukian Kaneklin *Conoscere l'organizzazione*, La Nuova Italia Scientifica.

MACCIÒ M., D. VALLINO (1996). Note sul complesso fraterno nei gruppi. *Psiche*, 2.

NAPOLITANO F. (1999). *La filiazione e la trasmissione nella psicoanalisi. Sulla consegna transgenerazionale del sapere*. Milano, Franco Angeli.

PETRELLA F. (2006). Freud's style: terminology, metaphor and textual strategies. *The Italian Psychoanalytic Annual*, 2007, 107-129.

REEDER J. (2004). *Hate and love in psychoanalytical institutions*. New York, Other Press.

ROCCHI C. (2003). On the countertransference of the patient. Transformations of the psychoanalyst's "theoretical self" and their possible articulations with the vicissitudes of the analytic relationship. INT. J. PSYCO-ANAL., 84, 1221-39.

SPEZIALE BAGLIACCA R. (2002). *Freud messo a fuoco. Passando dai padri alle madri*. Torino, Boringhieri.

Original italian version:
Riv. Psicoanal., 2007, 3, 593-610

Laura Ambrosiano

Via Ozanam, 15

20129 Milano

(Translated by Janice Parker)

Ethics of responsibility and psychoanalysis after Auschwitz

VALERIA EGIDI MORPURGO

«Our tragedy and its memories drown in noise»
(ELIE WIESEL, 2000)

T hese heartfelt words of Elie Wiesel, the writer who survived the extermination camps, and a Nobel Prize for Peace laureate, point out the difficulties we unavoidably come up against when faced with the Shoah.[1]

Between noise and oblivion: defensive strategies. In my view, writing and talking about the Shoah involves risking a mere rhetorical commemoration in which words are merely empty, senseless sounds. Rhetoric is a defence against horror and therefore against awareness and against ethical responsibility. But the silence of forgetfulness – caused by splitting and denial – represents a real strategy of annihilation of the «drowned» and the «saved».[2]

The defence of noise and forgetfulness rob all mankind of the possibility to represent or «think» about Auschwitz, the peak of human suffering.

A discussion on the possibility to «think» about the Shoah involves thinkers belonging to different schools of thought. We must consider, among others, critical opinions like those of Claude Lanzmann, author of the monumental documentary *Shoah*, who believes that «explanations» about the Shoah could in some way «justify» it (1991)[3] and Moses Kijak who has vigorously pointed out the limits of the capacity of the human mind to work through the mourning of *social catastrophes*

---

[1] I am using the word Shoah (which means «devastation, catastrophe») instead of Holocaust. The word Holocaust («total sacrifice») contains a potential ambiguity, vigorously pointed out by Bruno Bettelheim (1981, 91-94), Primo Levi (1997), and Giorgio Agamben (1998), because its use might become an accusation against the exterminated people, and lead to believe that the victims of the Shoah are not the victims of human destructiveness but sacrificial victims offered to a god in expiation of guilt.

Indeed, the word has a story and a wide usage and it is widely used especially in the English-speaking intellectual world and will be used in quotations.

[2] See Primo Levi, *The drowned and the saved*, Little &Brown, London ,1991.

[3] See The obscenity of understanding: an evening with Claude Lanzmann, *American Imago*, 48, 473. See also Agamben's discussion on the paradox of understanding and witnessing Auschwitz (*Quel che resta di Auschwitz*, 92-93).

like the Shoah because the Shoah «has unveiled an aspect of the human being which completely changed mankind's ethical image» (2005).

And yet if psychoanalysis does not ponder over the Shoah, it runs the risk of rejecting it into silence, into nothingness and of failing its clinical and ethical purpose.

Even today, though historical events are removed in time, denial and silence prevent the «bringing into thought [...] through bonds with other individuals» (Puget, 1989, VIII, §2) of traumatic occurrences and hinder representation of catastrophic events which, if not worked through, tend to pass on, in a pathogenic way, from one generation to the other.

THINKING ABOUT THE SHOAH. A CHALLENGE FOR PHILOSOPHICAL THOUGHT

The Auschwitz theme is indeed «petrifying» and seems to go beyond the mental capacity to work through and transform because *the Shoah is unique*, as pointed out by P. Lacoue Labarthe and Jean Luc Nancy in their books *La fiction du politique* (1987) and *Le mythe nazi* (1991). As:

• the Final Solution has represented an ideological, unheard of assault on the *identity* of a people. What makes the Shoah unique is that «the extermination of the Jews cannot be explained in political, military or territorial grounds» (Lacoue Labarthe, 1987) (my translation from Italian edition).

• the Shoah was carried out industrially: «The Jews were "treated" like industrial waste or a proliferation of parasites. As Franz Kafka understood a long time before, the "Final Solution" interpreted old abuse and contempt metaphors to the letter [...]» (Lacoue Labarthe, *ibid.*).

• the extermination plan was carried out worldwide: «This pure hygiene or health operation (not only social, political and religious but also symbolic) has no historical equivalent» (*ibid.*).

The Shoah is also unique:

• due the material and metaphysical silence that weighed on Auschwitz. «At Auschwitz everything developed, came to an end and burnt out for weeks, months and years in absolute silence, at the margin of history and adrift» (Neher, 1970).

• due to the regression to *concrete* thinking. Isn't what Lacoue Labarthe defines «to interpret a metaphor to the letter», perhaps, the regression to *concrete* thinking ? or to Hanna Segal's symbolic equation, that is a psychotic mechanism for which the human being «decreed» as subhuman, a parasite or refuse *becomes* waste material to be eliminated?

Can we affirm Shoah discontinuity with the historical and intellectual worlds of yesterday's and today's West? and with its psychological background?

In *Modernity and the Holocaust*, Zygmunt Bauman, the theoretician of post-modernity, affirms continuity remarking that «The Holocaust was born and executed in our modern, rational society, at the high stage of our civilization and at the peak of human cultural achievement» (Bauman, 1989, X). In other terms, the Shoah *is a problem for us* and *is a present- day problem.*

So as not to reduce these words to pure abstraction, we must recognize that on the scenario of a catastrophe such as the Shoah, there are victims as well as persecutors, accomplices as well as witnesses. Sergio Quinzio, a Catholic philosopher, invited the non Jews, the Gentiles, for the very reason that they were spared extermination, to tackle the theme of the Shoah, starting from the position they held on this tragic scenario. This also concerns the *capacity* for thinking the *unthinkable* Auschwitz:

«We, who have not experienced what the Jews have lived through, will never know. But we must listen to their voice, the voice of the witnesses of the inaudible» (Quinzio, 2002, 164).

These considerations still concern us closely because anti-Semitism is not a ghost of the past. Auschwitz still questions us; it even concerns those of us living in Western countries where an easy-going, self-acquitting morality risks clouding the historical responsibilities of the past and exhausting present ones. Shmuel Erlich has clearly referred to creeping anti-Semitism in today's Western world and to Europe's responsibilities:

«The risk and danger of my discussion so far is that it may lead you to think that anti-Semitism, especially in its perverse Nazi form, is a thing of the past, a mere historical phenomenon. Such a conclusion would indeed be dangerously misleading if not delusional. Anti-Semitism is alive and well, particularly under its new guise as anti-Israel sentiments and hatred» (2005, 11).

THE DISAPPEARANCE OF ETHICS

In her work *The Ego Ideal* (1973) Janine Chasseguet Smirgel has stressed the role of anti-oedipal phantasies in Nazi mental universe. She remarks that the Nazi cult had a mother-God as its object (*Blut und Boden*, 'blood and soil') bringing about a *real uprooting of the mind both of the father and of the paternal universe* together with all that derives from the Oedipus complex. This assault on the Oedipal norm leads to a reversal of ethics: Nazism is recognized as the universe of perversion, a sadistic-anal universe, «the opposite in every detail to what is described in the text we base our Judaeo-Christian civilization on» (Chasseguet Smirgel, 1984, chapt. 1).

Niels P. Nielsen also studies the disappearance of natural ethics in depth. He reminds us of the upside down world metaphor in the specific form of the perversion of truth, morals and rights implemented by Nazism and the terror regimes (Nielsen, 2004, 195).

Janine Puget recalls *ethical perversion* during a dictatorship. The aim becomes «the annihilation of law. Transgression is set up in all fields. The individual takes possession of the new rules of the game» (Puget, 1989, VII §4).

In the perverted upheaval of values caused by Nazism and violent regimes, we notice what has been defined by many thinkers as the *disappearance of ethics*.

Bauman's remarks concerning the situations in which the principle of individual survival has caused ethics to disappear stress that it has been and is always a choice: «The lesson of the Holocaust is the ease with which most people separate themselves from a situation that does not contain a good choice [...] argue themselves away from the issue of moral duty [...] adopting instead the precepts of rational interest and self-preservation» (Bauman, 1989, 206).

There is also another agent attacking ethics and reducing it to silence: the individual and social pathology of moral indifference and *ambiguity*: «What will tomorrow bring to our children and to yours? What is going to happen? What is going to happen when hatred emerges once again? What is going to happen when indifference, the worst danger of all –I believe – prevails? [...] indifference to other people is blasphemy and the only way to fight indifference is by sharing our knowledge, our thirst for knowledge and friendship» (Wiesel, 2000, 152).

Psychoanalysis has often reflected on the pathology of indifference which is, first of all, moral indifference. *Indifference and duplicity* characterize the ambiguous position and personality identified by José Bleger (1967) and developed by the Argentine psychoanalysts who have experienced State violence and deepened the pathological consequences of a social situation of extreme abuse and violence. Silvia Amati Sas has transposed Bleger's conceptualization of the mechanisms of exporting the undifferentiated or symbiotic part of the mind onto the plane of group psychology (trans-subjective space) and onto the relationship between the individual and a totalitarian regime.

In intra-psychic space, we can see a primitive «agglutinated» nucleus of the Ego containing incompatible and opposing aspects, not experienced as clashing. In this sense, the symbiotic Ego nucleus is «ambiguous». This nucleus is «deposited» on an object which is originally the maternal object, but then extends to the environment and to relationships with family, religion and society. In this ambiguous nucleus deposit key, Amati Sas described the phenomenon of the slow build up of acceptance of State violence, writing of mass acquiescence to the Argentine military regime which left thirty thousand dead, the *desaparecidos*, at the end of the 1970's. (Amati, 1989).

A contribution to the study of the individual and the social pathology of mimetism also comes from Z. Bauman's theories. He defines our culture as the time of Proteiform identity or liquid identity (2003). Though Bauman does not refer to the psychoanalytical theories of mimetism, we can notice that his concept of *Proteiform identity* is in many ways similar to the pathology identified by José Bleger and by Madeleine Baranger.

In different forms and languages, all these thinkers and psychoanalysts point out two dangers which might lead to «other» social catastrophes: The danger of expelling the oedipal Super Ego which took place in the Nazi mind (and in the totalitarian mind or in the authoritarian personality), and the, perhaps less recognizable, danger of indifference and ambiguity. They all refer to «natural» ethics or to Judaeo-Christian ethics as a bulwark against the two dangers of the totalitarian and the ambiguous mind.

Although these references to ethics are immediately and intuitively understandable, we may further analyze ethical implications by distinguishing between «motive» ethics (in our contemporary world this concept has its origins in the Enlightenment) and «purpose»[4] ethics. Following the latter, respect of laws or of an ideal is good. These laws/ideals are to be considered the purpose mankind is aiming to achieve. This kind of ethics has its origins in the classical world. [5]

One of the best illustrations of the ethics of purpose, and one of most moving illustrations of the ethical principles which are denied in the universe of ambiguity and violated in the universe of perversion is Socrates' choice.

In Plato's dialogue *Gorgias*, Socrates says to Polus: «For I certainly think that I and you and every man do really believe, that to do is a greater evil than to suffer injustice (*Gorgias*, 474,b).

Socrates' ethics is the ethics of purpose. Unjustly accused of violating the laws of the polis and condemned to death, Socrates refuses to run away.

His attitude of respect for the law was interpreted by Franco Fornari (1970, 72-75) as a sign of *ethical ideals typical of the depressive position*. The respect Socrates had for the laws of his community expresses the ideal of saving his love object, that is the laws, the paternal law, even beyond self-preservation.

FROM THE ETHICS OF MOTIVES TO VALUE

In *Civilization and its Discontent* (1929), Freud outlined the concept of the «Cultural Super-Ego», which «deals with relations of human beings with one another [...] under the heading of ethics» (142). In his text Freud seemed to suggest an ethics of motives, aimed at describing, not at prescribing; indeed he appears sceptical about the possibility that ideals and moral values may have any power to modify human

---

4 In German: *Zweck*.

5 The two visions cannot always be separated. Kantian ethics, for instance, can be seen both as ethics of motives and as ethics of purpose, as pointed out by Nicola Abbagnano in *Dizionario di filosofia* (1964). The so-called natural ethics, when it defines the good as respect for the laws (human and divine), or for an ideal, is an ethics of purpose.

aggressiveness, and he has a critical attitude to «natural ethics»: «[…] anyone who follows such a percept in present-day civilization only puts himself at a disadvantage *vis-à-vis* the person who disregards it […]. "Natural ethics", as it is called, has nothing to offer here except the narcissistic satisfaction of being able to think better than others « (S.E, XXI, 143).

In spite of appearances, however, Freud's position cannot be called hedonistic, being as it is pervaded by realism, with a reference to the principle of reality and to Ananche as pointed out by Philip Rieff (1959, chap. 6)[6] who established the bounderies of a vision of psychoanalysis understood as ethics of motives. Besides which, the *Todestrieb* theory contradicts Bentham's utilitarianism [7] based on which human behaviour is caused by the self-preservation principle, by awaiting pleasure or pain or by balancing the two motives. But there is more. Some years after *Civilization and its Discontent*, while the Nazi storm was brewing, Freud in *The Man Moses and Monotheistic Religion* (1934-38) vigorously asserted the importance of *Geistigkeit* (spirituality/intellectuality) which means «pre-eminence given to intellectual labours» (115) but also *instinctual renunciation*. Describing Jewish monotheism, Freud shows how ethics and religion originate from instinctual renunciation: «Ethics is a limitation of instincts» (118). The development of ethics represents, in Freud's words, the «worthier alternative» (115) a civilization may reach, superior even to the Greek ideal of harmony «in cultivation of intellectual and physical activity (115). It is difficult to deny that the ideal of instinctual limitation is dealt with by Freud as a real value even if he does not refer explicitly to an *ethic of values,* that is to the neokantian position [8] Leon Grinberg summed up his own position and the positions of several analysts on ethics of psychoanalysis noting its similarity with *the ethics of science itself*: «psychoanalysis as a science shares, as such, the ethics of science in general for which the value –the "good that characterizes it"– is the discovery of truth, its assertion and its defence. The analyst must make both the repressed good and the repressed evil conscious» (Grinberg, 1971, Part I, § 3). For Money Kyrle: «Analysis is a rational process which accomplishes the only discovery of error and replaces it with truth» (quoted by Grinberg, *ibid*.).

Following this definition, the ethics of psychoanalysis would be, once again, an ethics of motives because reaching the truth would be a good producing wellbeing or a diminution of pathology in the individual. As regards the study of society, ethics would be, in Freud's opinion, a means through which society tries to master instincts and, above all, human aggressiveness. But Grinberg suggested, as we shall see further on, a reinterpretation of the concept of reparation which cannot be linked with the ethics of motives.

6　See Rieff, *Freud, the Mind of the Moralist,* chap. 9, § 4; Freud refers to *Ananche* also in *Discontent,* 625.

7　See Nicola Abbagnano, *Dizionario di filosofia,* 375.

8　In which values are expressed in historical ages as *Weltanschauungen* (Visions of the world). See Viano, 1975, 131-32.

Moreover, if we strictly follow the ethics of motives, as pointed out by Rieff, we still face a problem: a science that positions itself *neutrally with regard to the concept of value* easily becomes subservient to the aims of power and authority (Rieff, chap. 8, § 6).

If we relinquish the concept of value, we must ponder over how to safeguard, ethically and psychoanalytically, the right to have a critical viewpoint of society, especially in the light of the massacres of the 20th century.

RESPONSIBILITY AND CAPACITY TO REPAIR

Responsibility is a modern concept arising within 18th century theories of the contract between political representatives and citizens; first of all, it means that the individual accepts both *responding to the other,* and *responding for himself* before the other. There is no need for symmetry or reciprocity between subjects, or between subject and object, as pointed out by Hans Jonas (1979). Following this perspective, of Kantian origin, the subject draws the sense of its own existence from the acknowledgement of the existence of mankind, the others. Saying «I am» means saying «I am responsible».

Psychoanalysis is not only compatible with the ethics of responsibility but it may be considered a specific form of it: the work of remembering and reconstruction is based on the ethical principle of responsibility being, as it is, a way of bearing witness to truth and reality.

Moreover, if we interpret psychoanalysis as a discipline setting the foundation of subjectivity –a necessary foundation – in the acknowledgement of the duality Ego-other and in the dialogue, we find one of the grounds for the ethics of responsibility.

But there is still another psychoanalytical concept, the Kleinian concept of reparation which is even closer to the ethics of responsibility because it implies *that the subject finds its own sense in the respect of otherness.*

The capacity to repair is a result of the depressive position; the capacity to take upon oneself responsibility towards others is part of reparation.

What is the capacity to repair? According to Hanna Segal reparation or reparative capacity «Reparation proper can hardly be considered a defence since it is based on the recognition of psychic reality, the experiencing of the pain that this reality causes and the taking of appropriate action to relieve it in phantasy and reality» (Segal, 1964, 82) This, of course, applies to true capacity to repair, not to false reparation, maniacal or obsessional reparation.

«True» reparation is linked to the capacity for depressive guilt as Leon Grinberg has proved (1981). By the suitable expression «reparative vocation» of the analyst, Grinberg effectively describes the analyst's commitment not just towards the person being analyzed, but also towards society: «We analysts have implicitly, in our vocational choice, a tendency towards reparation. [...] I think that such a tendency towards reparation manifests itself not only in relation to the individual but also in relation to society» (*ibid*, 278)

It seems undeniable that through this concept Grinberg moves from the ethics of motives to the ethics of purpose. The expression «vocation» may be considered an assertion of the principle of responsibility implicating a reparatory potential. And the extension to the family and to society means extending the possibility of the subject (starting from the analyst) and the reparative ability (meaning the capacity to feel guilty and to feel loss for what has been damaged) even beyond what depends on or is easily controlled by the subject itself. *This implies recognizing that the destructiveness may come from other subjects, groups or society itself*, and rethinking ways to re-elaborate it.

A discussion that could be compared to Grinberg's is that of C. Fred Alford who introduces the concepts of reparative reason and reparative morality [9] in his work on Klein's theory of society. Alford stresses that Klein considers *altruism*, and therefore the concern for others, a primary human motive but not the self-preservation instinct and searching for pleasure as Freud had done. Following this consideration, he points out that Klein's is ethics of motives because there is no external ideal: «We feel guilty because we love the other yet have wished to harm him, not because we feel we have violated an ideal standard of our own, such as "do not harm those whom you love". The guilt of the Kleinian lover has nothing to do with violating a categorical imperative» (175-76).

Alford remarks in addition that «[…] reparative impulse is not automatically moral. It becomes moral only when it is applied in the right circumstances to the right people, standards that cannot be derived from the reparative impulse alone» (173-74). For this reason, he concludes: «[…] reparative morality is incomplete, because it cannot tell us when, how and toward whom we should direct our reparative impulses» (173).

So he points out the inadequacy of the ethics of motives, motives that are, in his interpretation of Klein, overlaying values.

But Freud's pessimism and the *Todestrieb* theory may be considered an extreme warning which human beings meet in every action guided by Eros, that is in building links. More than an explanation of the origins of destructiveness, *Todestrieb* is a warning against the threat of individual and group destructiveness, and the recurrence of such destructiveness. Above all, however, Alford stresses the critical and pessimistic character –which he calls «tragic» – of the Kleinian theory of society based as it is on the «fragility» of reparation at all levels.[10]

---

[9] Alford uses the word «morality» as will or good subjective intention, without, however, linking it explicitly to Hegel's theory of morality.

[10] See pp.10-11.

We may conclude that it is necessary to stress the ethical nature of Freud's and Klein's positions based on a choice of values: «With the *Todestrieb* Freud [...] more than asserting a scientific principle, asserts, in my opinion, an ethical value [...]. From this point of view, Kleinian theory of the more mature character of the depressive position compared to the paranoid-schizoid one is truly faithful to the spirit of Freud and *Todestrieb*» (Morpurgo, 1996, 215).

Let us now consider reparation, at a cognitive level, as a tendency to symbolization, and at the level of aggressive and destructive tendencies towards the object, not only as description of a mechanism but also as a process of *restoration of the structural parity of dignity between subjects.* Then reparation would be an unwarranted restoration process or perhaps a goal towards which the process tends. The same could apply, if we refer to Freud's conceptualization, to the process through which Eros, not accidentally defined «eternal» (as every goal) by Freud, tends to union and link.

In this sense reparation becomes a path and a process tending to infinity, with both a psychological and an ethical meaning as it warrants the attempt to keep or restore the structural parity of dignity and of value of the «Ego» and the «other».

After Auschwitz, after the tragedies of the 20th century, considering how easy it is to pervert truth and science itself which may be put to the service of bloody ideologies, we may wonder if in the mind of the analyst there should not be the consciousness of Kantian ethics (or derived from Kant as ethics of responsibility) giving equal dignity to the subject and to the other. This does not imply accepting principles or ethical theories external to psychoanalysis or questioning the autonomy of psychoanalysis as a science. It is enough to keep the assumptions alive, implicit in psychoanalysis, concerning the ethics of responsibility and to safeguard the ethical significance of Freud's and Klein's theories of society.

A CHARACTER FOR MAKING THE SHOAH THINKABLE: JOB

Psychoanalysis, faced with the trial of making the Shoah thinkable and with the horror of a trauma which had been repressed for two generations (Kaes, 1989), among its basic conceptual instruments, turned to the concept of the working through of mourning. René Kaes has stressed how the process of mourning, which deeply engages individuality, also has a collective, group aspect: mourning always has «a collective, social, cultural or religious inscription» (Kaes, 1989, II, § 6).

To suggest a way of working through mourning and imagine a way of thinking Auschwitz, let us consider Wiesel's moving words on the biblical story of Job in *Sei meditazioni sul Talmud* (Six Meditations on Talmud)(2000).

Job is the just man to suffer for terrible evils that he cannot understand, and he turns to God asking for an explanation. Job is personally involved but he also calls upon God to fulfil *his responsibility*, and God, in his answers, which pose questions on the origin of the world, admits his responsibility towards the human being.

With the story of Job, Wiesel represents the path of mourning in processing depressive guilt, and reaching a reparative position because he stresses Job's ability to overcome his desperate protest. Job calls upon God without revolting against him, that is «he does not accuse him of the loss of the object, holding him responsible for it» (Grinberg, 1971),[11] and he does not split the image of God into a holy figure and a demonic one. And since he does not split the Super Ego, he does not make the Super Ego a persecutory agency. So, despite going through inexplicable suffering and terrible mourning, Job does not lose the good object.

He saves himself and lives a new life, he retrieves his possessions and has other children. But…nobody will give him back his lost children. *The reparative process does not have a happy ending*. Working through mourning ends in acceptance not in cancelling loss.

Through his words Wiesel voices the transformative aspects of reparation which does not abolish mourning, or deny loss. Thinking in reparative terms does not mean working through to conclude or annul mourning and loss, and not even guilt and shame. On the contrary, thinking in reparative terms and in ethics of responsibility terms means accepting the depressive burden.

Wiesel refers to a discussion in the Talmud: if two friends are lost in a desert and only one has enough water to survive, what will they do?[12]

«When the surviving friend comes out of the desert, he is no longer alone. He will have to live two lives, his own and the life of his dead friend. Does this viewpoint not count for all of us, Jews and non Jews alike? It does count for us who survived tragedies in which other people died. Once we have overcome the tragedy, we are no longer alone: we must continue to live for those and in the name of those who are no more» (Wiesel, 2000,150-51). The person who menages to escape from the desert, the survivor, has the duty to bear the moral burden, which is a depressive burden, also for those who are dead. Every individual is responsible, always, under all conditions, for other people. Thus Wiesel points out a form of capacity of thinking an unthinkable tragedy: it is not a question of «explaining» the anxiety of the «drowned» but of accepting the burden of their suffering.

---

[11] See the chapter on Jakob's mourning, in *Culpa y depresión*, Part III, chap. 23.

[12] Wiesel refers here to a discussion in the Talmud, in the Baba Metzia treatise, between Rabbi Akiba, the great scholar, and Ben Petura. The dramatic question concerns the case of two friends who are in the desert and only one has a supply of water sufficient to save himself and escape. The problem is: should they share the water and meet certain death or is it right that only the person who has the water uses it to survive and look for help? The question concerns the subject of universal love and of love for one's neighbour. Wiesel's solution is particularly interesting because it does not answer the anguished question with a solution once and for all, but it transfers the problem of responsibility to the survivor.

This is the burden, and this is the wealth of the survivor. But are survivors only the survivors of the Shoah or are they all of us witnesses? Aren't we, the «saved» responsible to the Other, the «drowned», even if they are distant in space and time, if they belong to the past or are inscribed in the future?

SUMMARY

To think about Auschwitz means trying to represent catastrophic events, which, if not processed, tend to pass on in a pathogenic way from one generation to the next. In different forms many authors (such as J. Chasseguet, S. Amati Sas, J. Puget) pointed out the risk of loosing the ethics. Freud himself in his last book pointed out to the capability of instinctual renunciation as an ethical value, which is at the basis of Jewish spirituality (*Geistigkeit*) We can look for clues of an ethics of the psychoanalytical treatment, the ethics of responsibility, that focuses on the subject and human subjectivity. The psychoanalytical concept of reparation implicitly contains some aspects of the ethics of responsibility. Reparation is not only a process with a certain outcome, but a working through tending to the reintegration of the damaged object and to the acceptance of loss and mourning.

REFERENCES:

ABBAGNANO N. (1964). *Dizionario di filosofia*. Torino, UTET.

AGAMBEN G. (1998). *Quel che resta di Auschwitz*. Torino, Einaudi.

ALFORD C. F. (1989). *Melanie Klein and critical social theory*. New Haven, Yale Univ.Press.

AMATI SAS S. (1989). Récupérer la honte. In J. Puget, R. Käes eds., *Violence d'etat et psychanalyse*, Paris, Dunod.

AMATI SAS S. (2004). L'interpretation dans le trans-subjectif. Réflexions sur l'ambïguité et les espaces psychiques. *Psychotherapies*, 24.

BARANGER M. (1963). Mala fé, identidad y omnipotencia. *Revista Uruguaya de Psicoanàlisis*, 2-3.

BAUMAN Z. (1989). *Modernity and the Holocaust*, Cambridge, UK, Polity Press.

BAUMAN Z. (2003). *Intervista sull'identità*. Bari, Laterza, 2003.

BETTELHEIM B. (1952). Holocaust a generation after. In *Surviving and other Essays*, New York, Alfred A. Knopf.

BLEGER J. (1967). *Simbiosis y ambiguedad*. Buenos Aires, Paidòs.

CHASSEGUET-SMIRGEL J. (1973). *The Ego ideal*. New York, W.W. Norton, 1985.

CHASSEGUET.SMIRGEL J. (1984). *Creativity and perversion*. New York, W.W. Norton.

ERLICH S. *Der Mann Moses* and the Man Freud: Psychoanalytic Identity and Anti- Semitism, Presentation for Italian Psychoanalytic Centres, May 2005.

FORNARI F. (1970). *Psicoanalisi della situazione atomica*. Milano, Rizzoli.

FREUD S. (1929). *Civilization and its Discontents*. SE, XXI.

FREUD S. (1934-38). *Moses and Monotheism*. SE, XXIII.

GRINBERG L. (1971). *Culpa y depresion*. Buenos Aires, Paidos.

GRINBERG L. (1981). *Psicoanálisis. Aspectos teóricos y clinicos*. Buenos Aires, Paidos.

KÄES R. (1989). Ruptures catastrophiques. In J. Puget, R. Käes (eds.), *Violence d'Etat et psychanalyse*, Paris, Dunod.

KIJAK M. (2005). Efectos persistentes de los traumas sociales en las nuevas generaciones. Cambios en la imagen ética del hombre. Paper read at the IPA Congress in Rio de Janeiro, 2005.

JONAS H. (1979). The imperative of responsibility. In *Search of ethics for the technological age*, Chicago, Univ. of Chicago Press.

LACOUE LABARTHE P. (1987). *La fiction du politique*. Strasbourg, Christian Bourgois.

Italian translation: *La finzione del politico*, Genova, Il Melangolo, 1991, 54-55.

LACOUE LABARTHE P., NANCY J.L. (1991). *Le mythe nazi*. La tour d'Aigues, L'Aube.

LANZMANN C. (1991). The obscenity of understanding: an evening with Claude Lanzmann. *American Imago*, 48, 473.

LEVI P. (1987). *The drowned and the saved*. London, Little &Brown, 1991.

MORPURGO E. (1996). *Chi racconta a chi?* Milano. Franco Angeli.

NEHER A. (1970). *L'exile de la parole. Du silence biblique au silence d'Auschwitz*. Paris, Seuil.

NIELSEN N. P. (2004). *L'universo mentale nazista*. Milano. Franco Angeli.

PLATO. *Gorgias*. In *The Dialogues of Plato*, translated by Benjamin Jowett, New York, Random House, 1937.

PUGET J. (1989). *The state of threat and psychoanalysis*, London, Free Association, n.13. Also published in *Violence d'Etat et psychanalyse*, Paris, Dunod

RIEFF P. (1959). *Freud, the mind of the moralist*. London,Victor Gollancz.

QUINZIO S. (2002). *La speranza nell'apocalisse*. Milano. Edizioni Paoline.

SEGAL H. (1964). *Introduction to the work of Melanie Klein*. London. Heinemann

VIANO C.A. (1975). *Etica*. Milano. ISEDI.

WIESEL E. (2000). *Sei riflessioni sul Talmud*. Milano. Bompiani.

Original italian version:
Riv.Psicoanal., 2007, 2, 515-527

Valeria Egidi Morpurgo

Via Uberti, 12

20129 Milano

(Translated by Romano C. Cerrone)

Freud's objects. Plurality and complexity in the analyst's inner world and in his «working Self»

STEFANO BOLOGNINI

In a touching and well-researched paper published in 1989, Lynn Gamwell, Director of the Art Museum of the State University of New York, wrote about Freud's sizeable collection of ancient art. She noted that Freud began to surround himself with valuable ancient artefacts (mainly small sculptures) after his father's death, in the 1890s, which were also the years in which his scientific and professional isolation was greatest.

At that time Freud set up for himself «an attentive audience of objects, including an Egyptian scribe, a Greek goddess of wisdom and a Chinese sage. […] These hundreds of human and animal figures were all turned to face him, in the manner of a large audience. […] He wrote thousands of pages under the watchful eye of Imhotepe, the Egyptian architect venerated in antiquity as a healer. […] Various accounts recount that Freud regarded these figures as companions».

However, these presences were not merely surrogates for the colleagues who, at the time, he was still without: despite the success of psychoanalysis, the ongoing conflicts over theory and among groups left him bitterly disappointed. Oppressed by such diatribes, the founder of psychoanalysis always returned to his desk and to his tried and trusted audience, who represented wisdom throughout the ages for him.

A constituent world of external/internal objects, therefore, a source at the same time of comfort and inspiration in a potentially creative, illusory middle-ground.

At the end of his life, after a long illness, Freud decided to die in his study, among his figures «his chosen ancestors, his most faithful colleagues and the personification of the truth of psychoanalysis which had been brought to light by him».

We are less alone today.

In the rooms of colleagues from other cities or nations, which I like to visit in order to be able to imagine them at work in my personal evocations during sessions, I have often come across at least one photo of Freud, and occasionally one of Klein, or maybe Winnicott, and in some cases portraits of the colleague's personal analyst and his/her supervisors; while quite rarely – appropriately – do I find likenesses of the analyst's family, clear rivals for the patient, best kept hidden in respect for the patient's temporary centrality, allowing him/her complete liberty to fantasise.

I must say that it is rare to find the indecipherable and spartan neutrality recommended up until some decades ago to ensure a «blank screen» in these rooms: today's analysts appear to have at least partially, and externally, given up the supposed ideal of the untraceability of their Self in the professional relationship with the patient, and, judging from the articulate language of their chosen decor, seem rather inclined to officially admit their existence as individuals as well as bearers/carriers of a mere function. Having the sense and good taste to limit themselves naturally to a perceptible, while at the same time usually sober, personalisation of the room, thereby avoiding the risk of narcissistically invading the workplace with a display of their private iconography.

The real presences in that room, however, those that actually count and make a difference, are not visible to the patient; even though they may cohabit in the space for years they will not be aware of them, for they are to be found in the mind and heart of the analyst.

The one *ex-officio* presence that patients always take for granted, *a priori*, is that of Sigmund Freud, well-known to all and of whom they have cultivated an entirely subjective image.

Generally speaking, it is «their» Freud, rarely that of the therapist.

The patient is unaware of who the other masters of reference may be, the best-loved authors, the colleagues with whom he/she has established an external and inner dialogue, or the cultural community in which the analyst plays an active part.

As I mentioned, we are less alone today, and our collective exchanges are both lively and frequent enough to obviate the need for such a quantity of interlocutors in effigy form as Freud had (I shudder to imagine the variety of comments we would hear today on an analyst's study furnished in the manner of Berggasse 19).

A century of psychoanalysis leaves us to address the difficult wealth of the complexity of theory models, and poses a problem of abundance: how to host, in our scientific-professional imaginary world, the plurality of foundation scientific presences along with the daily ones; an antagonistic plurality of that longed-for unicity which narcissism tends to defend at all costs as the dimension of choice. What still prevents us from recognising and appreciating such plurality and complexity at least a little is, at times, a problem of transference (Klauber, 1981; Rangell, 1982; Smith, 2003; Reeder, 2004; Spurling, 2003; Ambrosiano, 2005; Bolognini, 2002, 2005; Foresti and Rossi Monti, 2006), or, in any case, of *multi-object cohabitation* with inspirational figures considered at times less as equivalents to parental or family figures in the evolved sense of the term (and thus with their not over-idealised characterisations and limits), but more as «full parents» in the archaic, unique and pre-Oedipal mould: a parent not to be «disloyal to» placed in a broader family context, then growing and differentiating oneself, while at the same time belonging to him or with whom to identify completely rather than partially.

Freud, Ferenczi or Klein, Winnicott, Bion, Kohut, Lacan, no matter who: the transference script which may at times be played out – at a not very evolved level, in the unconscious area of the inner world of analysts or of analytical Societies – tends to be essentially similar, and the risk is that it may lead to parochial over-simplification of the inner self and a corresponding consequence in the professional and institutional fields.

Two preliminary points need to be set out: the first concerns the fact that many of the subsequent observations are to be read with reference both to the analyst's inner world and to the by-products and repercussions reciprocally flowing between the inner world and the institutional world which, while they do not coincide, are not totally independent of each other either.

The second point: the debate I intend to develop is not in favour of a generic theoretic-clinical eclecticism but rather, – I would stress – comes out in favour of recognition of the plurality and the complexity of our contemporary horizons, in continuous and demanding evolution, and of the usability of these in exchanges with colleagues and in the privacy of everyday reflection on theoretical and clinical issues.

Continuing the round-up of «the language of objects», this time in collective workplaces and studies, that is, in institutes and the offices of psychoanalytical societies in the three continents of psychoanalysis, what is striking is the manner in which official iconography as hung on the walls represents, in the majority of instances, two series of portraits: that of the super-national Great Masters, which officialises the historical branching off of psychoanalytic research, and a more home-grown and reassuring one portraying local predecessors (usually a collection of pictures of past Presidents), which acts as the point of junction between the ideal and family history, and as shock-absorber in the dilemma concerning plurality and the assurance of the institution's identity and continuity.

TRANSFERENCE UNICITY

It is quite natural that each analyst makes choices in terms of theory and choice, and that a given author may satisfy an individual's, or a group's, overall scientific vision requirements more than others, characterising his/her scientific identity, just as it is realistic (regardless of the choice of destination harbour) that a young analyst undergoing training may elect one author as a beacon to ships at sea, which requires a temporary, natural simplification of the theory field in order to lay the foundations of his/her emerging theoretical and technical subjectivity.

I wish to deal here with a *grey area* which may lie hidden behind certain theory over-simplifications, and which is due to an excess of transference on the analyst's part towards the parental or narcissistic equivalent as represented by the inspirational object, and which may represent a hindrance to exchanges with colleagues: the symptom of this grey area being an incapacity to communicate with the «Other than Self», which is unconsciously feared as being dangerous or too disturbing. This grey area does not coincide at all with the strong and authentic identification group which may well be established using a theory arrangement based even on a single inspirational figure, having a simple and authentic internal constituent identity (that is to say, clearly identified and separate from the inner object of reference); but it is distinguished by *symptoms «of closure» towards an exterior which does not provide immediate confirmation.*

It is the duty of a sufficiently mature therapist to remain vigilant, reflective and self-critical towards a possible tendency to implement an idealising, archaic transference towards a specific, hyper-possessive inner object («Thou shalt have no other gods but me!»), such transference operating as protection against the disturbing experience of a plurality of family presences.

In effect, plurality sounds offensive to our original narcissism which wishes us, underneath it all, to be in an intimate, exclusive and privileged internal and external union with one confirming, mirroring, parental or narcissistic equivalent.

My first patient in analysis springs to mind, a young engineer, the second of four children, who could not bear it when another player in his favourite football team (Inter in 1980) scored instead of his beloved Rummenigge, the symbol of a perfect and idealized narcissism and of invincible «German» technology which clearly represented the projection of his ideal Self.

This man found it unbearable that also in his field of work (civil engineering) there was not one only point of reference, one Great Master, able to provide a solution to each and any technical problem: there was, it must be said, a certain Leonhardt that he quoted to me incessantly and who appeared to be the *non plus ultra* in the sector, but who, tragically, was not up to dealing with the most disparate situations. To give an example, having been charged with designing footpaths in his town, this engineer discovered, to his dismay, that the great Leonhardt had had nothing at all to say on this matter, meaning that he would have no option but to ask the advice of an engineer by the name of Semenzato, a colleague just a few years older than him who had carried out similar work in a neighbouring town, and who would have been able to give him some useful pointers. The prospect of such a thing sounded offensive and narcissistically unacceptable to his ears: to sink from Leonhardt to Semenzato?!? … unthinkable! … «Why – he shouted during his sessions – why is it that in civil engineering we do not have a unique and absolute equivalent of Dante Alighieri, considered by all as unquestionably "THE SUPREME POET"???».

It goes without saying that at the time I was scarcely a few years older than him, and that I was at risk of appearing dangerously equivalent to the very provincial Semenzato, an older brother in professional terms who disturbingly interposed himself on the unique and mirroring relationship with his narcissistic Ideal.

It must be said, as an extenuating factor for my young patient, that complexity and plurality really do not constitute a restful circumstance: they require harder work and a much greater inner space than elementary functions of the «o – o» type do.

In a paper dealing with the area of training (*La famiglia interna dell'analista*, 2005) I underlined the need to broaden the family background of the working Self to include an extended structure in which the equivalent of analytical grandparents, uncles, aunts, cousins and siblings could be found, as it is these figures as a whole, these potential interlocutors, that constitute substantial wealth for the purposes of *inner consultation* during clinical pactice.

We well know that many authors, over these last hundred years or so, have provided a useful description of at least one specific aspect or portion of the workings of the minds of human beings. We are also well aware that many of them, be it for narcissistic, Oedipal or generational reasons, have given prominence to their own discoveries and acquisitions as if they felt the need to replace those going before them by invalidating them; others, more measuredly, realised that they were putting forward extensions, changes of perspective as well as additions and integrations rather than replacement theories, and stated officially (Klein and Kohut spring to mind) their intention to provide continuity of thinking with respect to the works that went before them: except for then dedicating the vast majority of their work to the presentation only of new aspects to which they could claim copyright. In this manner they effectively provoked the implicit conviction, in the minds of readers and of fellow professionals, that the old had been fully replaced by the new, with the foreseeable opposite effect resulting in rejection by some and absolute proselytism in others.

Just as in the past, some psychoanalysts today express themselves, in their writings, as if Freud (theoretically speaking) were no longer one of their fundamental points of reference, while in fact he still is, even if only as results from their implicit assumptions at starting point. They appear to deny, in any event, the fact that Freud was the first to bring up rather a large number of points, and launched explorative thinking on many issues well in advance of subsequent developments.

Others, vice versa, consider that Freud said it all, really, and that any further follow-up is not «derivative» (perhaps inevitable and appropriately integrative), but rather «drifting», with respect to his works, and they issue glowering warnings not to deviate from what they consider the straight and narrow, as if every new aspect were an expression of opposition (an assumption which – unless wielded selectively – runs the risk of becoming a vice-like grip).

In any event, our pre-conscious mind could not care less about either total *a priori* rejection or complete proselytism, and therefore, at specific stages in treatment or during a given session, cavalierly by-passing the barriers put up by our preferences, just when (and if) we least expect it, it reminds us of this or that author, perhaps even one we are not particularly fond of or do not hold in any particular regard, who has written a good deal on certain patterns or certain developments which at that moment – dammit! – certainly fit to a T, and which, to be honest, enable us to see or understand something new: just like an unloved relative providing us with useful tools in some unexpected and vaguely upsetting circumstance.

Although it is not that the pre-conscious is always to be taken literally: the central Ego is fully entitled to come up with its own observations and to make choices, drawing from them at a secondary level.

However, the preconscious is an interlocutor deserving of respect, and not simply because – if allowed to express itself – it has its own unforeseen and unsuppressible originality, and we would do well to listen to it: free association, at times, seems to gain access even to theory, through creative and thoughtful interaction with clinical practice.

It is up to us to integrate, or more modestly, to allow, certain unexpected and logically non-coherent connections which surprise us during a session to live together in an intermediate interlocutory area. At times, if one is patient, they may turn out to be less incompatible and contradictory that at first appeared: more or less as happens from time to time among families or groups, when contributions which seem to undermine the coherence of a certain way of seeing things then demonstrate an unexpected productiveness.

It must also be underlined that an assumed theoretical rigour on the logic front may in some cases be a sign of a certain rigidity and intolerance at psychological level, hindering contact and consultation with a number of inner interlocutors having diversified competences (like mother and father, originally, with their respective languages and mindsets, as experienced by the child during his upbringing and in the adult's inner consultations).

The problem that I am describing, in effect, is that of the *contactability and consultability of an extended inner group* which may (and I underline *may*, and not *must*) be part of the authentic inner world of the contemporary analyst.

I wish to add that I maintain with due care a distinction between the *working Ego* and the *working Self*: inner interlocutors are part and parcel of the latter while the workingl Ego consults them, and eventually, if it is sufficiently independent and mature, takes a position, chooses and reaches a decision.

The complex setting out of our inner organisation during sessions does not constitute an insurmountable obstacle for therapists: we are quite well trained, for example, in exercising suspension of judgement, in considering allocentered points of view, in identification alternated and crossed with a number of characters appearing on the stage, in dealing with continual flashbacks and flash-forwards, in moving from outer to inner and their being simultaneously present, in perceiving desire behind defences, etc; it is fair to say that on average we are tried and tested when it comes to setting up a complex mental scenario.

There are certainly others who outshine us in this sense: philosophers, to give an example, have an overriding, dynamic advantage, as they are more used to addressing abstract concepts than emotional experiences.

I would go so far as to suggest that usually, unlike us and with all due exceptions, they *travel without hand baggage*: the baggage of memories, emotions and sensations which we carry with us, for inevitable association, when each theoretical reference brings us back to the sessions, to our clinical and personal histories, to more or less painful and difficult situations under therapy.

The philosophers, our cousins in thought, specialise in conceptual exploration, which for the most part evokes other conceptual explorations, and this is why – at least apparently less weighed down by emotional loads – they seem better equipped to tolerate complexity.

Also in discussing our theories I believe that we analysts must frequently tolerate a complexity which is not yet rational, but evocative, somewhat greater than that requested of those who, in their reasoning, are legitimately unhooked from the continuous, intense evocation of experience.

The other highly specific point in which psychoanalysis can be seen to be a «science operating under special rules» lies, in my opinion, in its acceptance of the alternation *of primary and secondary process as a functional regime, specific to the mind of the analyst.*

The problem I place before you is this: *is this true only for clinical practice, or is it true also for theoretical reflection on the specifics of psychoanalysis?*

I can understand how, for a «normal» epistemologist, a reply which allows for alternating primary/secondary functioning *also in the manner of theoretical reflection* may sound unacceptable: in that by alternating functioning the principle of contradiction may be suspended, and in an assessment of the validity of two contrasting theories «Occam's razor»[1] may also not work, as it does not consider the *ability to cohabit* of two theories which are coherent within themselves, but not one with the other: a frequently occurring paradox, often proving fruitful in the *real* mind of the analyst (and not in the ideal mind).

---

[1] Occam suggested that among the various explanations for a natural phenomenon, it is preferable to choose the one that does not multiply useless entities (*entia non sunt multiplicanda*); usually used as a rule of thumb when choosing from among various hypotheses offering equivalent explanations for one or more natural phenomena observed.

Antithetic theories and models may therefore share a certain degree of «truth» (or more modestly, of usefulness) which each one would normally rationally exclude in the other: if it were not that in certain cases one perspective may appear more fertile and move liveable with than the other and in certain cases vice versa, as in effect it may happen that they co-exist not undeservedly from a clinical point of view.

The diversity of opinion on what in psychoanalysis today may be defined as «research» (there is a current of opinion which restricts the term to mean empirical research and another which extends it to conceptual research, and then there are those who see clinical practice as creative inquiry, those who demand objective, statistical or psychometric measurability of the variables observed, and so forth), is emblematic in this sense, and seems to suggest a degree of caution with regard to a possible categorical judgment on methodology. A good example is provided by the exchange of opinions between Otto Kernberg and Roger Perron (2006) published in the last issue of the *International Journal of Psychoanalysis*.

I am aware that I am treading on a wasp's nest, and so I will go no further than to simply make reference to the issue.

Let us return to complexity and plurality, and their effects on theory and clinical practice. A critical point for we analysts is, for example, linked to the theoretical-clinical decision either to «condense» the representations of the object into the unicity of the base transference relationship, or vice versa, to give voice to, tolerate and agree with a certain plurality of presences on the analytical stage, employing creative management of the session, oneiric level included, to deal with the «one», the «two», the «three», and the «more than three» depending on the situation of the moment.

The multiple figures present in a speech or a dream may be seen as the separated or fragmented products of a narcissistic portrayal (only images of parts of the Self), or of a binary situation (images of the Self and of the object); otherwise they may be deemed as pertaining to more highly organised spheres of the inner scenario, such as Oedipal triangulation, family set-up or a group situation which may be important and relevant to the subject at a given time, etc.

The multiplications and complexity of the representations of the Self, or of Self and object, may also depend upon the existence of a high level of anguish, which may produce multiple splitting as a defense mechanism, and therefore the degree of fragmentation of these representations may also be indicative of the patient's emotional state.

In such a case, however, we endeavour mainly to reintegrate the aspects of the Self that are split.

In other cases the dispersion of the representations of the object into many figures on the stage indicates a need to interpret this multiplication of representatives in terms of transference, re-connecting this apparent plurality of figures to the representation of the object-analyst.

In yet other circumstances we find ourselves required to decide whether or not to grant a certain degree of separate object dignity to a figure which may begin to exist in the patient's inner world in continuity with transference, and of which we are sure that it is an extension, while it begins to take on a progressively more different status, gaining the right to claim independent citizenship status in the patient's life as a result of its on-going existence and consistence.

A classic, in this sense, is the manner in which developments in the patient's love life are treated. Depending on the clinical context, the analyst may choose to give pre-eminent importance to the aspects of the patient's shift away from the analyst himself to an external object as defence mechanism; or those – more mature developments – of an evolutive moving to a new, realistic and possible object (the analyst becoming, in this case, a post-Oedipal parent capable of relinquishing); or again, at a much more regressive level, those which may grasp the opportunity, through the new entry, to «retrieve» some element of the patient which – after splitting, blasting from afar and exile well beyond the borders of the Self – had been waiting for who knows how long for an opportunity for introjective representation or reintegration in a Self which may still only be portrayed through an image of the couple, and so on.

What is important is that the therapist's perceptive qualities are finely tuned, that he has a sufficiently wide array of configurations and models at his disposal in his «working Self», and that he displays a degree of internal mobility in his «working Ego».

On the subject of possessing an adequate amount of models and configurations, a curious episode which occurred around forty years ago springs to mind.

At the end of the sixties, new habits, new cultural perspectives and new professions began to emerge in Italy as a result of the economic boom, including – in addition to psychoanalysts –sommeliers, i.e. advisors with refined tastes, introducing new drinking habits.

I was both struck and amazed one evening in an elegant restaurant in the capital, when one of these specialists approached our table with his silver tastevin around his neck, consulted the menu which we had chosen (based mainly on lamb) and after deep thought advised us that a Blauburgunder Sudtiroler from '65 was, in his opinion, precisely what was required.

Those were the years in which James Bond confidently ordered an exclusive millesimé champagne by the year and I was convinced that our expert must be a bottomless pit of knowledge.

I became somewhat perplexed, however, when, moving a couple of tables away, I heard him recommend the same Blauburgunder, with the same pretentiousness, to a couple who had ordered ham and melon. At that point I became fascinated with eavesdropping on his subsequent conversations at the various tables, discovering that he managed to offload a good case of Blauburgunder, regardless of whether the hapless diners had ordered Dover sole or game from the Italian highlands. And yet, judging from the way he moved and expressed himself, he had seemed to me to be an expert of the highest order.

Now, I suspect that it can be no easy matter to work with such inner mobility unless one is willing to collaborate at least to a certain extent with those diverse inspirational objects which, with introjective authenticity, have become part of our inner psychoanalytical family.

These objects may act as a third party with respect to the analyst-patient twosome, or even with respect to the dyad formed by the analyst and another over-englobing inner object – in any case with respect to a group of two, rather than to a couple.

I believe that at times the therapist runs the risk of forming a narcissistic dyad, instead of a differentiated couple, even with the aid of a master or a favourite author. In addition, as regularly occurs in the early stages of clinical practice, the inner identification regime may induce the analyst to *become* his own analyst or supervisor, *acting as them* and losing touch with his own Self instead of remembering them and consulting them while remaining himself.

The therapist's harmony and integration of theory and technical aspects certainly depend on his basic nature, the forming of his personality and his years of training. These underpinning factors go to make up a sort of «complex personal equation» for the therapist, making him unique and specific with respect to any category standard.

What I am attempting to point out here is how harmony is also the fruit of a relative (and in any case humanly precarious) acceptance of plurality and conflict in a sufficiently loving inner sphere, possibly being equipped with a good grounding of physiological narcissism.

The latter is provided primarily by mother and father and by their subsequent equivalents, then by analysis, and later on – let me add – by an adequate and not unrealistic overall enhancing of the family/institution from which one has grown, which constitutes an inner object of fundamental importance to the analyst.

PLURALITY IN PSYCHOANALYSIS TODAY

Although André Green in the pages of the *International Journal of Psychoanalysis* (2005) criticised Wallerstein's idea of *common ground* and of the «many psychoanalyses» with a certain vehemence, the IPA Congress in Rio in 2005 in my opinion in fact confirmed the progressive, substantial acceptance by the community of a fertile variety of currents of analytical thought in which the novelty is not in the *variety* (well-documented) but in *fertile*, as it has been clearly perceived that analysts have become tired of wars of religion and find it increasingly more normal to exchange ideas and organise panels comprising colleagues from different backgrounds holding differing views.

The fertility is provided by the fact that therapists of varying origin no longer restrict themselves to singing from their own hymn sheet on their own behalf, operating – as it were – «in parallel», but are beginning to *join in* with a certain curiosity, *without doing their best to «convert» the other, but rather with a view to setting up an exchange of ideas which is in no way threatening to their respective identities.*

This is what we see in international group clinical case discussion.

The «monochrome», panel, on the other hand, is considered less attractive than it used to be at congresses, and at times runs the risk of repeating self-confirming parochial atmospheres, although it comes into its own when re-examining a highly characterised cultural biotope which it may avail of in its internal references. These observations still hold true, without any great discontinuity, with respect to the analyst's internal and external environment, in particular, they do not refer so much to whether one has few or many mentors during one's training as to whether one has *few or many interlocutors* – possibly quite dissimilar one from another, in both the parental vein and the fraternal vein – *to converse creatively with, both externally and internally.*

By the way, our *mono-Leonhardt* engineer went to Semenzato in the end, with the result that the footpaths were given a collegial genesis, rather than an autarchic or divine one.

Like many of my Italian colleagues, for many years now I have had the opportunity to establish relationships for the exchanging of views with psychoanalysts of different backgrounds, training, residence and tradition.

I may say that (with what I have discovered to be a shared sensation) the first meetings recalled those with distant expatriate relatives of the third or fourth generation: mutual curiosity, some misgivings, the awareness of a common family history, while at the same time – powerful and undeniable – the experiences of a stranger.

A number of ghosts, some of them projective in nature, generated an initial and ill-concealed tension: and even the promising diversification of genealogical lines, which in meetings with foreign colleagues should have fostered the potential for cross-fertilisation without the foreseeable marching on the spot of reassuring and confirming reiterations well known in local environments, was in danger of being an early defensive bulwark.

Taking part in international discussion groups with colleagues of differing nationality, but more importantly, *from different schools,* has enabled me, little by little, to dispel some of these ghostly presences without having to give up my original family background identity.

I have met people keen to work on clinical material with authentic curiosity towards the contributions of others, perhaps sharing an implicit, spontaneous pre-selection process: these groups attract people who are well-disposed, regardless of their (often highly personalised) professional background, to taking advantage of contact and exchange in a climate of effective cultural otherness.

More complex has been the experience with CAPSA (*Committee on Analytic Practice and Scientific Activity*), the new initiative set up in 2005 by the President of the *International Psychoanalytical Association*, Claudio Eizirik, to facilitate inter-continental exchanges on issues related to theory and clinical practice, through an official network of specific invitations, by the Society, to colleagues who can present their direct experience of the different ways of working in the three large areas covered by the IPA. Briefly, I can say that the few cases of initial resistance to such cross-exchanges came from countries with a strong local characterization in theory terms, perhaps more used to self-confirming situations and, generally speaking, more inclined towards exporting their psychoanalysis rather than importing from others. The positive results emerging from the first year of meetings seem to light the way towards a new period in the history of our Association.

On the subject of «psychoanalytic families», I have no intention of foisting on you an update on «how much Freud», how much Klein, how much Winnicott, Lacan, Kohut, Bion, etc. one comes across at the various psychoanalytic societies on different continents, according to the local stock exchange quotations or considering the *impact factors* gathered by attending such meetings. I do wish, however, to share with you the lasting impression that I have formed over the years and through a growing number of interpersonal contacts, and which contributes to my overall analytic viewpoint today.

It appears to me that a process of actual transformation of a number of «incom-patibilities» is being undergone in many countries, not in the sense of a cancellation through denial of discontinuity and theory differences, but rather in the sense of a *recognition of the existence, of inter-consultability and of the dignity of the different psychoanalyses* (in marked parallel with the very recent official acceptance of the existence of different training models within the IPA), while at the same time a labo-rious yet progressive pacifying of the conflicts concerning the historical, scientific, institutional, family, theoretical and clinical figure of Sigmund Freud is taking place.

Do I run the risk of providing an over-simplified version if I say that Freud, in our collective imagination, is slowly and laboriously *becoming (also) a grandfather*? [2]

---

[2] I wish to refer here not to whether Freud is «passé» or not – an issue on which the press periodically interro-gates analysts in a summary and provocatory manner – but rather to the fact that others after him may have con-tinued the intergenerational chain with the characteristics and prerogatives of equally worthy generativity and parenthood, both original and their own.

I believe that this point – what we may refer to as Freud's possible grandfatherhood in the interior world of analysts – requires clarification: knowing how to become a good grandparent means accepting that others, after us, may also give birth; and that it is the procreative ability of our successors which proves the quality of the origi-nating roots.

May we believe that by virtue of his extraordinary (but not divine) fertility he now has many grandchildren, and that no one of them is, inter-generationally speaking, the *only* child having the right of the first-born and exclusive entitlement to inherit both title and estate?

We would not be doing Freud any great service, and even less to our internal Freud, if we were to imagine his children and grandchildren as mere clones of pre-scribed codes. On the contrary, in general terms, recognizing himself to be a descen-dant of Freud is for the therapist the natural product of deeply-rooted feelings of authentic gratitude and admiration.

And not only: quite apart from a recognition of common genealogical and histor-ical roots, the majority of therapists do not at all repudiate the importance and the soundness of Freud's discoveries. They feel – if not authorized– encouraged to take their research further, towards new areas, making use also of new theoretical and technical tools. I would tend to stress the word *also*.

Just as I consider the pole of selective rigour necessary and essential in scientific psychoanalysis, I hope to have contributed here to providing dialectical representa-tion also of the other pole within which the field of our discipline may prosper and fertilise itself: that of prudent, careful and no less selective confidence in its own potential developments.

I feel myself to be the son of classical psychoanalysis, which I treasure and of which «I throw nothing away», but I feel it to be a family type of relationship, and not holy or idealized, much less fetishistic.

This enables me, I feel, to approach the new with interest, without feeling overly guilty or fearful, under the watchful eye of my forebears.

Moreover, I also think that our past masters showed courage in exploring the unknown without restricting themselves to the «holy scriptures», and that this is just what we need to learn from them in the first place, while of course holding on to our appropriate critical faculties.

At the same time, I do not harbour any compulsive anxiety to get rid of the family paintings or library: I am not intolerant of my roots, if I am not hidebound to reli-gious repetition of the same without being allowed to add anything of my own per-sonal creativity or our shared, fraternal generational creativity.

That is the manner in which I see our «post-modern» state: as a substantial family-like appreciation, rendered human, not idealized, of our original psychoanalytical objects, giving full recognition to the inheritance that has been passed down.

From where, aside from our transference, but possibly using the energy of our transference, we may move forward through two poles: that of appreciation of a valuable inheritance which is not to be squandered, and that of having courage to face new frontiers to be conquered, just as Sigmund Freud and his pupils, the pioneers, did, at times alone and at other times as a group.

It is definitely true that we are not alone today, unless we choose to be so, and if we understand how to make good use of the presences and the resources available in our field.

Over the last few years, the most comforting notes I have heard have come from clinical meetings: banal as it may be, working together, among colleagues, driven by the pulsions and vicissitudes of the individual's narcissistic stock-taking, the inter-subjective implications in meetings and the over-assessment of the paths of transference, the re-introjection of divided elements, falling into rêveries and recovery of memories, are concepts which are less and less alien to each other, and increasingly less incompatible in the real mind (not in the ideal one) of analysts, who usually maintain a very clear idea of origin as distinct from the relevancy of concepts within the different models.

I may be describing a complex, long wave movement which concerns the evolution of the international psychoanalytical community in its scientific and institutional aspects (CAPSA is, in the end, an «emerging entity» in this complex process): *the movement for meeting and exchange while respecting difference and plurality.*

I would like to conclude by bringing this issue (which, given the geographical spread of psychoanalysis we see today, is at risk of taking on a planetary dimension) back to a more individual and possible more «housewifely» level: in unpacking (our «hand baggage» mentioned above) after a clinical meeting with our distant colleagues, we often return to our studies with a great quantity of paper.

Photocopied articles, books, and notes scribbled down during discussions will lie around on the desk for some time, later to be disposed of or placed on our bookshelves or filed away under specific headings for subsequent use, going to make up part of what Cesare Musatti referred to as *plankton* the analyst feeds on as he follows his wandering needs and inspiration.

However, another, less tangible gift will steal out of the bag as soon as it is opened, and will follow us, invisibly, to our work station: an effective expression, an unusual concept, a meaningful exchange between two colleagues, a surprising interpretation, maybe even a special way (to our eyes slightly «foreign») of creating a pause or maintaining suspense, will spring to mind when least we expect it, and will probably be a non-banal moment during a session.

It may even come in useful, provided we are not offended, provided it does not scare us.

BIBLIOGRAPHY

AMBROSIANO L. (2005). The analyst: his professional novel. *Int. J. Psycho-Anal.*, 86, 1611-1626.

BOLOGNINI S. (2002). *L'empatia psicoanalitica.* Torino, Bollati Boringhieri.

BOLOGNINI S. (2005). La famiglia interna dell'analista. Read at the INT seminar of SPI, Milano, 18 June 2005.

FORESTI G., ROSSI MONTI M. (2006). Teorie sul transfert e transfert sulle teorie. Relazione al XIII Congresso Nazionale della Società Psicoanalitica Italiana, Siena, 29/9-1/10/2006.

GAMWELL L. & R. WELLS (1989) (ed.). *Sigmund Freud and art. His personal collection of antiquities*, New York, Harry Abrams Inc.

GREEN A. (2005). The illusion of common ground and mythical pluralism. *Int. J. Psycho-Anal.*, 86, 3, 627-632..

KERNBERG O. (2006). The pressing need to increase research in and on psychoanalysis. *Int. J. Psycho-Anal.*, 87, 4, 919-926.

KLAUBER J. (1981). *Difficulties in the analytic encounter.* New York–London, Jason Aronson.

PERRON R. (2006). How to do research? Reply to Otto Kernberg. *Int J. Psycho-Anal.*, 87, 4, 927-932.

RANGELL L. (1982). Transference to theory. *The Annual of Psychoanalysis*, 10, 29-56.

REEDER J. (2004). *Hate and love in psychoanalytic institutes.* New York, Other Press.

SMITH H. (2003). Hearing voices: the fate of the analyst's identifications. *JAPA*, 49, 3, 781-812.

SPURLING L. (2003). On psychoanalysis figures as transference objects. *Int. J. Psycho-Anal.*, 84, 31-44.

WALLERSTEIN R. S. (2005). Will psychoanalytic pluralism be an enduring state in our discipline? *Int. J. Psycho-Anal.*, 86, 3, 623-626.

Original italian version:
Riv. Psicoanal., 2007, 1, 179-195

Stefano Bolognini

Via dell'Abbadia, 6

40122 Bologna

(Translated by Carol Carmody)

Reflections on psychoanalytic training

ADAMO VERGINE

Training is an issue that has never been settled from a theoretical perspective, even by Freud, and it has developed gradually throughout the history of the movement more as a political than a scientific matter. Over time, the concept of analysis and analytical function has become more and more coherently linked to the suspension of judgment and free association methods. On the subject of training, however, which increasingly represents the psychoanalyst's enactment within the social field, the necessity has arisen to express judgment and therefore to institutionalize a hierarchy of values, competencies and rules which are only apparently connected with the scientific criteria of the discipline, so as to reach an adequate degree of social consensus.

It is a knotty issue which is still very difficult to clarify and I think that possible solutions may be found only through concerted group effort. In my opinion, it must be borne in mind that each psychoanalyst today, regardless of how he has been trained, has in any event acquired a strong, deep, automatic and unconscious bond towards his Institution which may be greater than that felt towards psychoanalytic theory.

For us psychoanalysts, being part of the institution is an important defence; it represents a point of reference and an anchor as we venture into the search for yet another sense, and therefore it ends up representing perhaps the most stable and containing aspect of psychoanalysis itself, while the theory and its course have a fluidity that is connected to the mobility of the experience. Therefore, each of us is always the bearer of a good deal of conservatism which puts up resistance to innovation or to new approaches to the issue of training which do not also have reassuring margins of observance. So, starting from a distance, I shall begin by asking a question which may be of use in initiating debate on the topic.

With hindsight, is it possible in the field of psychoanalysis to have a scientific theory of training?

This paper originated in response to a request from Agostino Racalbuto to reactivate scientific debate on psychoanalytic training, with the aim of collecting the contents in a publication. A first draft had already been discussed, but then, before a final version had been prepared, his sudden and painful death occurred which put an end to many of his projects which were not at an advanced stage of development. Subsequently, once I had finished it, I presented an early version of the paper to the Centro Psicoanalitico in Rome on 17 January 2007. The current version contains some updates and reworking.

Or, considering the unconscious quality of the experience, its relative and partial inferability in objective terms, as provisional as our attempts at theorizing are when we try to make our subjective experiences objective and shared, *should we recognise that it is more or less impossible for us to foresee, generalise and then render uniform the training behaviour of analysts with regard to such a function?*

Or should we consider the unicity and originality of each training experience to be a quality of psychoanalysis? If this were the case, then why do we establish an institutional hierarchy of training competencies as if these could be foreseeable and capable of being generalised?

Thinking of everything that has happened in almost one hundred years of experience, we should say that reflection on training over that period of time has been influenced more by religion than by science and that therefore the institutional regulations that we have agreed upon are soaked in ideology or in that type of faith represented by the convictions of the school of thought in vogue at that time, in which thoughts themselves on that experience are not yet deducible, ready to be recorded, or open to criticism. A faith which, strangely, unites us more than it divides us until it progresses in its theorisation process. In fact, it often happens that when it becomes a theory it divides us.

If the need to believe, as Kristeva (2006) states, is an important crossroads in psychic processing, because the subject needs to believe in his experience in order to record it, then the moment of faith is a form of authorization towards an ideal, in an illusory attempt to pacify conflict on the issue of knowledge.

In the history of psychoanalysis, and especially with regard to training, we have entertained many positively utopian ideals which almost require a profession of faith, such as that of the healthy or neutral analyst; or the one which considers the analyst to be the possessor of objectivable knowledge and therapeutic technique; or the uncritical faith in the unconscious; or again, faith in an objectivable psychism. These radical points of view, in the end, represent defensive bulwarks which continue to offer support to the stability of the institution. If, however, idealistic thought and objectivating thought imply a hierarchy of modes of thinking which facilitate the pyramidal configurations which link us to the culture of our society, this hierarchy is certainly a hindrance to the accomplishment of the analytical function and to the construction of a scientific attitude coherent with our experience.

Over the years we have mulled over these issues on numerous occasions and it is beyond doubt that there is more awareness in the spirit underpinning the approach to psychoanalytical training today. Currently, throughout the psychoanalytic world as well as in our Society, an urgent need is felt for reflection on this experience and for a possible, consequential amendment of the criteria which govern it. We are all well aware that this is no easy task. An example of this enormous difficulty can be seen in the latest document from the IPA, drafted by the IPA Educational Committee in July

2006.[1] A very articulate and well thought out document, which felt the need, on a mandate from the IPA, to consider at least three models: the traditional Eitingon model, the French model which separates personal analysis from training, as well as the Uruguayan , which represents a middle ground between the other two,[2] pointing out, however, that within these three models innumerable differences in application are to be found in the various geographical areas adopting them.

Our Society, as a group, has already opened up a debate among all members on certain issues relating to the Articles of Association and rules, which naturally can not be unlinked to aspects concerning theory, and vice versa, with the result that many members found these to be so restrained in their need for conservation as to induce them to prefer the *status quo* for the time being, (approximately two years ago).

We have been made aware that certain shifts in psychoanalytic theory, such as, for example, those in technique and training, are formulated both on the basis of what we presume to know, and (particularly as far as training is concerned) on the setting out of the perceived dangers to be avoided with respect to what we know that we do not yet know well.

On the other hand, this awareness, which keeps us wading mid-way in the river of knowledge, also contains a grain of doubt which may become a suspicion and therefore a great need for control, naturally interwoven with logical ability, but which remains, however, as a feeling of persecution which is justified by the scientific requirement to clarify.

Now, avoiding supposed yet not really foreseeable dangers (perhaps guided more by the spectre of providing good treatment than by actual experience) has led us in the past almost always to put forward rules outlining «what not to do», almost in the same manner in which, in the sphere of religion, those who take care of the faith indicate what is to be avoided.

These types of rules have eased greatly over the years, despite which the need to be sufficiently certain of the suitability of the candidate remains primary in the minds of analysts carrying out training, who are at present the only people responsible for

---

1 Report by the IPA Training Committee, edited by S. Erlich, chair of the committee, dated 29-30 July 2006.

2 The Eitingon model is the first and most traditional model used for training, with four sessions both for the candidate's personal analysis and also for that which the candidate performs under supervision. Among its features is the aim of achieving a deep transformation in the candidate (eliminating his defences and resistance to the greatest possible extent), and therefore the Training Committee can exercise strict psychological control, and hence also has the possibility to manipulate. The French model is the one which inaugurated the separation of personal analysis from training. So, in admission to training, which can occur only after the end of personal analysis, great attention is paid to investigating possible personality disorders that candidates may have; the Training Committee's power is similar to that of a university. The Uruguayan model developed basically as a reaction to the concentration of power in training functions. Essentially it attempts to safeguard the psychoanalytic principle: training functions are divided into seminars, personal analysis, supervision and assessment, so that the person who exercises one function may not exercise another, and entry to training is allowed only at a very advanced stage of analysis. The range of teaching is very broad, as is the possibility to choose one's teachers, with the aim of avoiding dogmatism issues.

the training of psychoanalysts. This need is apparently dictated by the desire not to train a person who is not suitable. I say «apparently», because when with the assumption of such responsibility one is tempted to accomplish it through deeply anti-analytic methods such as reporting or even investigative questioning and diffidence to the point of suspicion, which are part of our history – this leads one to think that the idea of responsibility may be used to hide that of persecution or possible guilt. I am speaking, naturally, of unconscious guilt or persecution which may certainly touch each and every human being when he feels responsible for a transition from one generation to another. For example, it may be due to the fact that each act of judgement may veil its components of ambivalence, which are inescapable for all human beings, even those analysed. And so it may happen that contrasting drives are projected onto the person for whom one has assumed responsibility. This is a natural and unconscious mechanism which, on the other hand, has at times also come in useful for the vigilance which it has put in motion, for example in the contexts of selection and evaluation. On many occasions, however, in the past – and at times more recently – it has unfortunately been a religiously persecutory behaviour.

Naturally, this is a long way from the achievement of something that could be defined scientific, which, while it has been proposed, is extremely difficult to accomplish, particularly if one wishes to purify it of not only its integralistic expressions but also of the religious or moralistic aspects which are not easy to sidestep in a science which works on thought and on human behaviour. A good example of a historical calamity, perhaps necessary at the time and not yet completely eradicated, is given by orthodoxy.

To grasp an understanding of the current situation at international level it is sufficient to read the report drawn up by Mary Target (2001), head of the Working Party on Education, to which D. Tuckett makes reference in his Presidential Report to the EPF Congress in Sorrento (2003). From the investigations which this group carried out at European level it emerges that training is prevalently a political and bureaucratic matter, leading to Tuckett's deeply-felt appeal for all psychoanalysts to commit themselves as a group to drafting agreed-upon, scientific criteria. Because, as he states in his report to the EPF Congress in Budapest,[3] more transparency is required in order to address the problematic obscurity inherent in evaluation, being made up as it is only of implicit criteria. He exhorts analysts to give voice to their feelings and thoughts so as to build up an objective framework of evaluation criteria. In short, we should try to avoid the «anything goes» school of thought!

Personally, I am in total agreement on the call for transparency, but without an openness towards «anything goes» at least initially – the approach which, suspending any expectation, opens the door to the unthinkable – there cannot be transparency

---

[3] This paper was later published: cf. Tuckett (2005).

or sincerity. On the other hand, it is psychoanalytic experience which leads me to doubt greatly whether we may be able to say everything explicitly and therefore be able to construct an objective framework. I think that this can not occur in any immediate form but only in a more processed from built up from generation to generation.

Anna Muratori (1980), in a paper published many years ago, pointed out that the narrative and the history of psychoanalysis are only a small part of psychoanalytic experience, «therefore, in each of us (to a greater or lesser extent) two types of analysis coexist: a codified psychoanalysis and a secret psychoanalysis which develops in the shadow of the former and whose existence is based on its denial» (27). This idea has always made me think that we, as analysts, collude in fantasising about a sort of Super-Ego of the psychoanalytic group which allows certain experiences while prohibiting others, and therefore our empiricism and the setting up of our rules are continually determined by this code which, however, is slowly transformed over time and also through our acquisitions.

Otto F. Kernberg (1985, 1986, 1996, 2001) has spoken up at different times to point out what he considers to be serious errors in current training criteria. In particular, his essay on the *Thirty methods to destroy the creativity of Psychoanalytic Candidates* provoked heated international debate in which a number of Italian colleagues also participated [4] and in which the dogmatic and basically unscientific aspect of psychoanalytic training is criticised.

Russo, too, in his 1995 paper on training, complained of the scarcity of data and of the fact that this experience had been very little processed, considering, from his point of view, that this may have been due to the fact that training has always been an experience *in statu nascendi* and that therefore there cannot be a theory able to predict its developments. Then, in 1999, the *Rivista di Psicoanalisi* issued a stern warning on the topic of training in its third issue in which principally the articles by Di Chiara, Laplanche and Robutti stimulated much reflection on our function as trainers. Di Chiara (1999), while defending the need for institutional mechanisms in favour of training, cites a vast amount of literature which, starting from Anna Freud, shows how doubt has always been cast on the institutional mechanisms adopted for training as not being sufficiently grounded in psychoanalysis.

Laplanche (1999) actually uses strong words with reference to training analysis and with reference also to the so-called « training analysts». He calls it «analysis to order» and states that Lacan's split opened people's eyes to all the manipulative aspects of training, and as a result the Association Psychanalytique de France came to the decision to separate personal analysis from training.

Robutti (1999) also suggests that this function may turn out to be somewhat similar to an «as if» function, due to the candidate's tendency to conform to the mood and

---

4 See Ponsi and Rossi Monti (1997).

expectations of the analyst having training functions as a strategy to achieve concrete personal advantage – qualification as a psychoanalyst – and therefore is in favour of the separation of personal analysis from training.

The separation of personal analysis from the bureaucracy of training is, in my opinion, desirable even for another reason: because the «power to assess» should be separate from the «power to analyse» since one has to do with facts concerning the conscience and should ethically be limited to this sphere, while the other is an analysis of psychic, affective and ideational activity of the self and others. Mixing up these two functions, training analysis could become a contradiction in terms, as many analysts around the world now feel, and this is why we should address the issue of the distinction between evaluative and analytic functions, probably also with the separation of personal analysis from the rest of the training sphere: teaching, supervision and scientific activity.

All of this also makes one think of how many ideals have guided us in good faith and how our theories would have more to gain from that suspension which, in analysis, continues to check our every landing place. More often, instead, we are tempted to want to give not only an objective version but also the most exhaustive, without considering the psychological and affective difficulties deeply implicated in scientific dialogue. This is both because each individual thesis is unlikely to accept that it may suspend its own belief,[5] and because – as Chianese (2006) states, and I agree – in psychoanalysis just as in art there is a long process which allows us to train ourselves, and therefore along with the theories adopted we also defend those strong, vital and unconscious convictions necessary to live and to be able to express ourselves.

Each point of view is based on a different affective-theoretical implicit belief, and therefore scientific dialogue has great difficulty in developing in a coherent or convergent dimension. In psychoanalysis it is difficult to be able to abstract all the experience and process it, not least because our affections are a fundamental, constituent part of it. One is able only to compare conscious ideas, leaving aside emotional conflicts which, in any case, play an important role in resisting or facilitating comprehension and therefore real dialogue.

However, from time to time we take small steps, stimulated by the enthusiasm of reason or proceeding on the wave of emotions of the psychoanalytic groups, from time to time also through a few votes more or a few votes less, without ever introducing catastrophic changes. An example could be given by the way in which, in our Psychoanalytic Society, since 1994, despite all the battles, we have only managed, during the four years of the Chianese presidency, to allow associate members to vote only on matters concerning our statute but not on training and now, under the Riolo presidency, having taken this step, we have succeeded in definitively separating the

---

[5] As I stated more fully in the introduction to Il dialogo scientifico sull'osservazione e sull'esperienza psicoanalitica, edited by S.P.I.'s National Research Committee (AA.VV., 2006).

full membership course from training. Maybe, on this further step, we will finally be able to separate personal analysis from training. This way of proceeding has the delicacy and prudence which is dedicated only to very fragile organisms whose survival is at stake.

The regulations which govern psychoanalytic training, in reality, are almost always far from the personal convictions of the individual analyst, those which guide us in the privacy of analysis. We often find them constricting or they induce us to introduce religious argumentation into a scientific environment, as for example when we appeal to moral responsibility in order to train a good analyst, or when we find ourselves having to assess a person who does not share our ideas, without yet being able to articulate analytic mental behaviour with the mental need for reality and objectivity. In fact, if we wished to be severe, I think honestly that we would only manage to give credit to the fact of having completed an analysis, while one cannot fathom how, from an analytic point of view, we could ever certify with arguments which can be shared that an analysis may have been good or bad in the immediate term.

It is only *a posteriori,* when we are able to reflect on the performance of entire generations, that we can finally shed greater light on phenomena of past analytic experience.

We know that Freud suffered greatly from Ferenczi's claims regarding the incompleteness of his analysis, criticism which led to the idea of «good» or «bad» analysis being put forward. We also know that Freud did not share that conception of psychoanalysis, and we have a testimony of this not only in his correspondence (Freud and Ferenczi, 1993-1998), but also in his work on *Analysis Terminable and Interminable* (Freud, 1937). The question is still open. What good it certainly produced was that everyone felt responsible, and therefore one questioned oneself more and more rigorously: at first, that led towards strong institutionalisation to compensate for the difficulty to win over the unconscious; today I hope that awareness can lead us towards an inverse trend. The first tendency compensated with rules for the difficulty to control unconscious vicissitudes and the original manner in which these are organised by conscious thought in each human being, analyst and patient alike. Now, instead, entrusting ourselves to the on-going experience of the mind – which incessantly analyses itself and others, and then observes how others continue to analyse – we may be led to gain greater trust not only in reason and knowledge, but also in the unconscious dimension of the human being, so as to feel the need for rules less and less.

On the other hand, I have to admit that I have often found myself reflecting on how each of us who exercise training functions may easily project onto the candidates that lack of an ideal for which we all signed up in our personal analysis: as we did not manage to be ideal, we now expect it of the candidates, as if to silence one's own conscience as well as perpetuating the ideal.

It may be that we can no longer continue to use different weights and measures. On one side we theorise that the human psyche is ambivalent, that it feeds on love and hate, that to attenuate conflicts it always projects onto others what it dislikes for itself or what it is not able to achieve by itself. And so, if we state that we are aware of this, we should begin to recognise that we are all this not only when we analyse, but also when we evaluate. It is easier for us to recognise it in our analytic behaviour, but much less so when it concerns our institutional behaviour, seduced as we are perhaps by the idea of having to be teachers. We have faith in science more as a method of control than as a method of experience. In fact, we have communicated our clinical experience to ourselves, not as a personal experience which cannot but be original, but rather amalgamating it with some particular school of thought, perhaps in order not to feel alone and more often in that blend of morals and conformity to ideas which are for some reason current in our group and are shared by the majority at any given time.

On the other hand, it is not so easy to establish *a priori* with a technical approach, whatever it may be based on, what type of analyst we wish to train, not only because it is not humanly possible to decide which training of the psyche may be better than another. Among other things, in psychoanalysis the concept of training is already very different from pedagogic training, that training with regard to which one generation has no difficulty in proclaiming that it wishes to extend itself into the next one, and thereby to shape it in some manner in its own image.

That is not to say that this problem does not also concern psychoanalysis, and even its scientific nature which is achieved – at times even by plagiarizing – through extending itself down through the generations. But psychoanalysis sets itself another basic function, that of allowing the creativity of each single individual, and this is certainly neither foreseeable nor compatible with expecting scientific continuity.

It is true that, like all human beings who try to be able to predict the generative act, we would also like to be able to predict the result of acts of training. However, we must also bear in mind that the analyst we train is also a human being who through his analysis will be what he will be, especially if the analyst has been, let us say, «sufficiently good», in the sense, that is, that he respected as far as possible that person's potential.[6] And yet we always feel that, in any case, a responsibility of ours which we cannot evade is involved. How can we respect that responsibility without preventing the other person from being only as he can be? Some could say that it is precisely for this reason that there is selection, and if someone cannot be an analyst, in the way each of us tries to depict it to ourselves, then he will not do it.

I believe, instead, that today, at the stage we are at in the debate and at the point of construction we have arrived at, it is necessary to decide whether the postulate of the

---

[6] See Bonaminio (1996).

unconscious is a fundamental and necessary issue for us or not. I say «decide» because we are dealing with an alternative whose poles are either not demonstrable or not comparable, and therefore both may be legitimate.

From my point of view, the training process is fundamentally unconscious and only with time is it processed, verbalised and manifested in sufficiently observable human behaviour. Therefore, I am of the opinion that we do not really have instruments of thought, but only sentiments to decide whether the analysis has been successful and is over, or to understand whether that person will make «a good analyst».

And yet, at the same time, we observe both in our Society and at international level,[7] that parties are still being formed which place themselves more or less on this side or on that side of the hypothetical crossroads mentioned above: there are those who take the side mainly of objectivity, reason at all costs, academic instruction, examinations, and checks as well as technical and cultural competence; while on the other hand there are those who are more inclined towards subjectivity, imaginative creativity, learning from experience, dialogue without checks and examinations, as well as emotional competence. Or, as the previously mentioned, recent IPA document states, there are innumerable combinations of such criteria, connected to the differing cultural backgrounds and geographical areas of those involved.

My doubt is whether we may be only perpetuating within the area of our experience the competitiveness which we notice internally between primary processes and secondary processes, as if each one were supporting an aspect of one's experience, which, all things considered, we have decided to make prevalent. If once we were obsessed by analysing at all costs, I have the impression that today, based on our further experience, we may be more inclined to consider a correct blend of analysis along with not necessarily analytic reflection efficacious.[8] This already appears to me to be a sign of an attempt to follow an intermediate path, functional but not polemic, more ego than super-ego, and also because experience suggests that not only analysis, but also the ability to defend oneself from this mental exercise, or the ability to hold back unconscious emergencies depending on the ability of the Ego and therefore also to be able to use the work done in the secondary processes for real aims or to better defend ourselves are important for the functioning of the mind. In other words, our attention is greatly focused on safeguarding the Ego rather than on demolishing its defences.

The affective and theoretical constellations of psychoanalysis are quite diversified and at times irreconcilable. Now, even if there is scientific dialogue, this is never fully put to the test, there is always a margin of pacific co-existence which at times seems to be almost a conspiracy of silence. This also depends on reasons of policy as

---

[7] See for example the recent debate (2004) in The International Journal of Psychoanalysis, between César Garza-Guerrero and Eglé Laufer on current issues in training.

[8] As it seems to me that Russo (2006) also suggests in his excellent book Le Illusioni del Pensiero.

well as of institutional power, because the pyramid of institutional power in psycho-analysis is a truncated pyramid which sees all analysts having training functions as equals at its highest possible peak. There can not be a person who can lay down the law more than all of the others, and this involves a certain official diplomacy among peers, either deferring battles to scientific dialogue – when one feels up to sustaining it, given that it requires more effort – or deferring more probably to policy, i.e. to a vote or to the decisions to be taken in assessment contexts.

Coming to the *what to do,* in principle I agree with Russo (1995) when he says that training is an experience *in statu nascendi* and that therefore a theory of training should be developed each time and from time to time. In concrete terms, however, we have an institution to run, for which we have responsibility, while scientifically we experience the paradox that no-one knows exactly what any other analyst colleague is doing or thinking, despite all our rules of reciprocal cross-checking. It appears that the training functions are a type of consecration, due to which everything deriving from these functions is more or less accepted as sacred, perhaps also so as not to be obliged to enter into scientific discussion.

If, instead, we wished to move towards an attempt to regulate our subject according to a scientific order, then I believe it would be necessary to have greater transparency on reciprocal experiences – as the previously mentioned Tuckett (2003) stated – and this, naturally, should be in a position to not be continuously checked and invalidated *a priori* by the prejudices of someone who manages to set himself up as a judge by his own will, drawing on the consensus of the moralism of the others rather than on scientific reasoning. Since psychoanalysis makes its scientific choices not only on the strength of reason but also on the strength of emotions, through our self-same experience we should be able to build and to continue to invent our scientific nature, as Freud had begun to do. I do not think that this can be achieved outside of a group effort committed and co-operating to this end, which should certainly be based to a great extent also on an institutional collegiality, albeit more lay in nature. I believe that more widespread laicity would attenuate the conspiracy of silence and, at the same time, may increase scientific honesty and transparency.

If we wished to search for some common denominator within the array of the many shifts of psychoanalysis, with the exception of that common ground inaugurated by Wallerstein (1988 and 1990) and taken up by many analysts as a very vague, reassuring criterion,[9] I think that we would find very little.

In fact, if we try to expose those cores of psychic functioning which appear to be generally agreed upon and capable of being agreed upon, the inventory, even if simplified, would in any event be very short.

---

[9] Taken up again also in the latest report from the IPA (previously quoted) it refers to the fact that essentially all the training institutes pursue a tripartite model: personal analysis, supervision and teaching.

– One thing that we can generally agree upon is that the psychic events of an analytic experience are gathered quite clearly by both the patient's and the analyst's conscious Ego.

– That this Ego, however, is also aware of the fact that psychic phenomena occur in parallel which are not immediately conscious, which are perceived to be there and concerning which we note that they may also cause different psychic responses: either of fear and hence of defence or resistance, or of interest, and hence of mobilization towards better knowledge by both sides of the therapy relationship.

– At this point the paths may now divide: a) if it is felt that the unconscious must become conscious and that interpretation may confer this power on the analyst, this path may be tread omnipotently, as was done in the past; b) if, instead, it is felt that secondary thought is only processed and slowly transformed by primary processes which are experienced and define us in the analytic relationship, then one must also think that the primary processes are not known in themselves and that therefore it is useless to pursue interpretive fancies at all costs. One feels oneself committed instead to continually reprocessing conscious data in terms of free associations and drifting attention. It is true that experience, in order to be processed, is in any case modelled on some earlier or necessarily new form of theory. But in such case the interpretative moment does not originate from a technical or theoretic preliminary intention, rather it naturally derives only from the work of psychic transformation carried out at a pre-conscious or unconscious level which is then partially reported in consciousness.

I wonder why we should not be confident that continuity in psychic training is assured, as biological training is, simply by observing the analyst that is emerging, without knowing exactly what he will be like, but being certain that everything possible has been done not to try to make him something that he himself is not, and therefore that he has in fact been allowed to express his potential.

If we consider that the fundamental postulate of psychic functioning is that of the unconscious, the primary processes and the secondary processes interacting as a result of the destiny of urges, transformations, achieving of pleasure or displeasure, and therefore of the performance of experience and its being played out, then I think that if we are coherent we can only accompany, assist and be participating witnesses to the training process but not decide what it will be. We place our knowledge at the disposal of the analytic context – such knowledge actually being essentially our own experience in analysis and a knowledge of the history of psychoanalysis – along with all our psychic patrimony, made up of our personal history and analytic history and of how these have been transformed through the experience of continuous analysis.[10] Such patrimony, also psychically active and determining, in my opinion, is still a

---

[10] As Chianese also states (2006, 119-120).

mainly unconscious patrimony and is therefore unconsciously usable in the analytic relationship.

The problem arises when collegial use is made of those qualities experienced, because they may have taken a different path in each person and therefore they may have got as far as comparison, and then to dialogue and debate, in different forms, making it unlikely that they may immediately constitute a common value or shared theory modulation. It seems to me that we need to work on this point and I am convinced that we psychoanalysts cannot pretend that what other colleagues think does not concern us at the same time. We are fond of the institution precisely because it allows us to be able to separate something of ourselves, knowing that there will be someone else who will be interested in playing the other part.

Certainly, if we found ourselves in large numbers sharing the opinion that this is the way things are, we would have to deduce for the moment that any type of evaluation – whether for admission, or election to associate membership, or to full membership or to the status of training analyst – could certainly appear to be arbitrary. If the person in charge of assessment does not have at his disposal any objective element on which to base such an evaluation, then in order to be able to reject or accept he can only use his own fantasies elicited by the encounter with another human being in all his complexity.

I do realise, however, that a large institution such as ours can not all of a sudden wipe out a situation of this type, because it would be like demolishing a dam and destroying everything. So I would be the first to oppose such a move, I would not propose such a thing and I feel that our Society is right to go forward one small step at a time.

However, if we wish to make the most scientifically of the experience carried out since 1994 with the new Articles of Association and rules drawn up under the Di Chiara Presidency after the 1992 crisis, and if we wish to be coherent with this important experience, we should at least address the issue. For example, we could begin to work (I do not know whether on the rules or discussing the matter with the colleagues who are in a position to exercise these functions) with the aim of pruning (perhaps autoanalytically) each assessment setting of those religious, debatable and coarser aspects which only produce wars of religion or narcissistic beatifications. The co-option criterion undoubtedly favoured these aspects, but evidently it is not so easy to expunge them only because it has been decided to pass on to a critical evaluation.

Clinical practice and technique are perhaps the two fundamental focuses of the friction which occurs in evaluation contexts, be they those of candidates who apply for associate membership or those of analysts who apply for training functions. Clinical practice and technique are the temporary processing of thought, and therefore they may be a topic for scientific discussion only among peers in the Society, but not examination subjects, as there is very little of an objective nature to discuss, to object to or to defend. It seems to me that the subject of an examination should have to do with a candidate's intentional and conscious activity, such as, for example, a knowledge of the history of psychoanalysis and also of the possible manners of clinical and technical observation, but should not concern an activity of which only a small part can be perceived at a conscious level, knowing also that it takes years for a process of processing to produce greater awareness. That being so, we had also considered the idea of «permanent training»,[11] of which I have also been a staunch supporter, not thinking that it could at times slip, along the way, towards permanent control of all members.

We could, in the meantime, limit the evaluation to ascertaining the extent of the candidate's awareness with regard to his own experience, while that «extent» should also be processed jointly with the candidate, unless we wish it to become an expression of a discretionary judgment.

The urge to know, along with the urge to dominate, must be very strong in analysts, not only due to the fact of having to deal continuously with mystery and madness. However, if we had greater trust in psychic life, analysing our behaviours as well – both the analytic and the institutional – even ghosts and ideals could be recognised and could cooperate towards greater sharing based on experience. There would be more space to think and each person could feel responsible for our progress.

SUMMARY

Over the years, the concept of analysis and analytical function has been linked to the suspension of judgement and free association with increasing coherence. However, if its scientific knowledge is also to be Institution of knowledge, as regards the culture of our civilized society, it must also share an objectivizing and idealistic thought that consequently becomes a hindrance to the creation of analytical function and the construction of a scientific order that is coherent with our experience.

The author believes that if one is to be able to work around such a paradox that generates considerable institutional tension, far removed from scientific activity, the decision must be made as to whether we believe the postulate of the unconscious is a fundamental scientific issue or not. The starting point is the consideration that each analyst makes his own knowledge available in the analytical context – which is essentially a personal analytical experience and a knowledge of the history of psychoanalysis – together with the entire psychical patrimony that is the result of personal and analytical history and of how it was transformed by the experience of continuous analysis.

KEY WORDS: Psychoanalytic training, psychoanalytical associations, unconscious.

[11] In consideration of the fact that we psychoanalysts can never have a scientific and definitive idea of training, many analysts have felt that training could have permanent and collegial aspects and processes in the sense that each colleague, in discussing the experiences of the others, helps each one to better process his own. This was set up in Italy by Roberto Tagliacozzo when he was national secretary of training in the 1980s.

REFERENCES

AA.VV. (2006). Il dialogo scientifico sull'osservazione e sull'esperienza psicoanalitica. Roma, Borla, 2006.

BONAMINIO V. (1996). Esiste ancora uno spazio per l'individualità del paziente? *Riv. Psicoanal.*, 42, 97-110.

CHIANESE D. (2006). *Un lungo sogno*. Milano, Franco Angeli.

DI CHIARA G. (1999). L'inconscio e la formazione psicoanalitica. *Riv. Psicoanal.*, 45, 445-463.

Freud S. (1937). *Analysis terminable and interminable*. SE, 23.

FREUD S., FERENCZI S. *The correspondence of S. Freud and S. Ferenczi*, 3 vol. Boston, Harvard University Press, 1993-2000.

GARZA-GUERRERO C., LAUFER E. (2004). Reorganisational and educational demands of psychoanalytic training today: Our long and marasmic night of one century. *Int. J. Psycho-Anal.*, 85, 3-13.

KERNBERG O.F. (1985). Changes in the nature of psychoanalytic training, structure of training, and standards of training. In Wallerstein R.S. (ed.), *Changes in analysts and their training*, London, Int. Psychoanal. Assn.

KERNBERG O.F. (1986). Institutional problems of psychoanalytic education. *J. Amer. Psychoanal. Assn.*, 34, 799-834.

KERNBERG O.F. (1996). Thirty methods to destroy the creativity of Psychoanalytic Candidates. *Int. J. Psycho-Anal.*, 77, 1031-1040.

KERNBERG O.F. (2001). Alcune considerazioni sulle innovazioni nella formazione psicoanalitica. *Riv. Psicoanal.*, 46, 551-565.

KRISTEVA J. (2006). *Il bisogno di credere*. Roma, Donzelli.

LAPLANCHE J. (1999). La didattica: una psicoanalisi «su ordinazione». *Riv. Psicoanal.*, 45, 559-569.

MURATORI A.M. (1980). Il non comunicato in psicoanalisi. *Riv. Psicoanal.*, 26, 23-42.

PONSI M., ROSSI MONTI M. (1997). A proposito dell'articolo di Otto Kernberg: «Trenta metodi per distruggere la creatività dei candidati psicoanalisti». *Riv. Psicoanal.*, 43, 91-97.

ROBUTTI A. (1999). Analisi personale e formazione psicoanalitica. *Riv. Psicoanal.*, 45, 537-557.

RUSSO L. (1995). Riflessioni intorno ad una esperienza di formazione. *Riv. Psicoanal.*, 41, 637-653.

RUSSO L. (2006). *Le illusioni del pensiero*. Roma, Borla.

TARGET M. (2001). Some issues in psychoanalytic training: An overview of the literature and some resulting observations. Presentation to the *II Joseph Sandler Research Conference*, London, University College, 10 March 2001.

TUCKETT D. (2003). Allocution présidentielle: Une initiative scientifique européenne sur dix ans. *Psychanalyse en Europe*, 57.

TUCKETT D. (2005). Does anything go? Towards a framework for the more transparent assessment of psychoanalytic competence. *Int. J. Psycho-Anal.*, 86, 31-49.

WALLERSTEIN R.S. (1988). One psychoanalysis or many? *Int. J. Psychoanal.*, 69, 5-21.

WALLERSTEIN R.S. (1990). Psychoanalysis: The common ground. *Int. J. Psychoanal.*, 71, 3-20.

Original italian version: **Adamo Vergine**
Riv. Psicoanal., 2007, 4, 977-994   ———————————————
                                                              Via Paolo Segneri, 1/b
                                                       ———————————————
                                                              00152 Roma

(Translated by Carol Carmody))

The experience of supervision

LOREDANA MICATI

Follow the fox. If we allowed candidates to speak more openly and if we knew how to listen, we would learn much. I have not found a great deal in the literature on the experience of supervision from the supervisee's point of view or on their assessment of it (Martin and coll. 1978). I haven't found anything at all on how the supervisor prepares himself for the initial meeting with the candidate. The desire to be a good supervisor is disturbing to the supervisor just as the desire to be a good analyst makes it difficult to be an analyst.

All authors agree on the need to respect the supervisee, to consider him a younger colleague, to favour, or at least not to hinder the development of his potential, qualities and creativity as well as on the best techniques to be employed in order to achieve such results. There is so much insistence on these aspects as to lead one to conclude that supervisors feel the need to guard continually against the pitfalls created by their own insecurity, by an uncertain narcissism and by the subsequent possible risk of being subtly arrogant and insufficiently respectful in training.

This is never discussed openly. A pleasant-mannered leg-pull is to be found in Levenson (1982) who quotes an aphorism of Oscar Wilde's on fox hunting, «a marvellous example of the unspeakable in pursuit of the inedible». According to Levenson, «with a very slight shift, much the same might be said about the process of supervision. It is a marvellous example of the infallible in pursuit of the ineffable!»

The esoteric aspects of analytical training give room to some unwitting abuse, which accounts for so much insistence on the need for caution.

ANTICIPATION AND THE FIRST ENCOUNTERS

Like analysis, but in a different way, the first meeting is preceded by imaginings and expectations.

Here, too, initially there will be two scared people in a room, but they will be scared for reasons of a different nature than those of the two people who meet for analysis. It is likely that one of the two, the supervisor, is more inclined to deny his share of fear and hide it under the cloak of his institutional role. The candidate is more willing to admit to this state of mind, considering it natural, given the circumstances, and he usually has his analysis at his disposal in order to work on it. The supervisor, on the other hand, should rely on his intellectual honesty and his habit of self-analysis.

The supervisor will meet a candidate that he may have come across at seminars, but this occasion will be completely different. Is it a first or second supervision? Or is it a candidate whose application for membership had been turned down, or who has been asked to undergo another supervision? Or may he have been asked to write up his cases again and decided of his own volition to start another supervision? In these last cases the supervisor will be meeting people at a later stage in their training, they may be gifted people who have been misunderstood or who have not found the right circumstances under which their abilities may be appreciated, or again it may be people with problematical aspects; they may often be embittered and disappointed or frustrated and resentful.

In order to lead the discussion into the area of experience I shall have to make it more personal. I wouldn't like to overemphasize by saying that there is something akin to birth in the lead up to the first meeting: it is the start of couple relationship which has creative potential and its development will depend on the quality of the meeting. There is curiosity. A human being, at a particularly intense stage in his training, is going to bring part of his world into my study. That human being has another one in his mind, or rather contains an incipient relationship and fantasies about it. What will be born out of the play of these intelligences and sensibilities? We are setting off on a new experience, with many unknown aspects, which may harbour surprises, from which there may be much to learn. This is how I feel prior to meeting a candidate.

To date I have mainly met supervisees over forty years of age, in some cases well into their forties, who had gained other experience in the fields of psychiatry, psychology, the social services and clinical practice. They were at a stage of life which may be described as mature, in which certain choices and experiences had already taken place. However, I have also worked with supervisees in their thirties, and this may become more frequent from now on. When I started following supervisees the waiting period was taken up also by thoughts of a narcissistic nature. All candidates judge their teachers, including during seminars, and at times they show a sharp and deep grasp of aspects of their personality, qualities, limits and lacks. Candidates make comparisons and exchange opinions.

A corollary of these thoughts is the other, superegoic in nature: «will I really be able to pass on something useful in this experience, or at the very least not hamper progress?

Years ago, at first meetings, at times the persecutory [1] and superegoic anxieties seemed to me to be clearly palpable in the room. I felt those of the candidate, as well

---

[1] The persecutory aspect of the institutional requirements and rules is often discussed, while the protective and reassuring aspect of working within an institution which gathers within itself a high level of knowledge, both technical and theoretic, and which can provide tools with which to address difficult situations is neglected.

as my own, which naturally enough were more attenuated. Aside from the cordiality and the pleasurable aspects of the start of a task being undertaken together, there was always an overhanging presence, slightly laborious and disturbing. I knew that we had to take our time and that there was work to be done in order to allow sufficient confidence in ourselves and in the relationship to develop. Over time I became more benevolent and less persecutory, more trusting and less worried – I mean of course with myself, and therefore with my object in that couple relationship. That is not to say that there were no worries or that they were insignificant. It is as if, before the start, I had to do a sort of implicit inventory of the resources I would need on the trip.

The run up and the first meetings are laborious, although interesting. There are times at which uncertainty and doubt are greatest. If I am able to avoid having too much recourse to the already known and the reassurance of previous experience, this new situation will offer me new opportunities to learn.[2] If this were to happen the conditions could be created in which the candidate, too, might learn something from our common experience (cf. Yerushalmi, 1999).

THE INEFFABLE AND THE COMMUNICABLE

When we organise our reflections on supervision we are forced to give a schematic representation of a complex reality and this is disturbing because what takes place in the study is much more than we can express, which is why Levenson speaks of the ineffable, which includes, however, the risk of the infallible.

Multiple levels of complexity are to be found in supervision. It is a scene which brings us back to another scene (the study where the candidate meets his patient) which in turn brings us back to other scenes. But also the first scene (the study in which the supervisor meets the supervisee) brings us back to many other scenes.

We might be tempted to say that the supervisor's study is too crowded and there are too many relationships criss-crossing there.

a)   The patient: the supervisor will need to build up a mental image of the patient's personality organisation. This will certainly be an image in a constant state of evolution, and not a diagnosis. Great attention is placed on all the elements of supervision which enable access to new insights on the patient and to a better overall understanding. Within the experience of supervision it is not really possible to separate the deeply interwoven aspects of the patient's treatment and the candidate's training. The candidate's training is central to supervision; however, from the perspective of psychoanalytical ethics, the patient's treatment occupies a central position. The patient is the most important person in this context, the one most deserving of attention.

---

2 On resistance to the influence of others and on the necessary conditions required for constructive exchange in training cf. Slavin e Kriegman, 1998.

b)   The patient-candidate couple: it presents itself as a duo from the outset, since, as Nissim states (1980)[3], the supervisor listens to (and then works upon) the transformations made by the candidate on the analysis he is carrying out.

The study in which the patient-candidate couple meets is the place, the only place is which the analysis is performed. That is where the experience of that analysis is played out live. I have seen from the literature that this obvious fact is not quite so obvious after all.

c)   The supervisee: the organisation of his personality, his capacity to listen and to relate to the other, ability to learn to use oneself as an instrument, insight, sensitivity, tact, intelligence and willingness to change within the experience as well as weaknesses and closure.

d)   The supervisory pair: these are two colleagues of different ages and knowledge who are sharing the aim of learning from the experience in which both are involved, but with a different degree of responsibility. The supervisor's work is carried out at a level of abstraction of the second degree compared to the often chaotic complexity of analysis. In supervision, how well the couple works obviously depends on the personality organisation of its constituent members. Regression is not encouraged; in any case the manner in which they relate to each other is intense and profound, while the exchanges may occasionally be of a primitive type. Perhaps even in an attenuated form, ways of communication which have to do with what is taking place in analysis may be reactivated (cf. Gediman and Wolkenfeld, 1980).

e)   The supervisor: what was said above in relation to the supervisee also goes for the supervisor. We shall see how, in my opinion, the assessment comes into this process.

f)   The relationships in which supervisee and supervisor are engaged on a personal, professional and institutional level (training analyst, other supervisors, training section, SPI, etc.)

IN THE STUDY

The candidate arrives and presents a patient that he has seen one or more times. What is the best approach for the supervisor to take? To look and listen. He has achieved a condition of sufficient inner serenity, has learnt to have confidence in his ability to listen and in the functioning of an inner world which, sooner or later, always surprises him, and wrong-foots some of the attempts made with a view to

---

[3] Cf. also Yerushalmi, 1999 who wrote: «Jacobs, David, and Meyer (1995) focus on the supervisory pair's constructions of the therapeutic material. Although, according to their argument, the supervisee presents a truth that is grounded in and supported by facts, it is still the supervisee, as teller, who constructs this truth and chooses those facts. Supervisees' formulations of their therapeutic hours combine subjective and objective knowledge. These are constructions of meanings that relate to, but are in no means identical with, the reality that is being described. In effect, they claim, supervision is a creative and imaginative activity».

understanding. He knows how pleasant and at times amusing the experience of being wrong-footed is. It is completely unpredictable, includes the slight discomfort of tolerating doubt and the opacity of communications which do not resound. Then, at times, an insight connects the material and imbues it with meaning. On the one hand, one must allow the so-called resources of the Ego to come into play, let the active and lucid mind form a general picture of the situation, carrying out the extremely useful and reassuring function of clarifying. At the same time other levels of functioning are also at work, those from which valuable insights and images not dissimilar to dreams are created. The most fascinating part takes place within this experience, which is very familiar to the analyst. It is here that insights which suddenly give meaning to the jumbled-up material which had occupied the supervision session up to that moment make their way into the supervisee's or the supervisor's mind, or as the fruit of their verbal or non-verbal exchange. We may say that the chosen fact arrives by way of field effects. Who the insight belongs to, or who got there first, is of no great importance, as competition and narcissism have taken a back seat at this point and the couple is operating within a creative exchange. It is similar to when two well harmonized tango dancers glide to the music using their imagination and technique creatively. At times they dance to the rhythm and are clearly differentiated, they allow each other to act and they act together, while at other times they dance within the melody and merge into it and in each other, in a creative and intense functioning which is the fruit of reciprocal trust, experience and understanding.

The work of supervision takes two people and at times it is of no relevance to know who is giving and who is receiving. The supervisor does not resound with certain supervisees, or in certain moments he is switched off or obtuse and without insight. Other candidates activate a process of reciprocal fecundation which gives birth to ideas, making the supervision a very lively experience.[4]

Years after the end of official supervision, having been an associate member of the SPI for a long time, a colleague recounts:

«Right from the first supervision encounter I had the sensation, confirmed and lasting over the years, that I was in the presence of a «tractor»: that is to say, a powerful machine, implacable in a certain sense, which used the harrow to break up the hard ground and turn it over in long, straight, parallel lines, the agreed-upon final aim being a well-ploughed field, but there was to be no breakdown, for whatever reason.

---

4 This is a delicate issue, parallel to that of the analysability of a patient. When the the supervisory pair does not work, it may mean that the supervisee is seriously lacking in the skills required to become an analyst, on whose difficulties the entire training section must reflect, or that these two people do not have the characteristics which would enable them to work toge ther in a beneficial manner.

And that is how the long supervision wound its way, session after session, even years after the end of the mandatory time: material in order and rigour in examining it. The clearly felt sensation that nothing important was overlooked, be it an unspoken thought, a lapse, something glossed over, a moment of boredom or tiredness – even though the patient in question obliged us to live in an asphyxiating climate in which boredom was a constant. Interest and curiosity enlivened the heaviness of the material and mitigated the superegoic aspect, slowly revealing the value and importance of paying careful attention to the slightest detail in each session. The rigour of the method, however, was balanced by complete freedom of thought and speech: I always had the distinct feeling that I could express myself with real sincerity, with no need to fear any type of judgement. No judgement on my theoretic orientation, in any case still being developed and consolidated, no attempt to influence it, but especially no judgement on me as an analyst, or, even worse, as from time to time one hears from other colleagues' experience, on me as a person. Any mention of the connection between the material being supervised and my personal analysis was always made with respect and tact, stimulating my interest to go deeper into the matter and never, ever, perceived as intrusive».

I would certainly not be flattered to hear myself described as a tractor or as a type of scrupulous and diligent clerk. It is clear that also the supervisor's personality traits put their mark on any supervision. I would, however, like to draw attention to other, less variable and rather interesting elements for our discussion.

Let me take a step back: candidate X had struck me, when I first met her during one of the informal assessment colloquia [5] we hold in our institute every year at the end of the seminars, for her sharp intelligence and for her ability to relate to others and grasp, with sensitivity, the shades of meaning inherent in the conversation. And so I was pleased when she asked me to supervise her and I prepared gladly for the experience. X arrived at the first encounter and spoke to me of the patient she had begun to see.

The patient was a man of forty, foreign, well-off, who had arrived in Italy in early adolescence and both of his parents were alcoholics. His life appeared to me to be hanging by a thread. He was crushed by feelings of guilt, which caused him to lead quite a miserable existence, spent mostly at the beck and call of people who tyrannised him in the most absurd manner. He seemed to be floating over an emptiness of which he was deeply fearful, and perhaps similar to that which his parents had tried to avoid with alcohol and destructive gestures. He was an alcoholic as well, without admitting it. He was measured in his speech, composed, contained and polite, he

---

[5] *End of year colloquia*: a great deal of attention is paid to them. In June every candidate has to present a short report on a theme of his choice, related to the seminars he attended. During the colloquia the paper will be discussed by the candidate and by two training analysts.

never made a scene, or asked openly for help, never expressed his suffering in dramatic terms, never spoke of plans to commit suicide, or even expressed fantasies about it.

He showed great and endless self-control, but had implicitly communicated to the analyst that he felt trapped, with no way out, that he lived in a state of deep anguish, of real desperation. There was a palpable sensation that an unconscious plan could lead him to seek a solution in a fatal accident. He led a life which exposed him to a risk of this type. When he began to speak of his dreams they featured excruciating pain, Christs crucified and punishment expected or sought through death.

On the other side there was candidate X, a woman of forty, mother, wife, medical doctor, used, in a different specialisation, to taking on responsibility even in situations involving risk and urgency. Another type of risk, naturally. Here was a highly sensitive woman, lively, full of the energy and resources of mature youth. Even before the dreams revealed it, she had felt all the patient's unstated desperation and the danger he was in; she was extremely receptive towards the state of mind of this person who was so reticent and «buttoned up», able to spend almost entire sessions in silence. It was as if the analyst was able to feel and follow her patient's mood, or at least this was how it seemed to me. X had in some way enabled me to breathe the emotional climate of that relationship. However, I could take advantage of the observer's external position, which operates on a second level.

I mentioned the analyst's liveliness as a positive quality. The other side of the coin of this liveliness was a sort of restlessness, a tendency to consume the experience and move on to another, more interesting one, a touch of impatience. Too much rapidity. My task was not to understand why she needed to run so fast and to analyse this with her (though there was no reason why I could not discretely avail of my insights). My task was to seek an effective working method which would enable us to work well together.

Our common task filled me with interest, curiosity and pleasure. On the one hand the patient's personal history deserved our commitment, while on the other I was deeply interested in X's good training. I wanted X to get in touch with and develop other resources in addition to those which she already had. Referring once in an aside to her experience with her first supervisor (who I appreciate and have great respect for) X used the succinct expression: «genius and intemperance». Her personal analysis was over. There was good reason to think that this may have been her last institutional training experience.

It seemed to me that the patient's great slowness deserved respect, that he did not want to be overtaken by an over-intuitive analyst and that it was necessary to learn to tolerate the wait. On the other hand, I had the feeling that the analysis had «taken», that for the first time in his life the patient felt contained, and borne along by a great, vital energy. We could take as long as was necessary.

This was hard, patient, tenacious, quiet ploughing, and was exactly the part that the highly gifted candidate X was lacking.

I think that there is more, and here we need to find the poor words which, stating part of the ineffable, let the fox go free.

The patient was lucky enough to find an analyst trained to grasp the slightest changes in mood of the other, even when that other is closed and silent. He would also have needed to find an analyst so able to understand his obsessive defences as to make him feel sure that he would not be outdone. He would therefore have wished for a person able, for example, to wait for him to come out of his eternal circular time spontaneously. The patient's sense of precariousness and fragility made this need for suspension a priority. It may be that X brought me her counter-transference reaction to something that her patient asked her and which she was not yet fully able to accept. I received the message at two levels: I have already spoken about the first; and the second was preconscious and had a counter-transference response. I think I did respond to what the supervisee brought me of her difficulty in relation to a part of the patient's requests.

In other terms, patient and supervisor worked, each on her own front, to get the analyst to develop the capacity to suspend the speed of insight in order not to antici-pate events. The patient wanted to be understood *intus et in cute*, but asked especially to be contained by an analyst who could share his experience without rushing him and who could tolerate the lethally asphyxiating climate of the sessions without going further. He also wanted the analyst to share, for as long as necessary, his way of functioning.[6] What did I learn from this experience? Very much, and we come back to the ineffable. I remember one aspect most vividly: my admiration for the great del-icacy of X in dealing with her patient, just brushing him lightly, but being at the same time a solid presence.

AN EXAMPLE OF FUNCTIONING

J, too, is a very gifted candidate. Almost fifty, a veteran of many supervisions, high-ly-educated, intelligent, and lively, J is a person with whom I work with great pleasure.

J tells me that her patient, Rita, remained in silence for an entire session, the first of the week. It was a quiet and thoughtful silence, says J, and she had not felt it right to interrupt it. Then she tells me about the material of the following session. I am very attentive, not tired, in a good mood, and even still I feel a growing discomfort, as if I

---

6 Cf. Lussana (1999, 472): «In analysis, from the single session to the entire week, slow time and movement prevail over the lively and cheerful. The former require the most detailed diction and denomination to animate and contain them, «patience» [...] which tolerates the suffering and frustration of them, until a configuration emerges and evolves from that state of dispersion».

had been hit by too many stimuli. I wonder: «Why is she speaking so fast, with this breathlessness which leaves me no time to think?».

The material piles up and I have no insight at all, can see no meaning, not even sectorial or provisory. I feel a sudden tiredness. Too much stuff, it is hot, I am uncomfortable. I rearrange myself on the chair. Then J tells me about a dream of Rita's, featuring a friend of hers, Maria, an impulsive girl who loses no time between thinking and doing or saying. «The type of person who, if she thinks she recognises an old school-friend, would not think twice about crossing the road and asking: – Are you by any chance …? – Just as I do» says the supervisee and adds, repeating the expression twice: «Rita and her friend incite each other». Then she goes on to tell me some detail of the slightly hypomaniacal function that the friend plays in the relationship with Rita. In taking her notes, the candidate makes an error in writing, from which she understands that she has associated the patient's friend's name with that of an incongruously seductive female character taken from literature.

I have summarised greatly and, from the entire supervision session, have chosen the elements which, being organised into meaning, allowed me to get out of an uncomfortable situation. Rita kept quiet for an entire session to indicate to her analyst that she needs a non-excited situation and she speaks to her of their relationship through the dream. The contents are clear and I will not dwell on them.

What is of interest for our discussion is the manner in which such contents arrive at my door. I do not choose how to carry out the supervision, based on my theoretic-technical arsenal; it is the situation which chooses how to use me. In this case I feel something which is probably not very far from what J's patient feels when she takes refuge in silence to have a bit of space and then, through the dream, tries to indicate to her analyst her discomfort at the defensively excited way in which the analytical relationship is working at that time. I did not choose to focus my attention on the patient, I just found myself in an experience which led me to an understanding of that passage. I can draw a theoretical-practical conclusion, the one I spoke about in the third paragraph «the ineffable and the communicable»: my interest is in the patient and at the same time in the analyst's training. Apart from being an ethical, theoretical and technical choice, this is the way in which I can work.

I had confirmation in the following supervision session. The supervisee tells me that the patient was able to bring herself to talk about separation, bereavement and loss. She also tells me that, during Rita's silent session she, the analyst, had been painfully absorbed in thoughts related to the recent death of a close relative, and in the complex emotions of pain and ambivalence provoked by the bereavement. Both analyst and patient had attempted to defend themselves through reciprocal «excitatory incitement», then the patient had indicated her need to get in touch with her pain and the analyst lived it through her own experience, before being able to give room to sessions in which pain could be shared and spoken about.

CLASSICAL DISCUSSION THEMES:
SYMMETRY, ASYMMETRY, TRAINING

«The supervisor at work listens and observes two people speaking in a room, or rather the transformations made on all this by the young analyst's account, and analyses them in the conviction that this is the way in which the candidate communicates even that which he does not wish to, or is unable to communicate, as well as that of which he is unaware in the patient» (Manfredi and Nissim, 1984, 592).

An interesting experience is that in which the supervisee relates with embarrassment about times in which he intervened in a manner which he considered to be useless or inappropriate or incongruous. The supervisor listens, slipping in and out of the story. He is obviously following a subterranean plot. The candidate's intervention or interventions appear to him to be on the mark, but not with respect to the manifest content of the exchange. The candidate had perceived the patient's unconscious requests, pressure and injunctions and had reacted, often in the most opportune manner, without being aware of it.

A process of this type is quite transparent to the supervisor, if not only because he observes it from afar.[7] The solicitations he receives are usually attenuated as he is not in the front line. He operates on a second level of abstraction. In cases of this type it is very interesting for the supervisor to go back over the exchange between the supervisee and his patient as it had been presented during the supervision session. It comes as a surprise to the candidate to realise that he had seen, felt and responded with certain areas of the mind, that his response was not spurious, that on the contrary it made sense and was useful. What the supervisee learns above all is that he can begin to place more trust in his ability to listen and communicate.

Tagliacozzo (1989, 941), quoting Fleming and Benedek (1966) writes: «The supervisor must help the candidate to develop himself as an analytical instrument», And later: «Supervision has the aim of verifying how the candidate organises his analytical functions [...] under pressure, under the tension provoked by the patient, under fire from projective identifications» (946). Yet again: «properly speaking, supervision is a specific part of personal analysis» (948).

I believe that Tagliacozzo gave these words a fully inner sense, meaning that the supervisee uses the supervisory experience in his personal analysis, or if this is over, that he uses the supervision to continue his self-analysis. Human relationships of a certain depth are opportunities for growth and change and therefore, in a more general sense, may be a part of each individual's personal path. Supervision is a privileged experience and a concentration of change because it is an intense relationship

---

[7] The same supervisor in a similar analytical situation may find himself, despite his experience, replying in an «incongruous manner» even with a degree of ingenuity, and realise this only later or not at all.

between two people who work on the inner world of a third, on their own and on the intertwined relationships. Part of this work relates to the analyst's personal work of analysis, self-analysis and re-analysis. Supervision discretely stops at the threshold to the sphere of the candidate's personal analysis.

Supervision may also be useful to sharpen the ability to realise that the patient-candidate couple is touching a delicate area in the candidate, but may not enter in that area. That is a highly private sphere open only to one's personal analyst.

WORKING ALLIANCE

Slavin and Kriegman (1996) maintain that, outside the family sphere, a person normally grants to another the possibility to influence him only when he feels that he is inside an honest, stable and reciprocal relationship. Suspicion of others and resistance to being influenced are natural, the authors maintain, until the nature of the relationship has been carefully examined.

I feel that this is what usually occurs during the initial phase of supervision if it is possible for a good working alliance to be set up.

Frijling-Schreuder (1970) was the first to use this expression, observing that: «Supervisor and candidate work together at an adult and highly sophisticated level» and «The candidate, however, should be made aware that the supervisor's attention is centred on the way in which he conducts his patient's analysis and not on the candidate's own personality problems».

«Actually – say Frijling-Schreuder – it is not a contact between equals only, because the supervisor has a second task, namely to evaluate the candidate's aptitude to become a psychoanalyst».

ASSESSMENT

Each one assesses the other, but the supervisor's assessment may have (but often does not have) a different weight. In any case this is what the supervisee thinks. «If you find that I am an extraordinary supervisor, I will find that you are an extraordinary candidate» declare Manfredi and Nissim (1984, 589) ironically of the narcissistic contract.

We are speaking of human beings and not of angels, although it is possible that the relationship is sufficiently clear and transparent and that collusion, reciprocal seductiveness and the play of crossed narcissisms [8] may be at quite a low level, while

---

8 The different work styles depend on personal variables, on the qualities which an individual may have at his disposal, on the compromise between narcissistic needs and the capacity to relate to the object. It is unlikely that the supervisor's narcissistic needs have all been dealt with, and so one may hope that the use he may put them to will not hamper the work too much. There is, for example, the supervisor who needs to be loved and is uncon-

estimation and reciprocal respect are substantial. In this case the evaluation element is not particularly to be feared, not least because it is not a figment of the imagination; it is explicit. Personally, I prefer that there be the utmost clarity in the relationship with the supervisee. What I will say officially corresponds to what I have said to the candidate during our journey. A problem clearly arises when the evaluation is negative.

This is a particularly difficult area and I am aware that my thoughts on the issue are different to those of many of my colleagues.

Let us go back a step.

There are candidates for whom analytical training is possible and others for whom it would be unadvisable. The latter are the consequence of an assessment error during selection. In theory it would be preferable to identify the error early on and remedy it. And this is where institutional lack of intervention is most apparent. Of course I am not saying that we are looking for «healthy» candidates. We would wish the candidate's personal difficulties to be sufficiently elastic as to allow his mind to address dangers and changes. We would wish him to be able to use them to understand the patient better. A candidate who has personally experienced the anxiety, anguish and depression which are habitual companions of the mind is more than welcome. We are in difficulty with a candidate who is over-rigid, paranoid or not open to insight, who is no longer working on his personal analysis and does not appear capable of evolving in self-analysis. In such a case we see a candidate who only has ears for the external reality and apparent speech, who refuses to enter into a relationship with the patient, who misses all opportunities for insight, who simply does not have what it takes to become an analyst.

The issue is not whether and how much the candidate still needs to work on his personal difficulties, but whether these are amenable to processing and can be used in working with patients. Certain personalities are simply too rigid and in these cases it would be the supervisor's duty to be clear on the matter.

Let us take a look at the situations in our institution which give rise to reflection and assessment on how the training of each candidate is progressing.

Personal analysis: the personal analyst may under no circumstances speak of the candidate in analysis.

End of year colloquia: The colloquia are seen as a moment of reflection for both trainers and candidates involved in the work that is being carried on. The aim of the

sciously seductive, without any malignity on his part; then there is the supervisor who needs to love, and continues to offer the candidate what he wishes to receive; or the one who neither wants to love nor be loved, being taken up with reassuring himself not so much that he is the best but rather that he is the one and only. He dispenses his knowledge as if it were divine rain and does not bother himself with learning if and how it is used. There are, of course, many variables and different combinations.

colloquia is to check on how well the seminars are working. At the end of the colloquia the two training analysts express careful assessments to the candidate and write up the minutes.

Opinions given by lecturers at seminars. When these exist, they are in any case fragmentary. On the other hand, a candidate seen in a group of people, on a limited number of occasions, may make an insufficient impression or even an impression which does not correspond to his real self. At times lecturers' assessments are highly discordant.

In our training who takes on the unpleasant responsibility of making assessments?

Is making assessments not part of the responsibilities of a training institute? I believe it is, and especially the assessment the candidate should receive during his training so as not to arrive at the end of it having to face the spectre of being incomprehensibly failed.

Being failed, as a consistent consequence, means a failure also for the section [9] of the training institute the candidate belongs to, which did not pick up on the weaknesses (was it myopic? careless?), which saw the weaknesses but did nothing about them (cowardly? sloppy? collusive? a case of beauty being in the eye of the beholder?), which did not see them because there weren't any, but did not prepare the candidate properly, or produce adequate and appropriate documentation of the candidate's merits. This is another delicate point as it concerns mutual confidence in the fairness of the training analysts belonging to the four different sections, and in the efficiency and efficacy of training sections.

What I wish to say is that if the members of the commission for qualification believe that they may trust the assessment made by the local training section, such an assessment should weigh heavily on the commission for qualification's judgment and the candidate would not be exposed to a type of roulette, depending on the commission he is called before or perhaps even on the mood of the commission members.

How is a correct evaluation made? In my opinion the candidate should be kept informed both during his training and at the end of it. The evaluation should include at least three aspects, the first being to protect the interests of the patients, the second those of the candidate and the third those of the SPI as institution.

To this end we must ask ourselves whether:

. the candidate who applies for qualification is able to work with his patient without causing harm and if he has developed adequate analytical skills;

---

[9] In the Italian Psychoanalytical Society the Training Institute is structured in four local sections spread throughout the country. The candidate's training is the responsibility of the local section; the committee for qualification is made up of five training analysts belonging to the National Training Institute, that is, by analysts belonging to the different local sections.

. he is capable of tolerating the stress of the profession without incurring serious personal consequences (in other words whether it would not be preferable for him to choose another profession which might be less taxing mentally);

. the institution may be damaged, in its organisation and prestige, by the aspiring member's unresolved conflict issues, by his rigidity or shortcomings in human, intellectual and analytical terms.

This assessment should be carried out during the candidate's training. In my opinion it should be worked through during the meetings held by the local training section, where the seminar lecturers and the supervisors, being the people who knows the candidate best, could propose their assessment to the training analysts of the local section.[10] There are those who believe that the supervisor's opinion should be taken with a grain of salt, as he is in such a close relationship with the supervisee as to risk, for any number of reasons, losing his objectivity and sense of distance.

However, exaggerated caution and suspicion lead to a paralysis in which no-one takes responsibility for anything in order not to run any risk, with the result that we put ourselves in a situation in which the risks are much greater. I have never thought that the supervisor's opinion is the only valid one, but rather that it can be a great help in knowing and assessing the candidate, within the more general assessment made by all the training analysts and the lecturers belonging to the local section, with whom he has come in contact.

The tutor should speak to the candidate. Roles and competencies have all been set up, but do they work?

Personally, as a supervisor, I take it upon myself to speak openly to the supervisee if I realise that he is lacking the requisites for him to become an analyst. I suggest that he take up his personal analysis again or, if his personal analyst is no longer available, undergo re-analysis. I tell him that I will be expressing my doubts to the training section. I speak to the training section of these issues as soon as I understand that the supervision can not work on levels which have to do with one's personal analysis, and I ask the section to shoulder its responsibilities. In any event the candidate is aware of the situation.

In my opinion this decision should not be left up to the will of the individual, but should become a shared and agreed upon practice, as otherwise it risks being over-zealous or even arbitrary.

I feel that the partisanship of local sections could be damaging to the institution. If we could let go of anachronistic partisanship and work better on the residual diffi-

---

10 Anne-Marie Sandler (1998) insists on the supervisor's responsibility. On the other hand, as this would be a responsibility shared with the training section there would be no risk of falling into the «pressing supervisee -supervisor bind, into the retroactive recovery of the dual relationship analyst-analysand, or into the marginalisation of the seminar and the Institute» to which Di Chiara (1999, 457) rightly draws our attention.

dence, we would be able to develop sufficient reciprocal trust in the fairness and reliability of the assessment of the candidate's section.

SUMMARY

The author reflects both on the supervisor's thoughts and emotions, which precede and accompany the first meetings with the candidate, and on the narcissistic worries and persecutory anxieties that are to be found in both participants. The two clinical examples presented show some of the ways in which the couple at work functions. Insight is seen as a function of the couple's creativity, being able to tolerate uncertainty and leave narcissistic competition behind. The classical themes of training, symmetry-asymmetry, working alliance and evaluation are examined. Finally, the subject of the Training Institute's responsibilities is dealt with.

KEY WORDS: Influence, respect, working alliance, evaluation.

BIBLIOGRAPHY

DI CHIARA G. (1999). L'inconscio e la formazione psicoanalitica. *Riv Psicoanal.*, 45, 3.
FRIJLING-SCHREUDER E. C. (1970). On individual supervision. *Int. J. Psycho-Anal.*, 51, 363-370.
GEDIMAN H. K., WOLKENFELD F. (1980). The parallelism phenomenon in psychoanalysis and supervision: its reconsideration as a triadic system. *Psychoanal. Q.*, 49, 234-255.
JACOBS D., DAVID P., MEYER D. J. (1995). *The supervisory encounter*. New Haven, CT, Yale University Press.
LEVENSON E. A. MD. (1982). Follow the fox. An inquiry into the vicissitudes of psychoanalytic supervision. *Cont. Psychoanal.*, 18, 1-15.
LUSSANA P. (1999). Introduzione alla teoria e tecnica della supervisione. *Riv. Psicoanal.*, 65, 465-473.
MANFREDI S., NISSIM L. (1984). Il supervisore al lavoro. *Riv. Psicoanal.*, 30, 4.
MARTIN G. C., MAYERSON P., OLSEN H. E., WIBERG J. L. (1978). Candidates' evaluation of psychoanalytic supervision. *J. Amer. Psychoanal. Assn.*, 26, 407-424.
NISSIM MOMIGLIANO L. (1980). Note in margine a un testo: la supervisione analitica. In G. Di Chiara (a cura di), *Itinerari della psicoanalisi*, Torino, Loescher, 1982.
SANDLER A.M. (1998). La transmission de la psychanalyse aujourd'hui. *Psycanalyse en Europe*, 50.
SLAVIN M. O., KRIEGMAN D. (1998). Why the analyst needs to change: toward a theory of conflict, negotiation, and mutual influence in the therapeutic process. *Psychoanal. Dial.*, 8, 247-284.
TAGLIACOZZO R. (1989). La supervisione. In A. A. Semi (a cura di), *Trattato di Psicoanalisi*, vol. II, «Clinica». Milano, Cortina, 1989.
YERUSHALMI H. (1999). Mutual influences in supervision. *Cont. Psychoanal.*, 35, 415-436.

Original italian version:
Riv. Psicoanal., 2007, 4, 959-975

Loredana Micati

Via Brunico, 6

00135 Roma

(Translated by Carol Carmody)

Disavowal of the erotic body, defects in primary containment and obsessional-autarchic shell in the analysis of two women

FRANCESCO CARNAROLI

> With every window that opens, I feel I am being attacked.
>
> (patient B)

In this paper I shall deal with the analysis (four sessions a week) of two women (A and B) who displayed a lack of psychic integration of the genital erotic body and a defect in their access (not only in reality but also in the internal world) to the erotic-genital couple relationship. These women were professionally successful and showed high intelligence. Patient B had never been in a relationship. Patient A had had a few but they had been short-lived and unsuccessful, in particular since they had been the result of a voluntaristic decision (without genital drive support), a wish to experiment, a sense of not wanting to be different from the others.

At the beginning and for a considerable part of the analysis, the sexual subject seemed to be something abstract and inconceivable to these patients. They had successfully managed not wanting to have anything to do «with that», with this thing that was not even named. During analysis, the hypothesis of secret masturbation proved totally unfounded.

The symptoms that had led A and B to seek analysis were depression, a sense of solitude and emptiness, states of chronic anxiety, and panic attacks.

As far as past depression was concerned, it seemed to be linked – amongst other things – to the psychic devitalization that originates from the lack of psychic integration of the erotic body. «Everything that provokes anaesthesia encourages the generation of melancholia», Freud observed and then added: «Melancholia consists in mourning over loss of libido» (1895, 199-200). However, the missing integration of the erotic body aside, the lack of meaning and vitality (vital depression) appeared to be linked to the missing introjection of the «elementary forms of contact and resonance» in the primary relationship (Fédida, 2001, 212).

During analysis it was observed that these patients had implemented a precocious disavowal both as regards their own genital feelings and the existence of a sexual tie between their parents. I believe that the activity of disavowal does not exclude the presence of displacement but that it influences the nature of the contents it acts upon. Indeed, the *disavowal (Verleugnung)* of the reality of the erotic body and the related *foreclosure (Verwerfung)* of the symbolic transcription of the disavowed content[1] act on the prodromes, on the initial outlines of an incipient fantasy. I therefore believe one can state that if disavowal mechanisms towards spontaneous genital feelings were put into effect in the beginning, the later oedipal fantasies will have characteristic traits: the form of a rudimental outline, lacking in development, sudden disavowal. Above all, however, there seems to be a «missing link» constituted by the sexual relationship between the parents (Britton, 1989). As a result, when this displacement takes place, the unconscious representations that ensue also have specific characteristics – scarce symbolic expression, a prevalently persecutory nature and the parents (and their genitals) are kept separate in them.

During analysis, *the problems these patients had as regards their genitality were shown to be the distant consequences of problems they had had during their early childhood.*

THEORETICAL-CLINICAL OUTLINE

During A and B's childhood there were defects in primary containment. Here I would like to outline three developmental objectives of such containment that are pertinent to the psychogenesis of the problem in question.

A) The infant needs to perceive relative continuity between the uterine and the postnatal environment and it therefore needs to experience a *sensual-epidermic containment*[2] that, according to Gaddini (1987) offers it, «a boundary-environment [...] in which to function simply and spontaneously». The perception of an Ego-skin (Anzieu, 1985), of a membrane that acts as the border of the Self, develops through the introjection of this sensual-epidermic function of the container. The formation of such a boundary triggers important developments: 1) the progressive elaboration of mourning as regards the initial perception of being a narcissistic unity with the caregiver; 2) the sense of one's own internal space and of an internal space within another; 3) the progressive embodiment of the mind, by means of a symbolic assimilation process of the sensorial input this results in. Winnicott (1962, 58) says: «The ego is based on a body ego, but it is only when all goes well that the person of the baby starts to be linked with the body and the body-functions, with the *skin* as the *limiting membrane*». If the baby is sure that it has its own boundaries, within them it can start a

---

[1] For the definition of the concepts of disavowal (Freud) and foreclosure (Freud and Lacan), see Laplanche and Pontalis (1967).

[2] Amongst others, Winnicott (1962, 58), Bick (1968), Anzieu (1985), Marcelli (1986,68), Ogden (1989, 30, 53) have studied this *sensual-epidermic function of the container.*

spontaneous process of psychic integration of the psychosomatic Self, the sensorial input and the drives coming from its own body.

B) Vygotsky's hypothesis (1930-31), which claims an infant has a *primary sociality* that precedes identification,[3] has been confirmed more and more by infant research. We now know (Trevarthen, 1997; Beebe and Lachman, 2002) just how many skills both members of the mother-child system are capable of – empathic, reciprocal miming and acoustic mirroring. Although the infant does not yet differentiate between Self and object, in the primary relationship, if things go well, it develops a «playful relationship» (Fattirolli, 2007), which I believe is the first prototype of the *creative intimacy* between two partners, characterized by the ability to play and by vitality and emotional spontaneity. There is a reciprocal game of communicative projective identification with a constant changing of roles so that each partner influences the direction of the other's later emotional and cognitive expression.

C) Depending on the extent to which the caregiver begins to be represented in the infant's mind, 1) as a separate subject, 2) as a container that is able to think and with an affectively charged memory towards the Self, the child is then able to experience *emotional peaks consisting of moments of symbiotic abandonment to the caregiver.* In his description of the symbiotic relationship between mother and child, Pine (1985,41) does not describe it as a stable characteristic in a specific phase of the child's life, but as high-intensity, affectively significant moments of the infant's day, in which it experiences the loss of boundaries, without a feeling of anxiety, as part of a rhythm of letting itself go and returning to itself. An example of this kind of experience are «the postnursing moments of falling asleep at the mother's breast».

Such pleasant and emotionally intense experiences are the prototypes of later experiences of the loss of the boundaries of the Self, including *passionate falling in love* and the *orgasm.*

If one is to be able to appreciate the experience of their loss, one needs to be able to perceive one's boundaries with a sense of security. As Kernberg (1977) says, «There is a basic, intrinsic contradiction in the combination of these two crucial features of sexual love: the precondition of firm boundaries of the self [...] and the sense of transcendence, of becoming one with the loved person. [...]. Loneliness, one might say, is a precondition for transcendence».

On the basis of the infant's history and the analytical transference history, one can hypothesize that as infants, patients A and B experienced a premature sense of separateness and the consequent traumatic sense of the fragility of their own boundaries. In the face of this experience, they reacted by creating a specific defensive organisation, in which this *clinging to the object* (Hermann, 1935; 1943) to patch the hole in the membrane of the Self played a key role. Such a relationship mode was estab-

---

3 For more on the subject see Carnaroli (2001).

lished when possible towards the external object, but prevalently and more constantly in the internal world – in a secret psychic world I shall call *obsessional-autarchic shell,* in which there is a *clinging to the object trapped inside the Self.*[4]

I believe that the relational configuration that is established in the obsessional-autarchic shell can be described as the *anal organization of object relationship.*

In anal autoerotism there is «a sort of object love» (Ferenczi, 1914, 321) towards the captured, incorporated object (Freud, 1915, 248). In this kind of object relationship, «the desired person is conceived as an object of possession and as a result is associated with the most primitive form of possession, that is, bodily content, excrements. […] And for the unconscious of the patient, the loss of the object […] therefore means an expulsion of the object in the sense of the bodily expulsion of excrements» (Abraham, 1924, 425-426). In the phantasy of anal retention, there is «the wish to preserve the object on condition that it be totally under the subject's control» (Heimann, 1962).

In the girls A and B, the construction of the obsessional-autarchic shell primarily had the function of creating an internal space marked by boundaries, to ward off the anxiety of un-integration that was linked to *defects in the sensual-epidermic containment.* The sense of cohesion that the Self achieved in this manner was, however, guaranteed by shutting off the other, and could therefore only be preserved at the price of reducing to the minimum inter-subjective relationship. From the very start, there was therefore a *defect in the playful relationship,* not just because of the problems the mothers had in adapting, but also because of the difficulty the young girls had in making their own contents come out, since they feared they might fall into a space with no boundaries. In the context of such an internal operational model it was therefore impossible to develop the ability of experiencing a deep emotional *abandonment* of the self to the *caregiver.*

The two girls had a docile attitude towards their mother, even if it was clearly *avoidant*; they were both praised as «good girls».

At a certain stage during analysis, both the patients showed me some photographs of when they were young. I took notes of the impressions those photographs had on me: the two descriptions are very similar, so I shall overlap them here, in search of a «model».

In some of these photos the girls were around their mothers' necks, but in a very strange position. It was as if they were fending something off – their bodies were rigid, removed from that of their mother, an outstretched arm to keep their distance, and a twisting of the back so they were looking elsewhere. Their faces were grim, expressionless, and ashen in appearance, with a blank look as if they were looking

---

[4] For more on the subject see the Abraham and Torok's description (1987, 125-131) of a crypt in which there is clutching to an incorporated object. The concept of *claustrum* formulated by Meltzer (1992) also proved useful on this subject.

inwards. They seemed totally self- absorbed, as if they could only make contact by concentrating on an object they had captured within themselves.

I felt that these photographs were the plastic expression of a specific internal operational model, at the border of the avoidant (trying to achieve the perceptive disavowal of their own needs for love) and ambivalent (clinging to the external caregiver by meeting their expectations but above all, the internal object they had captured inside).

I also felt that such a complex relational model (avoidant external behaviour but also one that is satisfied and accommodating, with the secret possession of the primary object) could probably constitute the first infantile prototype of a later *hysterical conflict*.

The object to be possessed is inside me, and I shall deny my interest in it in the external reality.

The possible origin of the hysterical conflict in the primary relationship with the mother was already been pointed out by Fairbairn who believes that the child develops a two-fold attitude in response to a mother who is both an exciting and a rejecting object. According to Fairbairn (1954, 24), «an infantile situation in which the mother plays both these roles would appear to provide the basic nucleus round which the hysterical personality is characteristically built».

Depending on to what extent the defensive organization in the form of the obsessional-autarchic shell was able to ward off the anxiety regarding the fragility of the self boundaries and the lack of self integration, this conditioned in a way I could call *tyrannical*, each later developmental stage, leaving behind a truly destorting mark on the various stages of the developmental process.

In particular, as far as psychosexual development is concerned, there were two consequences in the minds of the two patients that are the subjects I would like to concentrate on in this article.

A) Disavowal of spontaneous vaginal feelings

Both Freud (1924, 173; 1931, 225, 228) and Deutsch (1925) claimed that vaginal feelings occur during puberty. In particular, he believed (as he stated in his letter to Abraham dated 8th December 1924) that in young girls there are anal expressions of the libido. «The vagina, as we know, is a later acquisition through separation from the cloaca» (Freud & Abraham, 1907-1925, 528).

I believe, however, that in female psychosexual development any anal overinvestment has defensive origins following the disavowal of vaginal feelings – in phantasy, the anal orifice may be kept closed once the object of desire has been captured and kept.

This is on the assumption that there are spontaneous vaginal feelings in girls, as claimed by Horney and Klein and more recently by Lichtenberg (1989, 283): «The occurrence of erections and vaginal engorgement from infancy on during both REM sleep and awake states indicates that the lived experience contributing to the sense of self emerging includes genital sensation that triggers some level of sensual pleasure».

Horney (1924, 1926, 1933) and Klein (1928, 1932, 268-269, 287-289) claimed that genital anxiety in young girls, consisting in the fear of harming their own genitals,[5] is derived from phantasies of penetration (from their father's large penis) and from retaliation (from the mother).

While I agree with Horney in particular as regards the fact that disavowal of the vagina[6] is derived from damaging fantasies, I believe that *the anxiety of damage that sparks off the disavowal of female genital feelings does not refer to the vagina, but to the boundaries of the Self.*

If the boundaries of the Self are perceived to be fragile as the result of defects in containment, there will be difficulties in the integration of the psychosomatic Self. Potentially, every orifice can be perceived as a fault. In particular (as was the case with the young girls A and B), there was a *precocious disavowal of vaginal spontaneous feelings* because of the earlier and immediate meaning attributed to those sensations – there is an orifice there, *an opening which might allow an intrusion into one's own boundaries and the object of one's own desire may then later part from them.* In such a case, the incipient phantasies caused by such sensations (the desire that that internal sensitive area is the object of a penetrating contact that arouses sensual pleasure) immediately assume an agonizingly persecutory meaning. The idea that a penis enters is just as intolerable as the idea that it leaves and detaches itself from one's own body. The most tolerable fantasy is that of a faecal penis, captured and kept inside oneself.

B) Disavowal of the sexual relationship between one's parents

If it is to be able to create the premises to allow its full access to the genital erotic-emotional relationship in its own internal world, the child needs to experience all three sides of the Oedipal triangle, including the fantasies regarding the relationship of its parents as a couple.[7]

If development is relatively good, the oedipal preconscious[8] is confirmed in the fact that each parent is thinking of the other – the mother refers to the father,[9] and

---

[5] In 1933 Horney wrote an article entitled «*Die Verleugnung* [*disavowal*] der vagina». However, in the English translation of Horney (1967), it appears with the title «The denial of the vagina ».

[6] And not in the observation of the lack of male genitals as Freud claimed (1925, 254-256; 1931, 229-234, 241).

[7] David (1971); Money-Kyrle (1971); Meltzer (1973); Britton (1989).

[8] See Freud (1914): he speaks of «phylogenetically inherited schemata, which [...] are concerned with the business of 'placing' the impressions derived from actual experience. [...]. The Oedipus complex, [...] is, in fact, the best known member of the class. Wherever experiences fail to fit in with the hereditary schema, they become remodelled in the imagination» (119).

[9] Depending on the extent to which there is a trace of Oedipal love in the mother towards her own father (Ogden, 1989, 109-110, 123) and the libidinal tie with her own partner. In this manner, the mother not only indicates the presence of a third person, but also gives her own blessing to the young girl's entrance in Oedipal interest.

vice-versa. If nothing else, the primal scene is marked by signs of intimacy between the couple.

The perception of such intimacy, in which there are characteristics that differ from those that each parent has in his/her relationship with the child, have far-reaching consequences:

1) It «involves relinquishing the idea of sole and permanent possession of mother and leads to a profound sense of loss» (Britton, 1989, 84); furthermore, it is also a source of frustrating feelings of exclusion.

2) However, it is also a source of reassurance. Indeed, it contributes to the creation of clear, protective boundaries between the area of sensual tenderness and the area of genital sexuality.[10]

3) It takes on a propulsive meaning (David, 1971) – the intuition of an arousing, gratifying and forbidden relationship that binds the parents and excludes the child, activates the desire to become familiar with this exciting forbidden knowledge, albeit by means of the necessary process of mourning. This relationship of the couple is a trail mark that is internalized in the psychic place of the ideal and becomes a desirable developmental achievement.

4) It contributes to the process of signification of genital sexuality, which takes place in two directions – from the sensual-sensorial to the relational and vice-versa – and there is therefore a *reciprocal relationship between bodily sensations and phantasies about relationship* – a) the genital feelings activate phantasies that give a meaning to the sexual couple; b) the introjective identification with the parental genital couple (Meltzer, 1973, 115) is a decisive factor in the attribution of a meaning to genital feelings, fuelling the imagination of desirable scenarios of growing up in a *potential exogamous space*. If things go well, the latter begins to be fuelled during phantasies in childhood and then takes root in inter-personal relationships outside the family during adolescence.

However, in the patients A and B since this clinging was working in function of the non-recognition of the separation from the primary object, from a psychological point of view this meant that the sense that two people exist did not completely form; on such a basis it was impossible for the idea to develop that there were three people and as a result there was no representation of the primal scene or any psychic elaboration of the Oedipal triangular space.

The relationship between the parents was also disavowed (with the *environmental compliance* of one of them, as we shall see). The absence of any psychic elaboration of the affective-erotic relationship between the parents therefore becomes a gap, a «missing link» (Britton, 1989) in the young girls' psychic apparatus.

---

10 See Ferenczi (1932) for the distinction between tenderness in infantile eroticism and passionality in adult eroticism.

The disavowal of genital feelings and of the sexual relationship between the parents reinforces one another in turn, thus obstructing the development described above.

It can be observed that: 1) this disavowal of the parents' relationship is reflected in the perception of one's own body, and a *horizontal split* takes place – above the relationship with the breast, below the relationship with the penis. The erotic attraction towards the breast is allowed since it is a sensual object that refers to a still unsatisfactory and not yet introjected containing primary relationship. The relationship «below» with the fantasies of the penis is much more hidden; 2) both relationships (with the breast and with the penis) are destined to remain «trapped» in autoeroticism since they are carried out with an object that has been captured inside the Self. The breast is one's own breast while the penis is a faecal penis.

EXTRACTS FROM THE BACKGROUND OF A AND B WHEN INFANTS

Within their families, A and B found no environmental support towards the entrance into the oedipal triangular space; on the contrary, they experienced an anti-Oedipal developmental hold up that had trans-generational meaning.

What had happened was that one of the parents had *formed a couple* with the young girl, excluding the other parental partner, thus contributing to the child's phantasy that there was no third person, that there was no primal scene, that there was not Oedipal stage and that the desired goal – in the present as well as in the future – was to seek refuge in a closed space, to create a fusional union that was both salvific (since it enveloped) and desperate and claustrophobic.

Racamier (1995) called this kind of relational configuration *incestual* – incest without enacted sex, but rather with the sharing of a *disavowal pact* (Kaës, 1992) in which the genitals do not exist.

In the creation of such a an incestual pact aimed at disavowal, there is a determining contribution by the parent, who sees in the daughter the completion of a narcissistic fault and therefore will be unable to support the separation-identification process, which is perceived as a catastrophic wound.

It is as if the two partners wanted to preserve their lives and therefore remain immobile and the psychosomatic emergences that herald growth can therefore not be metabolized and integrated in the young girl's Self. Above all, the third person is expelled and a single cocoon that contains both partners is idealized, thus hindering the process of separation-identification and the creation of the individual boundaries of the Self.

Patient A

The patient described the relationship her mother had with her as avoidant, both from the point of view of physical contact and of empathic playful exchange. The mother sought refuge in her job. The care she took of the child focused on food.

A remembers that as a child she felt the *need to have a secret,* something her mother should not be told – but it was done in such a way that it was always possible for the mother to discover it. For example, there was a period when she used to *wet herself,* and would then hide her dirty underpants in places where her mother was bound to find them sooner or later.

A would look at her mother hoping to find recognition, but what she found made her feel a sense of emptiness. For many years, from adolescence until after starting analysis, A had a *phobia of mirrors,* because she could see the reflection of that rejecting gaze.

From the very start the patient's father had a very affectionate relationship with her, and it seemed to save her from the emotional poverty of her relationship with her mother. With great resourcefulness the patient filled all the spaces and roles her mother had left vacant. She and her father formed a couple that excluded both the mother and the younger sister.

A described her father's behaviour to her as follows: «My father made me feel that *if I was separated from him, I would loose everything. He would say: You'll only be fine with me, nobody will love you as much as me*». A's father was very sweet to her when she met his expectations, but if she appeared to be separated, he withdrew his affection.

For several summers (until A was 16), her father would take her on holiday with him, just the two of them. In the hotels they would share a double bed. There was no active sex. «I am sure his intentions were good. He just wanted me to remain his little girl, so he just *did not perceive* that I was growing».

When A was 12 she had her first period. Her mother said to her: «It's a nuisance; it's something women have to put up with. There are *things one does to please men*, because you know, they have strange needs … you *have* to do them».

When she reached puberty, the predominance and strength of this tie with her father led to a (renewed) rejection of genitality. The preservation of this tie had the upper hand over the mentalization of her erotic body.

During adolescence the patient suffered from *anorexia* for a while and she would blatantly leave the table to go and vomit the food she had just eaten. Apart from the anger she felt towards her mother «who was only worried about food», it is possible that this behaviour was also an expression of not wanting to grow up and wanting to remain her father's little girl for ever.

Patient B

Patient B slept in the double bed with her mother until she was fourteen. The father was sent to sleep in the bedroom that had originally been furnished for the daughter, and he was constantly belittled.

B's mother had also shared the double bed with her mother (excluding the father), and had always wanted to be fused in a single entity with her mother; in addition, she had always found «the mere idea» that her parents might have sex disgusting. She would often say to B: *those kinds of things are just not for me.*

This mother's behaviour towards her daughter was that of a constant appeal to share absolutely everything since they loved each other so much. B, however, did not have particularly pleasant memories of her childhood. She remembers that the atmosphere at home was tense and gloomy. Her mother would express her affection in a pointed, brusque and intrusive manner, with sudden changes in her behaviour that seemed to happen especially when B mentioned detaching herself, not being at one with her mother.

B remembers that ever since she was tiny, she withdrew, avoided contact and gave signs of being a separate person («I stayed on my little rug», she said), so as not to feel violated, to protect herself against what she experienced as intrusion and control by her mother. The latter had isolated both herself and her daughter in their own little world, one that excluded everyone else and she encouraged absolutely no kind of development of B's relationships with others. In such circumstances of total affective isolation, B was forced to cling to the very person who was controlling and intruding in her (considering her as a part of herself), and she would freeze in terror every time she saw her frowning.

When she reached puberty, her genital feelings – and the very existence of her vagina – were once again disavowed by A and also B. They could only wash themselves without any direct contact with their genitals, by immerging themselves in the bath. Later, for obvious reasons of hygiene, they came to a compromise – they concocted the use of a *little sponge* to wash their genitals, so that there was something between their hand and the genitals so as to avoid any direct contact.

DURING ANALYSIS

Both patients decided to go into analysis when they were on the verge of a breakdown. What they were looking for was a container to put their pervasive anxiety in and to help them metabolize it. During the first session patient A said, «I'm looking for a uterus». However, faced with a patient who clamoured for containment, I soon had the occasion to observe that there were two traits emerging in the analytical relationship. First of all, neither of the patients had assigned me with a function of deep containment; on the contrary, I found myself functioning as an epidermic container, of a *placating mothering*. Secondly, it seemed that they were guarding their own private, autarchic relational world, with a function of self-containment, a phantasy world that had to stay secret, so it would remain the source of a little vitality and self-cohesion.

Their discourse was characterized by a low, uniform tone and the use of abstract terms that were far-removed from any emotional experiences. They described their experiences by taking them apart, bit by bit. Abstracting and taking to pieces seemed to be the means to keep emotional intensity low, as if emotional peaks would have resulted in pain and disorganization.

It is this obsessional aspect in particular that I refer to as their way of preserving their sense of Self in an autarchic shell. Since there had been no primary inter-subjective field of sharing and elaboration of emotions, the latter were only bearable if they were subjected to various processes that made them less dangerous.

Such discourse modes required the lengthy working through of counter-transference reactions. Although I felt myself becoming more and more bored and sleepy, I realized that such reactions risked taking on a ruinous role and therefore confirming what was a vicious circle – you *make me angry because you are so distant and distracted, so I'll have to carry on containing myself alone.*

Patient A

In the first (lengthy) phase of analysis, in the transference the diffidence towards the reliability of the analytical partner was very clear. There were frequent moments of anger because of what she felt was an imbalance between her efforts to *activate* the analyst's mind and the lack of commitment by the latter to adapt actively to her needs. Her dreams frequently expressed her anger that I was busy with something else. For example: 1) «I came back to my office after the holidays and found that my things had been taken away, someone else was now in my office». 2) «I had an affair with a man who had had lots of affairs. So he was unreliable. I said to him: «Look! That's enough!». And I fell down, I slipped and I broke my ribs».

While I felt that her commitment to analysis expressed her *need to cling to me*, at the same time I had the feeling that, basically, she was still *withdrawn in herself.*

Schematically, during the initial period of analysis and in the transference in particular, I seemed to have represented her impermeable, impenetrable and withholding mother, who had not given her any space where she could feel welcome, and which had therefore exposed her to the risk of falling to pieces. Within such a relationship (and within the transference), it was as if she felt she could only stay alive by seeking refuge inside herself since, if she peeped into the inter-subjective field, she could feel her emotions sliding on the surface of the mother (and analyst) without leaving any marks.

Later on, the analytical relationship prevalently took on the traits that had characterized her relationship with her father – *a reliable relationship, unique in the way she had been able to portray it during her life – a relationship without the presence of any third person on the horizon, in which she dedicated herself to the other person, she was his prisoner and he her keeper.*

I was aware of the risks of a dead end (and the interminability of analysis) that were entailed in letting oneself be carried away in such a narcissistic fusion.

In this transference context, A described a dream she had had when she was 12, just after she got her first period – «I went into my parents' bedroom, where they were sleeping in the double bed; I cut off my father's penis and I took it away, going down the corridor that led to my bedroom. While I was walking down the corridor the penis grew bigger in my hands, and the bigger it got, the more anxietyr I felt – so when I got to my bedroom, I thought 'I don't know what to do with it' and I threw it away, in the corridor».

On that particular occasion the young girl was angry with her father because he had made her bedroom into his study and she had had to go and share a bedroom with her sister. The dream described the expulsion of the paternal penis («it's useless») in a moment of anger. However, this made me think that usually, *the father's penis is one of the parts of the other that is trapped inside the Self.*

I told her what I was thinking and also asked: «And does the same thing happen with me, you take my penis, take it inside yourself or do you throw it away when you are angry?».

She answered: «I start with the idea I have in my head about my experience with my father. I can't have a normal emotional life – either I steal something or I won't have anything».

The entire meaning was concentrated on the father. The mother had been deprived of (and she had deprived herself off) a sense of her own value and true role. The result: the mother was not the mother and the father could not carry out the role of the father because he was being the mother.

She later described the following dream: «I decided to throw an atomic bomb on an island near the one where I was. Before I did it, I thought about all the possible dangerous consequences – would the smoke from the explosion reach my island? No, it was too far away. I dropped the bomb. Then I am on my island with my father. It was only then that I realized how stupid I had been because I hadn't thought about the radiation, the consequences of atomic fall-out, which has a much wider range of action. Always being alone with my father. I think the bomb was on my mother. It's her fault I needed my father so much».

The desired aim is a narcissistic attunement with a container, without absolutely any recognition of separateness, otherness, or sexual differentiation. The parents are kept rigorously in «isolation». The «bad mother» is assassinated in function of making sure the «good father/mother» remains close. However, there is also the realization of the radioactive fall-out on her: in the sense that she no longer has an adult object of the same sex she can identify with. She also no longer had the image of a sexual couple she could identify with, before separating from it and then having her own sexual life.

This fantasied attack against her parents' genitals implies an undoing, in the *après-coup*, of the daughter's capacity to integrate her own genitals.

The reinforced reappearance of genital feelings during puberty encountered no scenario of introjected internal object relationships that could confer it with meaning or legitimacy and it was therefore relegated to a confused a-symbolic private space.

I think the following dream is of importance in this respect:

«I'm sitting down and have a blanket over my legs; I don't have any underpants on. There is a man standing next to me, a geological expert. We are near a volcano, which is in a house on a hill, there's magma inside and it's dangerous. The man puts a hand on my leg, the blanket slides off and you can see the pubes. I look at the house; I can see it is being invaded by red-hot volcanic magma from inside. A sort of blob that is pushing as if it was going to flow out of the windows, but it doesn't. The magma is burning everything. The windows are already blackened. I ask myself: «Am I the only one who can see it?».

In the transference, the surfacing of genital sensations was just as it had been during the long trips with the father, without meaning and destructive since they were out of kilter with the desired object relation, and were therefore destined to remain only brief private flashes which would immediately be rejected and soon become invisible to her as well within a brief space of time.

During her fourth year of analysis, the patient described the following dreams:

«I was working in a hospital and I had to perform an operation on a small girl but she had the vagina of an adult. The operation consisted in removing a membrane and proboscis from this vagina … I just realized at this moment that they correspond to the hymen and the clitoris … Thanks to this operation the young girl would be able to suck at the breast … But what has the vagina got to do with the mouth that sucks the breast?».

Analyst: «It is as if you were telling me: "I was a closed child, I couldn't trust anyone and I put a membrane between my mouth and breast. The only thing I let out of myself was something I had controlled before. Now I would like a more direct and deeper contact". According to the sequence of the dream, it seems that the desired objective was sucking milk at the breast».

Patient: «The only kind of masturbation I knew was touching my breast».

Analyst: «In the dream it is you who is performing the operation – you want to have control of the situation».[11]

Patient: «Well, yes … otherwise I feel lost, in total chaos».

Patient B

In the first dream B described to me, she and her mother were flying in an airship («an elliptical figure in which two centres are enclosed in the same involucrum» – said the patient, a mathematician); far away, down on the earth, one could see some

---

11 Other interpretations of this dream were given «in stages» but they are too lengthy to go in to here.

animals (animals-instincts – she said – that cannot be accepted and integrated inside such a relationship).

I believe that at birth, B was caught up in the maternal phantasy concerning a single involucrum that encloses the idealized tie between young girl and mother-breast.

I believed that this incestual and anti-Oedipal phantasy incited a horizontal division of the body scheme. At the top the idealized tie between the child and breast and below – separated – the rejected instinctual tie between the parents' genitals.

The second dream B told me was as follows: «A man I like comes up to me and hugs me and I was frantic. He says. "I know the reason for your problems – I've never told you until now because I didn't want to be intrusive – when you were small, your mother introduced you to a man". Then I have the feeling that the inside of my body is transparent… as if you could see it with X-rays … my digestive system – mouth, oesophagus, stomach and intestines».

I told her that the dream expressed the emergence of her anxiety as soon as she began to rely on the analytical relationship – «It is possible that the intrusive man your mother introduced you to when you were small represents the intrusiveness of your mother. The watchful maternal phallus that reached your internal organs via X-rays».[12]

The relationship B had with her mother was the only container she knew and she could not live without it. This is why (but also because that modality had already been suggested by the incestuous maternal phantasy) the intrusive aspects of that relationship were projected onto the outside, to the bad-father man. Consequently, the infantile genital feelings had to be rejected due to the correspondence perceived between penetration and intrusion.

As Micati (1988) observed, «abandoning oneself to passivity in the face of an omnipotent mother can be the equivalent to being exposed to devastating irruptions in one's own body».

As a result of the fact that her mother did not adapt to the needs of her emerging Self, and on the contrary, she was enclosed within the envelope of the maternal phantasy, B had the distressing sensation of having no personal boundary. This led to the creation of an obsessional-autarchic shell inside her. This therefore did not facilitate separateness from the mother because the small shell had been created within the «ellipse» that also enveloped the mother – a small enclosed space within a closed space. During the intermediate stage of analysis patient B described the following dream:

«I'm in my bedroom, it's night time. I can hear a man coming up the stairs. He is a threat and I'm frightened. I see a shovel and I hit the man with it. After that he appears

---

[12] See further on for an interpretation of this dream from a different point of view in a different transference phase. Indeed, as Riolo (2002) observed, the analysis of the transference is decisive in the assessment of «the point of urgency on which the interpretation must be insisted on to unravel a meaning that would otherwise remain overdetermined».

two-dimensional and much smaller. I go to the window and want to ask for help but there isn't anybody out there. In the meanwhile another man is coming up the stairs».

I told her that the man coming up the stairs could represent her own split off desires that were projected into the man. This idea of mine seemed to be confirmed by the fact that there appeared to be an eternal fight – every time her desire surfaced and was made harmless, soon another desire, simingly another man, came up the stairs.

She then began describing something to me – it took a number of sessions – that had happened to her recently and which had led to an «obsessional thought». For years the patient had found it impossible to tell me about the obsessional thoughts that were tormenting her. She would mention them, but as if from a great distance and very vaguely, and I could not get the message. And I did not insist because I knew that in the transference I was constantly at risk of actually being perceived as the *intrusive x-ray man.*

This was the first time that the message came across – although with great effort, very long-windedly, with frequent outbursts of abstraction that made every contact with the concrete experience disappear, and which I responded to by asking her to try and stick closer to the episode she was trying to tell me about otherwise I would have no chance of understanding her.

The episode concerned the present surfacing of impulses to masturbate and a fantasy linked to them. I would like to quote a few extracts in which the will to talk about it prevailed over the other that was conflictually present of not talking about it: «I really feel like I'm being attacked … in an isolated room … by impulses that lead to a sort of auto-erotism … But then the bit that is connected to masturbation disappears … While it was happening, *I could smell my bra* … [she cries] … The fact is, that thought, the smell of my bra has become an "obsessional thought"».

It then emerged that around puberty, there had been a period when she was aroused when she saw photographs of women wearing a bra (in fashion magazines).

I told her, «But, to protect your boundaries you have to take anything good into your shell, you have to be able to think you have to do everything alone, and thus, the erotic object is none other than your own breast».

A short while later she described the following dream: «I was driving a car, I put my hand outside the window and a sort of sticky powder stuck to it, maybe it was manna. When I finally brought my hand back inside, a ball of this stuff was sticking to it. I shaped it a little and it became a small umbrella».

I said, «You take something from outside (the bare minimum of supplies), you take it into your shell and you make it into an umbrella to protect you».

Her description of these «obsessional thoughts» gradually became less arduous. In particular, she described two, one that emerged when she was four and another when she was twelve.

When she was four years old, one day she was in a garden with some little boys. At a certain point they began playing the game of showing each other their genitals. Straight afterwards, however, she was overcome with anxiety. What she called her first «obsessional thought» was *I've done something horrible and disgusting*. She wanted to confess what had happened to her mother, to expel it, to be freed from the obsessiveness of this thought returning.

«I said to my mother, "I have to tell you something" and I found it really difficult to say it, it took me ages ... I think what I found unacceptable was that I had been *curious*».

Analyst: «I think that the fact you recognized your curiosity is a positive aspect in your description of that episode. But that curiosity immediately turned into anxiety ... Why? Because it was a *betrayal* of the "airship" relationship you had with your mother? Or because the penetration phantasies immediately turned into frightening phantasies of intrusion? In fact, I believe that although you felt your mother was intrusive as a child and you saved yourself by creating a shell inside, there was still this really strong tie with your mother. And so there was the tendency to rebuild the relationship by projecting the intrusive aspects onto your father».

B had her second «obsessional thought» when she was twelve, shortly after having her first period, and when she was still sleeping in the same bed as her mother:

«After doing a crossword puzzle with my mother, the lights were turned off and I was suddenly really worried that my father could be accused of being the *Monster of Florence*, and I thought, "Has he got an alibi?"».

At that time the patient therefore knew what the monster of Florence did («He murdered young couples and cut off the female genitals»).

Analyst: «You are still sharing the double bed – "airship" with your mother when new genital feelings occur during puberty. They reawakened the fantasies that you had had for an instant when you were four years old, about the female and male genitals meeting. However, in view of the "airship" relationship, those phantasies must not be accepted in your mind: They have to be *cut off*, the way the «Monster of Florence» did with the women's genitals. But once again this violence is projected onto your father – and, in a vicious circle – this makes you stay in the airship with your mother, frightened, because you are afraid of the man who is intrusive and violent».

After describing this fantasy of the father-monster, she found it easier to describe the «disgusting obsessional thought», that had prevailed at that time, and which she had often mentioned but only very vaguely and elliptically – when she had the fantasy of optimistically letting herself go in a relationship with a man (physical contact, an embrace, a kiss – but never a fantasy of a genital relationship), she would say the word «Pacciani» (none other than the Monster of Florence) – and would immediately feel disgust and instant cooling off. Me: «Just the word?» «Yes. Just the word!».

But once, with great difficulty and in tears, she told me that that flash might also have been because Pacciani put his penis in their mouths. And sometimes she had also had this flash during a session … hence, this thought could also be elaborated as a transference fantasy.

One final dream: «I was at the railway station [Florence, where there is no subway just a terminal]. A Eurostar arrived but it didn't slow down and crashed in the station, people were injured».

This dream was interpreted by linking it to a reinterpretation of the second dream («I know the reason for your problems: Your mother introduced you to a man when you were a little girl»). We were now during the phase of analysis during which the transference relationship was experienced on the one hand – intensely and mainly pre-verbal – as an enveloping involucrum, while on the other, as a space in which there was the urgent need to make good the genital phantasy. The primal scene was starting to be mentalized, but with anxiety.

Analyst: «It is as if you wanted to remain in a tranquil, protective involucrum-mother and at a certain point an uncontrolled penis arrives and causes a load of problems».

CONCLUSIONS

I have observed that in the case of the psychopathological conditions that have been described in this paper (defects in primary containment and formation of the obsessional-autarchic shell) usually result in (as regards the erotic body) *gender-specific defence mechanisms*. While the male is psychically able to assimilate his erotic body as a narcissistically complete whole that does not open itself up to another, and the boundaries of which are not interrupted, in female genital experience there is a much stronger and *ineludible meaning of opening*. In the context of the pathology described above, the male therefore frequently masturbates, also too precociously, which ousts latency, and it appears that the objective is mainly one of sensual-sensorial self-containment. *Conversely, by associating the genital phantasy to a distressing sense of intrusion, boundary violation, and the loss of the desired part object, the female tends to disavow the genital sensations since the incipient phantasy of being penetrated is experienced as incompatible with the search for an involucrum in which she feels contained.*

The psychic structure I referred to in this paper is the result of the early experiences in the lives of two female patients: they reacted to a defect in sensual-epidermic containment and to a defect in «playful relationship» by creating an obsessional-autarchic shell and, once they had made this the main way to organize their experiences, they were no longer able to open themselves up to the «emotional peaks» of complete inter-subjective experience.

The anxiety of opening oneself up to and separating from another had been allayed by capturing the object inside themselves, according to an object relationship mode that was founded on anal retention.

Within this framework, the primary relationship is not mourned and therefore (the true quality of the parental relationship aside), there is no possibility to tolerate the fantasy of the triangular oedipal space and the genital relationship between the parents.

During the analysis of patients A and B, when the initial representation of an erotic object emerged, it was the breast. This therefore highlighted an *horizontal split* – the breast above, as a sensual object that refers to a unfulfilling primary relationship of containment that has not yet been satisfied or introjected, is psychically integrated; below is genital disavowal that is also reinforced by the disavowal of the sexual relationship between the parents. The paternal penis is clandestinely kept inside, but it is a faecal penis that has been captured and kept inside.

Furthermore, since any kind of separatedness is intolerable, each of these relationships is experienced at an auto-erotic level – in a kind of auto-eroticism that foresees the presence of the object on (in) one's own body and that can therefore not act as a intermediate step towards a relationship with another in the *exogamic potential space*.

I emphasized the fact that this disavowal does not allow the full development of of these stages of fantasy life (conscious and unconscious), which remain simply sketched – psychic scenarios which disappear soon after they emerge. There is instead a return into the real of the disavowed contents, which acquire persecutory and intolerable traits, thereby justifying phobic reactions and the recurrent return into the obsessional-autarchic shell.

SUMMARY

The Author discusses several hypotheses regarding the reasons that might lead a woman to disavow her spontaneous genital feelings. Particular attention is paid to her primary relationship with the mother and to the inability to find a space in her where the young girl feels she can project her own contents. In the presence of an inhibition of her own projective impulses, the female finds it difficult to codify her own sexual receptivity positively. There is a better intersubjective codification of the male genital aspects compared to the female ones.

KEY WORDS: Female sexuality, sensorial containment, boundaries of the Self, primary relationship.

BIBLIOGRAPHY

ABRAHAM K. (1924). A Short Study of the Development of the Libido. In Abraham K., *Selected Papers on Psychoanalysis*, London, Karnac Books, Maresfield Library, 1988.

ABRAHAM N., TOROK M. (1987). *The Shell and the kernel: Renewals of psychoanalysis*. University of Chicago Press, 1994.

ANZIEU D. (1985). *Le Moi-peau*. Paris, Bordas.

BEEBE B., LACHMANN F. M. (2002). *Infant Research and Adult Treatment: Co-constructing Interactions*. Hillsdale London, The Analytic Press.

BICK E. (1968). The experience of the skin in early object-relations. *Int. J. Psycho-Anal.*, 49, 484-486.

BRITTON R. (1989). The missing link: parental sexuality in the Oedipus complex. In Britton & al. (1989), *The Oedipus complex today. Clinical implications*, London, Karnac Books, 1989.

CARNAROLI F. (2001). Vygotsky e la psicoanalisi. Relazione, linguaggio, coscienza riflessiva. In *Psicoterapia e Scienze Umane*, 3.

DAVID C. (1971). *L'état amoureux. Essais psychanalytiques*. Paris, Payot.

DEUTSCH H. (1925). The Psychology of women in relation to the functions of reproduction. *Int. J. Psycho-Anal.*, 6, 405-418.

FAIRBAIRN R.D. (1954). Observations on the nature of hysterical states. *Brit. J. Med. Psychol.*, 27, 105-25. In David E Scharff D.E. & Fairbairn Birtles E. (eds), *From Instinct To Self: Selected Papers Of W.R.D. Fairbairn. Vol. I: Clinical And Theoretical Papers*. Northvale, NJ, Aronson, 1994.

FATTIROLLI E. (2007). *Sullo sviluppo della capacità di giocare. Un caso clinico*. Richard & Piggle. Currently being printed.

FÉDIDA P. (2001). *Des bienfaits de la dépression. Éloge de la psychothérapie*. Paris, Éditions Odile Jacob.

FERENCZI S. (1914). The ontogenesis of the interest in money. In *Ficrst contribution to psychoanalysis*, London, Karnac Books, 1994.

FERENCZI S. (1932). Confusion of the tongues between the adults and the child (The language of tenderness and of passion). In *Final contributions to the problems and methods of psychoanalysis*. London, Karnac Books, 1994.

FREUD S. (1895). *Draft G melancholia from extracts from the Fliess papers*. S.E., 1.

FREUD S. (1915). *Mourning and melancholia*. S.E., XIV.

FREUD S. (1918 [1914]). *From the history of an infantile neurosis*. S.E., XVII.

FREUD S. (1924). *The dissolution of the Oedipus complex*. S.E., XIX.

FREUD S. (1925). *Some psychical consequences of the anatomical distinction between the sexes*. S.E., XIX.

FREUD S. (1931). *Female sexuality*. S.E., XXI.

FREUD S., ABRAHAM K. (1907-1925). *The complete correspondence of Sigmund Freud and Karl Abraham*. London, Karnac, 2002.

GADDINI E. (1987). Notes on the Mind-Body Question . *Int. J. Psycho-Anal.*, 68, 315-329.

HEIMANN P. (1962). Notes on the Anal Stage . *Int. J. Psycho-Anal.*, 43, 406-414.

HERMANN I. (1935). Clinging – going-in-search. A contrasting pair of instincts and their relation to sadism and masochism. *The Psychoanal.Q.*, 1976, 5-36.

HERMANN I. (1943). *L'istinto filiale*. Milano, Feltrinelli, 1974.

HORNEY K. (1924), On the genesis of the castration complex in women. *Int. J. Psycho-Anal.*, 5, 50-65.

HORNEY K. (1926). The flight from womanhood. The masculinity-complex in women, as viewed by men and by women. *Int. J. Psycho-Anal.*, 7, 324-339.

HORNEY K. (1933). The denial of the vagina. A contribution to the problem of the genital anxieties specific to women. *Int. J. Psycho-Anal.*, 14, 57-70.

HORNEY K. (1967). *Feminine psychology*. New York, Norton,

KAËS R. (1992). Pactes dénégatifs et alliances inconscientes. Eléments de métapsychologie inter-subjective. Paris, Editions Apsygée .

KERNBERG O. (1977). Boundaries and Structure in Love Relations. *J. Am. Psychoanal. Ass*, 25, 81-114.

KLEIN M. (1928). Early Stages of the Oedipus Conflict. *Int. J. Psycho-Anal.*, 9, 167-180.

KLEIN M. (1932). *The Psycho-Analysis of children* . The International Psycho-Analytical Library, 22, 1-379.

LAPLANCHE J., PONTALIS J.-B. (1967). *Vocabulaire de la psychanalyse.* Paris, Presses Universitaires de France.

LICHTENBERG J.D. (1989). *Psychoanalysis and motivation.* Hillsdale-London, The Analytic Press,.

MARCELLI D. (1986). *Position autistique et naissance de la psyché.* Paris, Presses Univ. de France.

MELTZER D. (1973). *Sexual States of Mind.* Perthshire Scotland, Clunie Press.

MELTZER D. (1992). *The claustrum. An investigation of claustrophobic phenomena.* The Roland Harris Education Trust.

MICATI L. (1988). Sulla sessualità femminile: osservazioni sulle forze che ne ostacolano lo sviluppo e sulla loro risoluzione. *Riv. Psicoanal.*, 1.

MONEY-KYRLE R. (1971). The Aim of Psychoanalysis. *Int. J. Psycho-Anal.* , 52, 103-106 .

OGDEN T. (1989). *The primitive edge of experience.* New York, Jason Aronson.

PINE F. (1985). *Developmental theory and clinical process.* New Haven and London, Yale University Press.

RACAMIER P.-C. (1995). *L'inceste et l'incestuel.* Paris, Les Éditions du Collège de Psychanalyse Groupale et Familiale.

RIOLO F. (2002). La trasformazione psicoanalitica. *Riv. Psicoanal.*, 48, 4.

TREVARTHEN C. (1997). *Empatia e biologia.* Milano, Cortina, 1998.

VYGOTSKY L. (1930-31). The history of the development of higher mental functions. In *The collected works of L. S. Vygotsky*, 4. New York & London, Plenum Press, 1997.

WINNICOTT D.W. (1962). Ego Integration in Child Development. In *The maturational processes and the facilitating environment. Studies in the theory of emotional development*, The International Psycho-Analytical Library, 1965.

Original it alian version:
Riv. Psicoanal., 2007, 4, 917-939

Francesco Carnaroli

Via Fra Jacopo Passavanti, 17

50133 Firenze

(Translated by Tina Cawthra)

Is anatomy destiny?

Metapsychological proposals on the femininity of women

AMALIA GIUFFRIDA

«It is[...] in the "childish organism" that this knowledge is accumulated and expressed –a bedrock of "experience" which charges the most adventurous theories with a weighty truth. Childhood theories are therefore the structure superimposed on the bodily experience which represents its "origin". The *body* provides *theory* with its *basis of truth*» writes Assoun (1997, my translation).

In putting forward these thoughts I find myself in agreement with certain premises that Assoun's sentence puts so succinctly. It seems to me that Assoun provides a fruitful synthesis of Freud's legacy with regard to the mind-body relation. Such a view highlights how the instinctual body is an irreducible element, a «basis of truth», for childhood sexual theories. However, at the same time, it does not ignore that this selfsame instinctual body also imposes a boundary upon the phantasies to which the polyhedral nature of the mind lends its «body». I will come back to this point later.

For the moment I would like to re-propose the fateful and well-known question that Freud put forward with regard to the secret of femininity.

«What does a woman want?»

Both theoretical tradition and the 'dark continent' itself make this a difficult question, even for women.

However, I will attempt to offer a provisional answer without necessarily falling back upon the area of the maternal, as so many psycho-analytical responses have done. Not that I do not believe that this maternal aspect is of fundamental importance for female identity. In fact, in the near future I aim to go beyond the Freudian cliché of motherhood as a transformation of the original masculinity (with penis envy being centre focus) and the Kleinian notion of the child-breast-penis-faeces equivalence (as interchangeable objects of the mother's internal body), to investigate the intuitions regarding this matter put forward by a pioneer of psycho-analysis, Mack Brunswick

(1940), who would argue that the desire for motherhood long predates the desire for the penis. This was a claim that would tend to be ignored by the subsequent literature. Even Chasseguet-Smirgel – who in her 1988 speaks of the 'potential of motherhood' as something which all women share, something which brings together mother and daughter as a distinctive feature of femininity – would abandon closer definition of this theme with a mere «And [...] so what if by this I am referring to the old instinct of reproduction!» (quoted by Godfrind, 2001).

We must recognise that in the literature to date, the «maternal» – especially when seen in contrast to the erotic – is scarcely distinguished from primary fusion, from the longing for a return to a narcissistic fusion. Look, for example, at what Winnicott (1971) understands by the phrases «pure female element», an undifferentiated state of «being» that is totally without the presence of drives. Though he does not attribute such a state exclusively to women, the notion does end up pervading his concept of motherhood. However, this is not the subject I wish to discuss in this paper. I digress merely to point out that I will return to it in a later work. My aim here is to discuss the area of the «sexual» in femininity – something which, having been covered by theoretical repression, is only recently receiving the attention it deserves.

This work will focus on some aspects of this problem that are yet, in my opinion, to be explored.

As is well-known, «femininity» is that which challenges some of the assumptions basic to the coherence of Freudian theory. Firstly, it undermines the notion of a universal Oedipus Complex as the central core of all neuroses (Freud, 1931). Secondly, it seems to undercut the explanation of anxiety as 'castration anxiety' which Freud would adopt at a certain point (Freud, 1925). And, finally and most importantly for my discussion, it challenges the concept of anaclisis, which reveals all its limitations when applied to an analysis of the genesis of female psycho-sexuality (André, 1994).

With regard to the first point, Freud argues that women not only remain substantially anchored in a pre-oedipal phase, but also that – if they do enter into the Oedipal phase – their love of the father will continue for an indeterminate period and is worked through only quite late and imperfectly.

With regard to the second point, we know that the phallocentric theory cannot be reconciled very easily with the genesis of female anxiety: in fact, a woman can only have a castration complex not fear of castration, as the «castration» is to be considered as having already occurred. But Freud knows very well that women do experience anxiety (perhaps, he thinks, more so than men) and this awareness pushes him to search once again for the source of anxiety in an internal attack of the drives, in their breakthrough of the Ego boundaries or, alternatively, in the anxiety of object loss. This point of view is what would inspire Klein (1928, 1932) and others after her to adopt an interpretation of female anxiety linked (Klein argues) to fear of the destruction of the inside of the body – with the birth of a child or coitus serving the function of reassurance.

The third point, with regard to the theory of «anaclisis» is the one I wish to focus on here in particular detail.

Freud tells us that the development of childhood sexuality is linked with the vital functions of the body, the primary needs of the infant. Thus anatomy «provides» continuity to the libidinal phases of development. However, the question becomes more complicated when we take into consideration the female genital apparatus.

While the oral and anal phases are, obviously, similar in both sexes, the first discrepancies occur with the phallic phase – a phase at which (the power of denial!). Freud seems to find the similarities between the two sexes covering over and erasing the differences between them (Freud, 1932). In fact, if the urinary function of the penis, a reproductive organ par excellence, will later function as the basis for the development of masturbation, thus as a model for the subject's release and control of energy, things go differently with girls. In fact, neither the vagina nor the clitoris have any self-preservative function during infancy; the former only acquires such a function later with motherhood, and the latter never does so.

Thus, in order to explain the erotic awakening of female genital organs, Freud has to fall back either upon those spontaneous internal processes which, beyond a certain threshold, produce excitation, or upon maternal care, and the seduction of the object. Along with these – and this is a point I will return to below – there is the phantasy of both parents, which Freud mentions repeatedly (1905. 1919, 1931).

As we all know, an erogenous zone is a zone of the body inscribed within the subject's history, a history which confers symbolic meaning upon that zone.[1] However, I would argue that anatomy does set some limits to the subject's phantasy: the inscription of phantasy within the flesh means that this flesh imposes and defines bonds, in spite of the polyhedral potential of the human imagination. As Freud tell us, the formation of phantasy scenarios and childhood sexual theories is a direct translation – the (always incomplete) creative/defensive product – of the drives. «What is correct and hits the marks in such theories is to be explained by their origin from the components of the sexual instinct which are already stirring in the childish organism» (Freud, 193.1908).

I would like to offer a contribution to the reconstruction of the process of creation of female eroticism, starting precisely from this observational vertex, which I would locate in the interspaces of the irreducible osmosis between soma and symbol, considering it effectively as a fundamental point of strength in psycho-analytical thought. In other words, I see the body as the interface of clinic and metapsychology(Assoun, 1977), inasmuch as, «far from being underestimated or marginalised –

---

1 I take for granted knowledge of the contents of the phantasies linked, from Freud onwards in the literature, to the libidinal phases in the development of female psychosexuality: the oral, anal, cloacal and phallic. Rather than aiming to refute or replace these, my argument is complementary to the vast body of theoretical work that, in part, figures in the bibliography to the present paper.

as occurs in certain contributions to psychoanalysis, which are themselves revealing – the real of the soma is here actually situated at the very heart of unconscious experience (Assoun 1977).

I would argue that, for it to be formed as such, human psycho-sexuality draws upon the fruitful presence of parental phantasy. This invests with its own symbol-generative power the excitation linked to a part of or the entirety of the infants' body. And it is this investment which then in turn creates auto-eroticism, which in its turn produces phantasies. At the beginning of life, in fact, an erogenous zone requires both internal endo-perceptive excitation and external investment; the latter being the product of an adult mind which confers the meaning which the infant then inherits by sharing it. As Assoun (1977) points out, this imaginary material is forged at the border of the primal scene: it is that which, from the phantasied enjoyment of the activity of the parental other, passes-in pieces- into the child's body. The psyche is constructed on the basis of the gestures and words that the parents address to the infant. Amongst these one can clearly note the real and phantasied relations that these parents adopt with regard to the child's erogenous zones, to the orifices of penetration/expulsion, the elected *loci* for the exchange between the internal and the external.

Here I would like to recall what Salomè wrote in 1916, when she focused her attention on the mother's attitude towards the control of the child's vital and sexual functions, and the diversity of phantasies that can result therefrom. She contrasts what she calls the «fusional ecstasy» deriving from the nutritional function, with an excretory function which is «an experience of isolation» (1915). In the former function, Salomè sees the pure prerogative of the mother, the prototype of her omnipotent possession of the child, whilst the second function – the child's first autonomous «solipsistic» action – can generate very intense experiences of separation within the mother (Giuffrida, 1987).

It seems to me no one nowadays could deny that these intuitions are the necessary complement to Freud's own thought with regard to the genesis of human sexuality. The real other, Widlöcher tells us (*et al.* 2002), may or not facilitate the creativity of sexuality. The object relation gives form to the phantasy constructed by sexuality.

From this conjunction it follows that the phantasy attitude of the mother towards an organ – in this case, the clitoris – that is the seat of excitation, independently of the self-preservative level, necessarily has significant consequences. And probably foremost amongst these is the notion of female sexuality as a dangerous and excessive end-unto-itself, as something overwhelming.

Need links up with the possibility of satisfaction and fulfilment; the sexual, on the other hand, is insatiable. In fact, in the child's capacity for clitoral orgasm, a mother can already see a symbolic threat posed – that which will take the child away from her, just as her own sexuality might have taken her away from maternal devotion. Such a capacity is also that which will make of a daughter a sexual rival of the mother. So the phallic stimulation that accompanies care for the child goes together with a maternal phantasy that is already complex and – I repeat – never bound by the self-preservative register, as is the case with a male child. In fact, never again will the penis of a son belong to the mother as it does during the early period of «maternage», when the excitation of the infant's organ can be controlled, and even induced. The penis, nevertheless, is the mother's; and it can generate – for her – children, penises, gifts, etc.

The clitoris, on the other hand, is an organ dedicated solely to pleasure, with all the phantasy corollary of guilt or omnipotent defiance that that can imply.

As confirmation of this, we may remember how this idea, transformed in devaluation, infiltrated psycho-analytical theory – above all in the work of the pioneering women psycho-analysts who were Freud's contemporaries. Its result was a theory which (with only slight nuances) is linked to the phantasies of the phallic-phase of the child of both sexes. For example, Deutsch (1925) claims that the clitoris, a superfluous organ, exercises simply an inhibitory action upon the reproductive functions that are 'inseparable' from the woman's sexuality.

However, the clitoris has the advantage that it can respond to stimulation like the other erogenous zones. It has the same modes of releasing excitation which delimit it as a space, as a source of drives, and play a role in regulating internal temporality. From this point of view, just like the penis (and here we link up again with Freud's own thought), it reveals a continuity of the functional and phantasy processes of the erotic body; it becomes a symbolic instrument of control over the drives, whose circulation is felt intrapsychically and interpersonally.

Truthfully, however, a more detailed discussion here should be dedicated to what Alizade, following Freud, calls the «primary orgasm», which she links with oral satisfaction. I would entirely agree with her that, in both males and females, primary orgasm extends to the whole body; that, through the mouth-breast relation, it induces a sensation of fusion, thus re-awakening genital sensations. However, this oral satisfaction is one of those in which sexual and self-preservative drives work together. Therefore it is inscribed within a form of periodicity which moreover (see the above reference to Salomè) is regulated in part by the mother's own actions. Only auto-erotic sucking is not subject to the regulation of the object or to the vital needs of the infant (with the sexual thus totally detached from the self-preservative).

I would argue that the 'primary orgasm' is a bridge, which acquires a paradigmatic value, between pre-genital and genital sexuality of women, just as it is a bridge between male genital pleasure and the male potential for *jouissance*.

I will explain further this point of view.

Alizade claims that in the «primary orgasm» during breast feeding, three components come into play that have specific erotic links: the element of the depth of the orifice, the surface, epidermic element, and the element which involves the inside of the body. The element of the orifice includes the breast and the nipple through which the milk flows into the child's mouth. The sensorial, epidermic element includes all the stimuli relating to the child's skin and the world of its senses (sight, touch, muscular pressure, texture, smell, etc). The third component introduces the inside of the body and the sensations of satiety or fullness (1999).

But let us return to the sexual within girls.

With the vagina, things are different: its mis-recognition during childhood is undoubtedly determined by a variety of factors, and I will not go over what has been said on the matter. Referring the reader to the vaste literature of the subject, I would however like to investigate certain hypotheses that I think are less evident.

First of all, there is the obvious point that, in childhood, there is no correspondence between mother's representation of the vagina and (except in the cases of perversion) its stimulation. The result of this is that the vagina is not included in an erogenous zone at this phase.

The maternal phantasy regarding the inside of the body, of which the vagina is the symbolic prototype, does not at the beginning correspond for the child to anything that can be «represented», because it is not 'supported' by an excitatory trace which can be localised. From this vertex, such a maternal representation may be felt by the infant as a disturbing, invasive external impingement; a sort of primitive breaking and entering that is as de-structuring as it is necessary. Metaphorically, it is as if the mother's phantasy «implanted»[2] an opaque (if not blank) zone within the infant's body; indeed, in the worst cases, what occurs can be tantamount to a total erasure. This opaque or blank zone can vary in extension and blankness depending upon the intensity of the repression of the representation of the mother herself. However, below a certain threshold of maternal repression, that opaque zone can condense the *creative potential of female receptivity.* This is a concept which, I would argue, is linked with the «negative hallucinatory» and requires further discussion here. Green (1999) points out that the negative hallucination is «the representation of non-representation», a definition which highlights how this may be linked with thought, or that which can become thought, and also with the fading of perception which creates the area for the reception of representations. I would argue that this concept can be used to describe the knowledge-misrecognition of the vagina in the female body during childhood, and that obscure presentiment of a receptive possibility which is bound

---

2 The reference to Laplanche and the theory of *séduction généralisée* does not appear to me pertinent within this theoretical framework. Laplanche argues that such seduction is not an «implant of representation» nor the result of the unrepresentable within the Other erupting into the infant psyche, but rather a «sign». In fact, the theory put forward by Green (1992), on which I draw in this paper, and the theory argued by Laplanche are in some ways incompatible. Thus the negative hallucination that is said to invest perceptions and representations resulting from this operation of «implanting» does not seem to me to be the same as what Laplanche understands by the infant's reception of an «enigmatic message».

up with the existence of an internal space. Just as in Green's theory, it can be applied to a varied range of representative potentiality. However, it can also cover over endo-perceptive infantile traces and make them untranslatable. Thus, at one extreme, the potential involved can find expression in a blankness that is the equivalent of the evacuation of representation, whilst at the other extreme, it finds expression in a blankness that retains the creative possibility of representation. As one can see, I have chosen this concept to distinguish what I am describing from the mechanism of repression, which is directed against one or more already operative representations present in the psyche. Negative hallucination, on the other hand, can be taken as a cross-roads of sources which, depending upon the development of primary relations, can lead either to representation or to the «negativization» of representation.

A second, related, point of great importance here concerns the fact that the vagina is part of the excitatory activities of the girl's body *from the very beginning of her life*, and that this participation therein is felt as disorganising, due to the diffusion of exci-tation. Because it plays a part in excitation without however acquiring a fixed, and therefore figurable, location for the child, it has a blurring, de-structuring effect; it makes the constitution of other defined erogenous zones problematic. From the very start, it places the Ego in contact with a fading experience, with an inside of the body whose boundaries are not defined because of diffuse and undifferentiated percep-tions, and which can therefore become a source of anxiety. *This is one of the factors that can contribute to the strength of the «negativization» of these sensations and of the representation of the organ that is their source.* The mnestic traces surging from vaginal sensations are immediately linked up with experiences of emptiness and mystery, symbolically reinforced by the gap between the representation of the adult, as mentioned above, and the impossibility for the female subject to locate (unless, I repeat, as a negative hallucination) the topos within which to «place» such a repre-sentation. Spread throughout the body, these traces leave remnants that work to dis-organise the other erogenous zones, which are more circumscribed and therefore more controllable, and hence themselves play an organising role in the construction of psycho-sexuality. One cannot deny that the location of excitation always has a reassuring function; it makes it possible to «bind» endo-perceptions and thus trans-form them into representations.

As far as I know, sufficient stress has never been placed on the link between phantasy and the constant drive impulse which, *from the very beginning*, leans on the female anatomy. This omnipresent trace is also the trace of an absence. Perhaps, therefore, it is in this experience that we can find the first sign of the female castra-tion complex.

Furthermore, if oral excitation, which is a partial precursor of *jouissance*, is con-nected to the rhythms arising from the self-preservative needs (see above), female genital excitation is linked with the self-preservative drive only when the woman reaches the phases of procreation.[3] The consequence of this tardy link, occurring so long after childhood, can find powerful expression in the phantasy of 'excess' which is applied to female sexuality (Giuffrida, 2004).

For the mother, this sexuality appears uncontrollable because, on the one hand, clitoral pleasure lies outside the self-preservative register and, on the other, vaginal pleasure is outside the scope of maternal action: it is the preserve of the «third». From this point of view, maternal anality, a powerful force of control over what «enters» and «leaves» the sexed body – and over the drives of infant and adolescent (Torok, 1971) – risks being defeated, risks suffering unprecedented expropriation. It is this frustration which many mothers express in the form of ostensible horror at their daughter's sexuality.

Certainly, the existence of «primary homosexuality» (Godfrind, 2001) – and, therefore, the eroticisation linked with maternal care and nourishment – can mitigate the force of this last claim; particularly if these phenomena are modulated by a maternal phantasy capable of inhibiting drives in their aim. However, what I wish to stress is not the analogies between the two sexes to be seen in bisexuality and in the fantasies of the negative Oedipus complex, but rather the more nuanced parental representations that contribute towards the constitution of the «feminine in women». As Assoun (1997) stresses, the real body is the hidden locus of truly sexual movement; it is the place where «male» and «female» never cease to separate from each other, be it within the body of a man or the body of a woman.

When everything goes well, the paternal phantasy can provide that «safe *haven*» that Freud speaks of; it can be an auxiliary in the constitution of the girl's genital sexual body. Endowing it with the representational, it can gradually occupy the locus imbued with negative hallucination. I am referring here to the phantasy described in *A child is being beaten* (1919) which Freud formulated during the analysis of his daughter, Anna.

That work throws light on the theme of the mutual phantasy between father and daughter; it describes how the daughter's primary erogenous masochism, which is a custodian of life as well as a catalyst of violence and a prelude to the Oedipal complex, can be integrated with the father's penetrative, «structuring» sadism. Freud himself speaks of this as a recurring phantasy in women – and, more rarely, in men. However, I would like to stress that this Freudian insight was actually a parenthesis in his thought; there was no follow-up to it in his subsequent concept of female psychosexuality, the core components of which remain unchanging throughout his whole work. This absence is itself a sign of a repression that brooked no contradiction. Furthermore, one can see the difficulties Freud envisaged in the waning of the

---

[3] I will not dwell here on the phantasy contents connected with the appearance of the menarche in adolescence, nor on the link between soma and the feminine within the menstrual cycle. I consider that this subject has already been widely dealt with in the literature.

Oedipus complex in women as betraying the difficulties he had in separating from his own daughter. But the difficulties faced by the «Father of Psycho-Analysis» do not belong to him alone. They are paradigmatic of an «original» difficulty, linked to a more universal phantasy of the father, which oscillates between fear of and desire for seduction. And if that phantasy is to prove fruitful, it must go together, in an interplay with the protective psychic shield *provided* by the mother.[4]

Clearly, this phantasy concerning paternal seduction remains a key point that it is difficult to resolve. In fact, only recently has it been recognised that this is a necessary component if the little girl is to access full psycho-sexual maturity. For example, Pontalis (1997) would, with regard to the father-daughter seduction, argue that a father who defends himself against all forms of seduction by his daughter, who is not seduced by her femininity, is more mortifying than a «father-seducer».

In my opinion, the modulation of the paternal phantasy – in a certain sense the precursor of what Schaeffer calls the penetration of *l'amant de jouissance* – is a breaking of boundary that nourishes the Ego.

In childhood, even the paternal phantasy of Oedipal coition «leans on» the absence of a representation of the organ that can be cathexed by it – an absence which is defensively filled by the child with a «cloacal» representation, combining erogenous zone and the infantile sexual theory which organises the phantasy of potential female receptivity. At this point, however, one has to break with what is argued by such pioneers of psycho-analysis as Jones (1927) and Abrahams (1922). Theories of female sexual development must envisage the differentiation (which is certainly never definitive, never 'total', of the cloacal into the anal and the genital – a differentiation which implies (and this is the essential point) *a differentiated psychic function.*

In *Le refus du féminin* (1997), Schaeffer highlights the similarities and differences between the two functions, with regard to the confusion of zones, of motor functions and of control. In short, the author claims that the confusion of zones can enrich female sexuality with its «confusion-diffusion-effusion», whilst the confusion of motor fuctions and control are of a different order, just as the modality of orgasmic release and *jouissance*, pleasure, are of a different order. It is the libidinal overflow which makes the difference, and which, Schaeffer says, «creates the disparity between the motor function of *jouissance* and that of sexual pleasure, which is given over to anality, to periodization and control, to the release and satisfaction of the Ego. *Jouissance*, on the other hand [...] is the body made vagabond, wandering without boundaries in a sort of generalised erogenicity» (155, my translation). As I

---

4 Once again, I differ here from Laplanche's theory of *séduction gèneralisée* in that I attribute the infant with a hedonic, creative role in the deployment of the sexual (Widlöcher). This is to be seen not only as a response to the traumatic «compromised message» from the Other, but also as due to spontaneous endogenic psycho-physical excitation. For a review of the debate on this subject, see the volume «Sexualité infantile et attachement» (Widlöcher et al. 2000), listed in the bibliography.

argue elsewhere (2004) «Women take refuge in their orgasm, which actually defends them – or can defend them – from *jouissance*, from ecstasy, from the archaic anxieties regarding their own ability to «lose themselves» in *jouissance* […]. The sex of a woman wants what her anal and phallic Ego cannot accept.» But here what comes into play is the core of the problem of female being, where one has to see a relation between the seductive intrusion, as the very basis of sexual life, and the phantasy of penetration by the paternal penis (André, 1994). *Jouissance* is loss of Ego boundaries, and takes on the characteristics of the drive; this latter is constantly present, both disorganising and nourishing. *Jouissance* is the «solution» in which the Ego does not repudiate the drive that violates it but rather receives it within itself. It causes within the Ego a particular type of happiness, which is not a state but rather an ever-increasing ability to be open to the drive. Hence it is an enrichment, an extension of the Ego's own limits and boundaries (Schaeffer, 1998).

The breakthrough and awakening of vaginal sensations represent for both mind and body a total break with the functional continuity of the other erogenous zones. Once more, the Ego is not «master in its own house» but delights in being defeated by the constant drive impulse. As Schaeffer claims: «In spite of herself, the woman is obliged to "work through" the phantasy of the stranger who robs her, enters her body, enters her Ego […] and at the same time can also supply her with nourishment» (1998, 54).

Clearly, as Freud intuited, clitoral pleasure can often be a final physical and psychical bulwark against *jouissance*. And this explains why it is so reluctant to cede some of its privileges. When «the pinaster splint» refuses «to set on fire the harder piece of wood» (Freud, 1905), this occurs because *the Ego cannot accept the absence of boundaries, the diffusion of pleasure, the overwhelming excess,* to quote the terms I use in another work on this subject. «It is a phantasy of excess which is inscribed within the very special representatives of the drives which are closely bound up with the erogenous zones of female anatomy. And it is also an excess "informed" by the strength of the repression of representations of the inside of the body (M. Klein) and of the counter-investments that result from that» (Giuffrida, 2004).[5]

More than the pleasure caused by other erogenous zones, vaginal «jouissance» «leans» on the constant drive impulse; it can become the paradigm of the Ego's capacity to receive great amounts of libido. But precisely for this reason, it is, as we know, the function that can be most stricken by conflict and thus subject to repression and massive, sometimes irreversible, displacement.

Clearly, I am not, like Freud, arguing that the shift from clitoral sensitivity to the vaginal awakening occurs without leaving «traces». I would describe them as two

---

[5] I hypothesize that within the constitution of femininity we can recognize in addition, a phantasy of an «excess of the maternal» that is both complementary and antagonistic to the phantasy of an «excess of the erotic». This is an heir to the omnipotence of the archaic mother, which takes form in the myths of those chthonic maternal deities discussed by Green(1992) and,earlier still, by Freud in *The Theme of the Three Caskets* (1913).

erogenous possibilities that do not subtract from each other but can, on the contrary, be cumulative. Indeed, I would say a woman's full psycho-sexual maturity finds expression in the often reciprocal interplay of these modes of excitation.

It is true that the vaginal sensations that accompany the excitation in the oral, anal and phallic phases are negated because tending towards disorganisation. However, the encounter with *l'amant de jouissance* who, when things go well, reactivates these sensations, is an act of nourishing de-structuration for both the soma and the Ego which submit to this fecund disorganisation. And, as I have tried to show, things go well when the ground has been prepared at length by the breakthrough of the parental phantasies, conveyed in a modulated form through an action that is already partially nourishing and assimilable during the child's Ego formation .

Après-coup, penetration plays out what in early periods of childhood had been carried out by the intrusion of the power of parental phantasies. These make figuration possible; they inscribe a symbolically-legible trace upon sensations and representations that otherwise would remain silent forever. If the parental phantasy remains mute – or is, on the other hand, too violent and intrusive – this may result in a denial or, worse still, a foreclosure of the genital in the growing female.

It is the reorganization of the drives and phantasies in adolescence that allows, or does not allow, the Ego to accept the penetration of large quantities of libido and to establish the vagina as an erogenous zone that is both defined and unlimited; a zone that envelopes the penis but also is felt as diffused throughout the entire body. However, unlike earlier, this diffusion now occurs through a shared concrete and symbolic action.

This is the central point: *the acquisition of female genital sexuality marks a rupture, a change in register with regard to all the forms of excitation and release belonging to the pre-genital phases*. It is a precipitate that has great potency in the realm of reality and phantasy. As I have already said, it is an «excess». The eruption of vaginal representations institutes therefore a discontinuity with pre-genital sexuality. It is a discontinuity that is not to be found in male psycho-sexual development; however, the male can, through identification, acquire the ability to accept the constant breakthrough of the drives by participating in the *jouissance* and enriching his sexual life.

At a certain point in their analyses, various women patients have recounted this «passage» with a sense of amazement and satisfaction, due precisely to their perception that this marked a change in their approach to sexuality. Above all, it brought into play a phantasy that is inevitably enriched by scenes and images inspired by mechanisms of the surrender of the Ego to the constant drive and to *l'amant de jouissance*, by erogenous masochism, by passivity and by the capacity to wait.

Having said this, I would like to conclude with two observations regarding the male-female interplay in bisexuality.

1. The passive-penetration phantasy linked with the earliest oral sensations is that which, first of all, enables the male subject to identify with the receptivity of the

female sexual organ. This is precisely because of the very diffuse nature of that excitation, and because of phantasies involving the regulating and controlling activity of
the Object which accompany breast-feeding. These pre-genital phases converge in
continual interchange with each other throughout the entire life. However, I would
also argue that the possibility of greater identification with female pleasure is to be
linked with what Freud, in discussing oral pleasure, first described as «the prototype
of the expression of sexual satisfaction in later life». The oral and the anal are therefore two processes in the organisation of receptivity wherein different modalities of
excitations and phantasies predominate. This is an aspect that should be studied in
greater depth with regard to the choice of the sexual object.

2. When things go well, men identify with female *jouissance* and with the
excess of the constant drive impulse. But they also have the task of introducing the
temporal regulation which, at a certain point, is also needed by female sexuality. It is
not possible simply to tend towards the dissolution of the boundaries of the Ego; one
must also re-establish them, re-establish one's barycentre. Perhaps, together with the
other factors mentioned in the literature, this need for temporal periodization which
the penis and its pleasure introduces into the sex life of the couple contributes – via
both the phantasy of the mother and later adolescent experiences – in the idealisation
of the male organ (Torok, 1964) as an instrument of both pleasure and control.

Just as in infancy the appearance and disappearance of the mother's breast can
introduce into the infant's psyche those caesurae that then trigger the hallucinatory
satisfaction of desire, and thence the processes of thought, so, by analogy, the penis
inherits the phantasy prerogatives that belonged to the very first regulator of the constant drive impulse. Penis envy and envy for «the good breast» thus, for this reason,
belong to the same symbolic register.

These functional, regulatory mechanisms infiltrate the primacy of the phallic
order and «give it body». The phallic logic, the law of the father to which, as Schaeffer
writes, the mother submits her daughter through her own silence regarding female
genital erogeneity, which nevertheless hands her over to «the desire of the lover».

SUMMARY

The author focuses on the development of feminine psychosexuality in relation to the
phases of libidinal development, with particular reference to the theory of anaclisis. When
things go well, parental phantasies perform a necessarily violating, but also nourishing,
function for the infantile Ego. They confer a potential ability to represent, as well as tracing a pathway for sensations and representations of feminine genital organization. Moreover, the acquisition of the latter leads to a change in the symbolic register.

KEY WORDS: Feminine psychosexuality, phases of libidinal development, anaclisis,
parental phantasies, constant drive impulse.

REFERENCES

ABRAHAM K. (1922). Manifestations of the female castration complex. *Int. J. Psycho-Anal.*, 3, 1.

ALIZADE A.M. (1992). *Feminine sensuality*. London, Karnac Books, 1999.

ANDRÉ J. (1994). *La sexualité féminine*. Paris, PUF.

ASSOUN P.L. (1997). *Leçons psychanalytiques sur corps et symptome. Tome 1*. Clinique du corps.

BRUNSWICK. M. (1940). The preoedipal phase of the libido development. *Psychoan. Quart.*, 9.

DEUTSCH H. (1925). The psychology of women in relation to the function of reproduction. *Int. J. Psycho-Anal.*, 6.

FREUD S. (1905). *Three essays on the theory of sexuality*. SE, VII.

FREUD S. (1919). *A child is being beaten. A contribution to the study of the origin of sexual perversions*. SE, XVII.

FREUD S. (1923). *The infantile genital organization: An interpolation into the theory of sexuality*. SE, XIX.

FREUD S. (1924). *The dissolution of the Oedipus complex*. SE, XIX.

FREUD S. (1925). *Some psychical consequences of the anatomical distinction between the sexes*. SE, XIX.

FREUD S. (1926). *Inhibitions, symtoms and anxiety*. SE, XX.

FREUD S. (1931). *Female sexuality*. SE, XXI.

FREUD S. (1933). *New introductory lectures on Psycho-analisis. Lecture XLIII: Femininity*. SE, XXII.

GIUFFRIDA A. (1987). Narcisismo, mimesi e nucleo fecale. In Sollini A. (Ed.), *Narcisismo, sé e relazione*, Roma, Borla.

GIUFFRIDA A. (2004). Il silenzio di Giocasta. Read at the Congress l'Edipo oggi. Roma 4-6 June 2004. In press, Milano, Franco Angeli.

GODFRIND J. (2001). *Comment la féminité vient aux femmes*. Paris, PUF.

GREEN A. (1992). *La déliaison Psychanalyse, anthropologie et litérature*. Paris, Les Belles Lettres, Paris.

GREEN A. (1999). *The work of the negative*. New York, Free Association Books.

JONES E. (1927). The early development of female sexuality. *Int J. Psycho-Anal.*, 8, 459.

KLEIN M. (1928). Early stages of the oedipus conflict. *Int J. Psyco-Anal.*, 9, 167.

KLEIN M. (1932). *The psychoanalysis of children*. London, Hogart.

LAPLANCHE J. (2000). Sexualité et attachement dans la métapsychologie. In Widlöcher D. et al., *Sexualité infantile et attachement*. Paris, PUF.

PONTALIS J.B. (1997). *Ce temps qui ne passe pas*. Paris, Gallimard.

SALOMÉ L.A. (1915-16). «Anal» und «Sexual». *Imago*, IV.

SCHAEFFER J. (1997). *Le refus du féminin*. Paris, PUF.

SCHAEFFER J. (1998). La felicità nella sessualità? *Psiche*, 2, 54.

TOROK. M. (1964). «Signification de l'envie dul penis» chez la femme. In Chasseguet-Smirgel J., *La sexualité féminine*, Recherches psychanalytiques nouvelles, Paris, Payot.

WIDLÖCHER D. ET AL. (2000). *Sexualité infantile et attachement*. Paris, PUF.

WINNICOTT D.H. (1971). *Playing and reality*. Tavistock Publ. Ltd.

Original italian version:
Riv. Psicoanal., 2007, 2, 293-308

Amalia Giuffrida

Via N. Piccinni, 87

00199 Roma

(Translated by Jeremy Scott)

Towards tolerability of guilt and its precursors

MARIA ADELAIDE LUPINACCI

Conscious and unconscious guilt, their roots and consequences, are inevitably linked with the human condition and therefore have always been an area of interest for psychoanalysis. This work focuses on when a sense of guilt is so intolerable to be excluded from lived experience. It explores the destructive, disintegrating effects guilt can have in a person's life, and the psychical manifestations of these effects (primarily in the form of unconscious guilt). The aim is to discuss the origins of this experiential exclusion of guilt and its precursors (a discussion which brings to light certain paradoxes) and to investigate the ways in which a sense of guilt may be transformed and rendered tolerable. As a background to my reflections I will first outline their conceptual framework, which derives from the work of Freud, M. Klein and W. R. Bion.

With regard to Freud's vast-ranging investigation of guilt, I would like to focus on two key theoretical notions that are of important practical implications in clinical practice.

The first of these is the stress which Freud puts upon the paralyzing and destructive effects that the unconscious sense of guilt can have on a patient's life and on analysis itself (which is, in effect, a struggle to save that patient's life); there is, for example, particular focus on the notion of a negative therapeutic reaction in Freud's *The Ego and The Id* (Freud, 1922).

The other point is the key function of the Super-ego as an internal point of reference; nowadays, applying the concept of «unconscious fantasy», one might think of this in terms of an «internal Object» or as the «function» of an internal Object. Such a Super-ego as a paternal introjection rather surprisingly, but with striking human sensitivity and acumen, Freud criticises as troubling «itself too little [...] about the happiness of the ego» in terms of the satisfaction of impulses (Freud, 1929, 143). A parent, one might well think, should be concerned about the happiness, about the needs of a child!

In *The Ego and the Id*, Freud expresses himself in these dramatic terms «We find that the excessively strong super-ego [...] rages against the ego [...] as if it had taken possession of the whole of the sadism available in the person concerned» (1922, 53). He then goes on to say «The ego gives itself up because it feels itself hated and persecuted by the super-ego instead of loved… to the ego, therefore, living means the same as being loved» (*ibid*, 58) The result is a terrible mix of libidinal needs, with surrender and submission to the sadism of an Object that desires death, to the point of self-destruction. And the clinical manifestations of this mix pose a technical challenge to the analyst, who must dismantle this destructive paradigm.

Freud's pessimism with regard to clinical success here seems to me to be linked to two things: the problem of the duality of drives, of their fusion and defusion (1922), and the question of the very origins of the Super-ego.

The vital needs of the Eros which unites must, at least partially, be defeated by the requirements and needs of civilisation, of which the Super-ego is the representative. As a result of the de-sexualisation and sublimation of the paternal image which occurs in the Super-ego «the erotic component no longer has the power to bind the whole of the destructiveness that was combined with it, and this is released in the form of an inclination to aggression and destruction» (*ibid*, 54). And later still, Freud adds: «But since the ego's work of sublimation results in a defusion of the instincts and a liberation of the aggressive instincts in the super-ego, its struggle against the libido exposes it to the danger of maltreatment and death» (*ibid*, 56).

In the light of the notion of Object relation – which she considers to be present and operative from birth – Melanie Klein would, in my opinion, introduce a fundamental turning-point in the discussion of this theme. Throughout her work she explores the substantial link existing between libidinal impulses, destructive impulses and the Object, arguing that the relation with the Object is a dynamic presence from the very beginning of an individual's life.

This approach introduces into the discussion of guilt a type of dynamism that is intrinsic to the forces at work. The result is that the «working-out» and resolution of the psychical consequences of guilt becomes «natural», even if far from straightforward and painless.

The sense of guilt originates not in libidinal impulses *per sé*, but in destructive impulses (or in the sadistic component of libidinal impulses). From the very first months of life, the infant tries to work through destructiveness in its various forms in order to save, to protect the Object; and in doing so, it is driven by love of this Object and deep sorrow for its loss rather than by fear (of castration) or disgust (at non-civilisation).

An Object with the function of a benevolent Super-ego – an expression of the capacity for love of parents and child – develops and takes on existence alongside the strict and persecutory Super-Ego. This striving to protect the Object occurs as part of the child's development whilst he is working through what Klein calls the «depressive position». And the internal Object involved is one that concerns itself with happiness; that feels compassion in reaction to sorrow and pain. Hence guilt does not become excluded from lived experience (Klein, 1935, 1940).

That the Libido not only looks for release, but looks also for an object relation changes our point of view with regard to the resolution of psychical conflicts. And even today the full consequences of this change are difficult to evaluate in full.

Bion's theory of thinking and his use of the concept of the container-contained relation in the development of psychic life made a further important contribution to this discussion (Bion, 1962, 1963, 1967).

His work describes a model of the mind that originates in the first relations between child and mother. When rêverie activates her alpha function, the mother acts as a container that detoxifies the child's anguish. She gives meaning and sense to the sensorial data and crude perceptions that the child projects/communicates into the mother; she makes them both bearable and usable. And with the repetition of experience, such a container (and the functions it performs) is gradually introjected.

If the mother does not receive within herself these projections – if her rêverie is obstructed; if innate characteristics make the child incapable of putting it to use; if specific circumstances interfere with the mother/child relation - then the container-contained relation is also disturbed. The result is not only serious consequences for development in general,[1] but – I would argue –also for the origins and vicissitudes of guilt.

The application of Bion's ideas to the discussion of the issue of guilt forms the core of the argument developed in this paper.

My interest in the theme led me at a certain point to observe that guilt is in fact situated at the centre of a paradox. It is a paradox between the need for guilt to be recognised as such - the fact that an inevitable part of the passage to maturity is the raising of guilt to the surface of awareness – and the destructive, paralysing grip of guilt which Freud so accurately noted.[2]

Must we therefore think in terms of some sort of transformation if the destructive potential of guilt is to be defused, if it is to be «worked-out»? And what occurs at the juncture between this «bearable» transformation and the emergence into perception of the unconscious sense of guilt?

In their recent work a number of Italian analysts have investigated some features of this paradox.

If guilt – especially unconscious guilt – arouses such terrible and destructive feelings (Cancrini and Corrente, 2000; Cancrini, 2002), how can it be contained? Who would

---

[1] Developing upon Bion's notions with regard to the formation of pyschical life and mental development, A. Ferro recently (Ferro, 2002) provided his own original and ample contribution regarding the factors and dynamics at work in illness and healing in a number of different situations.

[2] This paradox bears out the well-known observation offered by L. Grinberg, which is of continuing relevance here. He comments on how some psycho-analysts focus their interpretations on the need to rid patients of a sense of guilt – considering this as a negative, pathological feeling to which they have masochistically submitted, an unjust burden that has been imposed upon them by severe and terrifying Superego images – whilst others consider that the core of all neurotic conflicts is precisely the denial of the guilt felt because of one's own aggressive fantasies against Objects (Grinberg, 1971).

want to contain it? And how can the process of transformation into more benign forms – the sort of forms Speziale Bagliacca refers to when talking about the development from the «logic of guilt» to a logic of «tragic responsibility» (Speziale Bagliacca, 1998) – take place without a passage through the sort of «transformational container» described by Bion?

These questions led me to consider the need for a dynamic transformational container for guilt. Thereafter came the problem posed by the integration of the Self, and the integration and quality of the Object insofar as they function as containers.

SECTION ONE. A CONTAINER FOR GUILT: THE SELF

As an illustration of the theme of the transformation of guilt in relation to the integration of Self, I have chosen a patient I will call Luca and a sequence of dreams which underwent significant transformation during the course of his analysis.[3]

A forty-year old, Luca was as unfocused and immature as a twelve-year-old, for all that he appeared to have a perfectly ordinary work and family life. In talking, he gave an incredible sense of emptiness and flatness. The patient experienced a powerful anxiety of non-existence; his sense of being under continual threat of reduction to nothing, of nullification, had, with increasing frequency, resulted in panic attacks. Later these feelings would become anxiety at not knowing «what is right or wrong», not knowing if «he was right or wrong». Overall, one could see enormous yearning and effort to be able to exist. However, these were juxtaposed rather than being internally integrated.

Luca was one of those patient who appear to be almost «historyless», who are initially incapable of providing an account of or recollections regarding themselves and their life.

He was clearly terrified at the thought of being touched by emotions, so he could not let others get close to him; nor would he let mental objects get close to each other. He could neither establish links with others nor allow such links to become established. Within the analysis, this resulted in such a powerful impression of obtusity that at times I wondered if he was not mentally «slow».

Then I thought of the possibility of a mother whose rêverie had not functioned properly, whose mind had perhaps been too occupied by the concrete and practical; a mother who could neither perceive signals from her child nor leave traces of herself. Or perhaps the origin was a child who communicated weak messages that were diffi-

---

[3] It seemed to me meaningful to try to trace the construction of conscious thought regarding guilt through the sequence and nature of dreams as they occur in the analysis of a borderline patient. I would agree with Roberto Tagliacozzo (2005) that the nature and sequence of dreams – together with the conditions within which they are brought into the analysis – reflect the mental state of the patient in relation to his or her Object; the possibility of maintaining integration or falling victim to disintegration.

cult to perceive or understand; a child who would too easily abandon such attempts at communication. Whatever the source, something had led to the development within Luca of a defective mental container and alpha function.

Our initial work on his need to be able to exist – to feel that he did exist and that I was aware of his need for existence – led to the appearance of his first dreams.

Dream 1 – The Dream of The Pope. The Pope searches him out for professional advice (him, of all people!). Whilst he himself doubts himself, the Holy Father (the good Father) searches him out and validates him. The dream and the associations (as if the dream referred to a real event) gave Luca enormous pleasure and a sense of vindication.

Thus, thanks to this initial formation of a relation with an Object (the mind of the analyst that, within the transference, is trying to understand him and hence contains him), Luca begins to exist. At this point, emotivity gradually emerges, with hints and snatches of disturbing violence.

Dream 2 – The Dream of the Doberman Puppy. Luca dreams he has a Doberman puppy which he himself eggs on to attack first one person, then another. The identity of the person remains undefined. Once the dog attacks, another time it does not. Then in the associations… But why did it once attack someone it shouldn't have, but then not attack the next time? Why the good person and not the bad person? But in the text of his original account of the dream, there was no such justification regarding the nature of the people.

As often happens, what he says becomes incoherent and difficult to follow, with the result that I myself feel disorientated, caught up in the mental fog that Luca himself sometimes complains of feeling.

It is inevitable: as soon as emotional links are formed, especially if insufficiently contained, violence erupts.

Starting from my own feeling of disorientation, I decided to look for interpretations which test out the ground and lead Luca towards mental explorations of ideas. What, I ask with regard to the dream, *is the puppy's act of biting?* As the patient offers no associations I suggest, after a certain wait: *One can bite out of anger.. out of impatience,.. out of hunger.. Is it to tear something apart? Or it is a determination not to let go, a form of determination to save oneself?*

Almost spelling them out, I thus try to offer a way of identifying emotional components, which will enable him to distinguish the components which are more or less life-giving from those which are destructive. In effect, this involves us in a mental digestion of reality.

Gradually during the course of the analysis Luca began to talk of the fog lifting slightly, of glimpses of light becoming visible. As he felt more solidly compact, the anxiety attacks decreased in number and the patient managed to become more autonomous within his profession, shouldering greater responsibilities.

Though Luca himself denied it, I began to see a projection onto secondary figures of a clash, a sense of rivalry, with his father, of the admiring envy of a child who imagines the power of the adult to be limitless – even the (narcissistic, pre-genital) power of dishonesty and violence. It now seemed more possible to separate hostile attack from the defence of one's own identity, with the result that the patient now had to deal with a perception of his own aggressivity.

It is the Doberman puppy that attacks; this is reflected in transference.

Whilst in the moments of recovered well-being , there is an intense idealisation of analysis, the patient also attacks me unconsciously for the power I have to make him feel better – a power which for him is good and restorative but nevertheless mysterious. For example, once the patient opens the session with the usual questions: *Why is there no longer the anxiety and the feeling bad?.. Is it possible that I am better?... So, what does it mean? etc. etc.* And then he begins with a whole series of organic/physical explanations, until he then starts talking about the fog again. I interpret this to mean that his questions are working to break down the positive experience of his work with me, to the point where they also deprive it of significance… and ultimately he doubts whether such positive experience actually exists. Hence the fog.

He responds with a dream (which at thus point strikes me as practically an hallucination).

Dream 3. The Dream of Anatomical Parts. There were remains, human body parts, scattered around the ground. Then a surgical operation on an open chest cavity … Some coloured liquid was being inserted into the intestine … they were putting some coloured liquid inside me that would show up my internal organs.

I was rigid in my chair, feeling an indescribable horror: the image of a sectioning-room, where cadavers are dissected, is overlaid with an image of an operating-room, where bodies are cured and treated. The anxious and guilty thought emerges that the interpretation of his condition had damaged the patient's fragile mental container. For a moment, it seems to me that Luca is hovering between dream – an unconscious explorative and curative insight of both him and I being taken to pieces (represented by the reference to radiography and surgical operations) – and hallucination (the evacuation of fragments, of the remains and body parts scattered around the ground, through the organs of sense) (Bion, 1967).

For one horrible moment I experience the sense of guilt which the analyst feels as a result of the fear that he/she is incapable of helping the patient, indeed may be causing harm. Perhaps I had committed some brusque gesture that had broken a fragile object?

It seems inevitable that if guilt is to be understood and included within the analysis, then it must also pass through the analyst; it must be part of the analyst's own experience and the analyst must show him/herself capable of bearing it and thinking it through. The fact that, within the lived experience of the analytic relation, an

Object can emerge that is capable of managing the horror of guilt in a different way, can thus become a factor of change for the patient as well. Such an Object accompanies the patient along his/her own path; its functions can actually be assimilated by the patient.

Later in the same session, Luca said: *Where do those pieces come from? We need to recognise them. Could they be mine? But if I am in pieces like that, I can't put the pieces together. So there is no solution.*

In a very dramatic, but very clear way, the patient was posing a fundamental problem. If he is in pieces (and his Object is in pieces), how can he put those pieces together? That is, how can integration and repair come about? If there is no prospect of such reparation, how can guilt be experienced – an experience that is a necessary passage towards putting the pieces together and recovering the (analytical) Object which he needs? Furthermore, why did the vision of analysis as fragmented and scattered – a vision brought about by my interpretation – result not only in persecution but in a veritable derailing of the mental process? Perhaps because the interpretation had arrived at the point where the patient depended so much upon my mental functioning, upon his relation with me, that a loss of them would mean that he himself got lost.

At its more primitive levels, the integrity of Self depends enormously on the integrity of the relational Object (Lupinacci, 1986), so that a perception of damage in or loss of that containing Object results in disintegration, with the fragments produced having to be evacuated. In effect, they are evacuated and I receive a sense of horror. I experience an almost intolerably violent emotional impact, whilst Luca seems rather detached.

Some months after this it was Luca himself who suggested the metaphor of Dr. Jekyll and Mr. Hyde. Though this suggestion was made with a deep sense of unease and anxiety, it was an indication that he had achieved a level of integration such that the mechanism of splitting no longer took solely the pathological defensive and offensive forms which result in disintegration. Now, splitting could also be applied in its vital (developmental) function to create distinctions and see things in order, with the result that at least something good is recognised and preserved. And without this latter function it would be impossible to face and tackle guilt.

Thanks in part to the work on Dr. Jekyll and his alter ego Mr. Hyde, there was a subsequent dream in which Luca tried to bring together in analysis the themes of ambivalence and guilt.

Dream 4 – The Dream of the Cyclists. The patient is driving a racing-car on a race track when suddenly two women on bicycles and a man on a motor scooter appear in front of him. He sounds his horn, but he cannot stop. He drives in between them, but one of the cyclists loses her balance and falls and his car drags her along for a short distance. He then goes up to her and plays things down;: «Never mind, no harm done». Then he is seized by panic and starts shouting that her spinal marrow has been damaged; her face and eye are horribly injured.

After having commented on how well the car worked and upon his own composure – his calm in real life, his ability to function, have now increased – the patient in his associations begins violently to put the blame on those who let the people onto the race track. At this point what he says becomes chaotic, the phrases produced in the dream cannot be distinguished from those he offers in the associations made during the recounting of the dream. It appears to be an explosion of «beta» elements.

If we look at the dream characters linked with the theme of unconscious guilt, they are initially a «puppy» and «undefined persons» (dream 2). They then become human beings that are partially identifiable, even if horribly dismembered (Dream 3). Now they are clearly visible people (the patient, a man, two women), who are alive, whole and functioning. Even the «fact/event» causing guilt is represented, but anxiety and panic then explode; the mind seems to disintegrate.

Once again, but here even more clearly, the fact that the Object (the woman, the mother, the maternal aspect of the analyst) is damaged – and damaged in its function of support (the spinal column) and receptive perception (the eye) – means that the mind cannot contain and tolerate guilt. The fall of the Object not only sets in motion annihilation and evacuation of persecution and guilt («no harm done»), but also seems to rupture the links of sense that had been established, which are sustained by the relation with the Object. It is the patient's very mental capacities that are negated and evacuated.

How is one to understand all of this? Giving meaning, establishing links leads more deeply into the world of affects.

Using the Bion's formulations with regard to the fundamental emotional links of love, hate and knowledge (L, H, K) which unite two objects in a relation (Bion, 1962), we might say that when there is a K function – for example, in an analytic situation when the analyst tries to understand and the patient feels that he/she is understood – one creates a movement that expands from K towards L and H and adds to them. But if in the psychic reality that is then called into play the Object appears to be destroyed, the affects may no longer be sustainable.

I am suggesting that in a fundamental, primitive area of the mind, if contact is established with a damaged container, what might result is the loss of the functions of thinking.

However, after some time Luca – the very same Luca who had very few memories of his childhood! – managed to talk to me for the first time about a dramatic episode in his life when, as an adolescent, he inadvertently knocked over an aged and much loved aunt who would die due to the complications resulting from the fracture caused by the fall. The recovery of significant memories is always an important moment in analysis. But this was particularly important, precisely because it showed guilt being felt and borne in a way which made it possible for it to find expression in conscious life.

SECTION TWO. A CONTAINER FOR GUILT: THE OBJECT

For a patient such as Luca, with a fragile, ill-integrated Self and problems regarding containment and the processes of thinking, the first perception of guilt can be an annihilating experience; it results in the content forcing the container to rupture, throwing the patient into chaos. In fact, such a patient cannot rely on an internal Object that acts as a centre core for the cohesion and aggregation of the Ego; which constitutes a benevolent and tolerant – even if objectively fair – presence. Nor can he identify himself with one of the main beneficent functions of that Object: the transformation of raw-state emotion and impulse *in statu nascendi* into an ordered fabric (Ferro, 2002).

Significant here is one of Luca's recurrent dreams, a childhood nightmare that consists of a single image: an immobile marble-like face with empty, threatening eyes, which he at one time associated with a nun at primary school who had terrorised him. This represents the alienating, inhuman (marble) threat of an Object whose eyes are empty; which absorbs (the eyes are nevertheless a cavity) but does not restitute, does not form images endowed with sense and meaning. Such an Object does not see, does not give meaning or existence to the child; it simply gives the sensation of an unchanging, unforgivable «mistake», of being oneself somehow «wrong».

At times I myself found myself experiencing the blindness and immobility of this Object, finding myself incapable of seeing or understanding, of doing anything. Above all, I felt that anything I said would sound empty and meaningless; and at the same time I experienced the patient's anguish and sense of inadequacy. I was identified at that moment with the blind Object and with the anguish of the Self when faced with this Object.

The feeling of guilt, in fact, places the psyche in a tragically paradoxical situation (another paradox of guilt). By its very nature it marks the destruction of the Object, which at a deep level is always felt as the primary Object which should transform raw and terrifying experiences through love; which should give a meaning to such things; which should contain and delimit them and therefore make them «thinkable», But in perceiving guilt as an emotional experience, the Ego simultaneously perceives the damage or destruction and loss of the containing Object. It is a moment of solitude and disaster. The emotional «K bond» which exists between people – the specifically human bond of «trying to know» – becomes almost impossible. The emotive experience is not «thinkable» because the Object is destroyed and such thinking is a function of the relation with it.

This perception of guilt which is not contained internally can only be expelled, evacuated; the resultant experience is therefore one of persecution, paralysis and breakdown.

What I wish to underline is that in the destruction of the Object there is both the dramatic loss of a good, loving and loved Object and the elimination of the hated, hostile Object (the hinge conflict which, together with integration, is at the heart of the emergence of the «depressive position») (Klein, 1935, 1940). However, the «good Object» lost is «good» not only in the Kleinian sense but also in the Bionian sense – that is, it is not only an Object that nourishes and protects (Klein) but also a mother capable of rêverie, of the K link. And it is this latter which is essential to establish the function of contact with one's own mind as such. If it is lost, what remains is a marble face with empty eyes.

In my opinion the critical point is the moment of (perhaps unconscious or pre-conscious) perception of guilt; of seeing and of being seen. It is the moment in which the mental apparatus finds itself at risk, precisely because of the destruction of the Object and because it is a function of the relation with that Object. This is what we have seen happened in the case of Luca.

Nevertheless, seeing, being seen and being able to see onself constitute one of the goals towards which analysis strives.

The exploration of the quality of the internal objects that the patient puts forward in transference – their transformation within the analytical relation – is thus funda-mental. It proceeds alongside the construction/reconstruction of an Object which contains the devastating experience of guilt, accompanying and nuancing the per-ception of that experience; an Object from which this function is learnt.

Within the process of the assessment and recognition of psychical truth, at the moment of risk when the perception of guilt is an overbearing, indigestible event, it is essential that one has someone at one's side. This presence conveys the fact that guilt has not destroyed all ties and bonds. And if for a moment we look backwards to the point in life when this internal Object originates, the significance and meaning of this is even clearer. Imagine, for example, the various possible scenarios of infant development, involving: a mother who obsessively assigns blame and guilt or one who unites scolding with a touch of benevolent irony; a mother who falls silent or one who gets agitated; or a mother who recognises that things are not that serious, who consoles and comforts.

With great sensitivity, Winnicott recognises the need for the real mother to offer the child the real chance to make things good (Winncott, 1958). As is well known, this theme of reparation had already been introduced by M. Klein. But the conces-sion of the chance to make things good involves something more; it incorporates as structurally-inseparable components of the same process both the reparation and the acceptance of that reparation. This constitutes another way in which the Object contributes to the working-through of guilt. To put in it terms of the experience to be seen in South Africa: alongside the truth there is also reconciliation both with oneself and with the Other.[4]

In the analytic situation, we as analysts must first of all be able to contain (to reconcile ourselves to) our feelings of limitation and insufficiency; to recognise (in both senses of the term) our errors, defects and limits of characters (psychical truth). Thus, «up-stream» from our relation with the patient, we have to create a container which is such that the work of analysis can direct the patient towards a similar process .

Bion considers truth as a nutrition for the psyche.

So I am interested in the conditions in which the need for psychical truth and the encounter with psychical truth are emotionally sustainable (Lupinacci 1991). This concerns both the conditions of infant development and the technique used in analysis.

Here I will cite a brief passage from the clinical report of the analysis of a patient I will refer to as Rosa. Within this patient was the sedimented experience of a mother who would not tolerate any form of protest. It seems that she even held the infant Rosa's dummy in place by means of a cushion, so that the girl could not spit it out; once the infant almost risked choking to death when she violently regurgitated food that she could not expel from her mouth. Gradually, the patient had developed an internal attitude of total surrender, of submission to any sort of event or demand – to the point where she seemed to annul her very Self. Guilt and shame at existing were blended together in a very dangerous cocktail.

After a few years of analysis, during which Rosa had slowly come to feel herself as existing, she would go through a rather long period in which she showed intolerance and belligerence in analysis, as well as at home and at work. The quality of this belligerence was the same as that of the old partial Object of the dummy/cushion: «obtuse», impenetrable and persecutory. The note of obtuse cruelty that emerged made me think of the anxieties, needs and sufferings that had been bound together with the impenetrability of a mother who had perhaps adopted a merely concrete/practical approach to the discomforts and needs of her new-born child.

In spite of a noticeable improvement – and of the care that I took over both the timing and the form of interpretations – it seemed that from the «treatment» with me the patient unconsciously expected nothing other that a «digging into» her guilt, defects and weaknesses, a process designed to make her «cough up everything».

---

4 The reference is to the process of pacification and peaceful social integration which occurred during the transition from an apartheid to a democratic system in South Africa in the 1990s – in part thanks to the work of the Commission for Truth and Reconciliation (Tutu, 1999).

The idea that reparation and acceptance of reparation are structurally part of the same process is, I discovered, surprisingly present in the concept of *ubuntu* as it exists in traditional South African notions of Justice. As explained by Tutu, *ubuntu* means a justice predicated above all on healing wounds, correcting imbalances and binding together ruptured relations. It involves striving to rehabilitate both the victim and the criminal, who is given the chance to become reintegrated within the community that his crime has offended (Tutu, 1999).

Having identified herself with an impenetrable Object, she could not manage too keep anything down (inside); she felt merely exposed, dug into.

Rosa could be very destructive; however, my noting of this fact only worsened the situation. I did not fail to realise that this climate of destructiveness was in part due to a negative therapeutic reaction which was predicated on envy (even if this reaction made itself felt in a far from straightforward manner).

I would like to describe an occasion in which this could be confronted.

Rosa had *a dream in which she was very agitated as she entered a house in which her mother was present in the background.* (She was often in this agitated, flustered state when she arrived for her session of analysis). *There were then confused scenes in which she argued with her sisters and then left, deliberately taking away something she said belonged to her.* In commenting on the dream she said with bitter belligerence (which nevertheless sounded like masochistic provocation): *my mother did not even look at me... I think... Otherwise, she would have called me back in* (meaning: to tell me off). I had a very strong sensation of countertransference, feeling that she was about to drag me into her usual (and pointless) talk of pain, anger and guilt, the form in which she had recently taken to voicing her irrational and destructive convictions with regard to her perpetual unhappiness: that was how things had to be; that was how someone wanted them to be; she herself neither could nor, at this point, wanted to receive anything different. It seemed to be a case of what Freud described as the eroticised surrender of the masochistic Ego to the persecutory Super-ego.

Engaged in worried reflection upon these points, I then had the vision (as described in her dream) of her mother in the background who, for once, did not call her back [*richiamare* in Italian could be «call back» or «reprove»]; who had «nothing to say back to her» [*ridire*: to «reply» or «to find fault with»]. I calmly pointed out to her: «Perhaps the mother in the dream had nothing to say back/find fault with». There was a moment of amazed interruption; then, contrary to what usually happened, Rosa replied readily with great amazement and immediate relief, almost as if made light-headed, knocked off balance, by this new view of things.

This was a moment when, within the *hic et nunc* of the session, two things came together: the possibility that Rosa's primary internal Object was present and yet had «no fault to find» (visualised within the dream, this was something that had had to be constructed over time in the course of analysis) and the experience that, in the same way, I had nothing to «say back» (with the exception of that small observation with regard to the verb itself: *nulla da ridire*). It was a sort of «selected fact» constructed by the two of us; a motif played four-handed which served to calm the vicious circle of pain, destructiveness, accusations and guilt which was finding a place in Rosa's analysis.

It was inevitable that, at some point, Rosa should enter into contact with the hostility, ambivalence and even envy that she felt towards the analyst who was managing to help her, whilst she herself had supinely suffered so much and for so long. But she could not do this without herself being received and contained in an Object that is present, that sees her without immediately beginning to criticise her.

What was it that made possible this «selected fact» constructed by the two of us»? One might say that I had re-dreamed Rosa's dream (my vision of the mother in her account of the dream), re-attributing the meaning of the dream. That meaning now included: the manifest text of the dream; the associations made by the patient, which identified a mother who saw her solely in order to criticise and annihilate her with an analyst who again would criticise her for such thoughts; and my own disquietude as felt in the countertransference, which perceived the projection of the sadistic, impenetrable Object of transference and the risk of my own projective counter-identification if I had accepted her masochistic offer.

The mother in the dream, therefore, «said [criticised] nothing». Perhaps she was a mother who could manage to see the vital component contained in Rosa's jealousy and avidity. Perhaps she was no longer such an incarnation of what Bion calls a «Super-ego… a superior object asserting its own superiority by finding fault with everything» (Bion, 1962, 98).

Thus, I too had little to say; the patient had unconsciously got there on her own. All I had to do was point this out to her without denying her any of the credit or merit (without acting as a envious Super-ego); clearly, however, her entire attitude had pushed me towards picking up on and offering a critical interpretation of her jealousy of her sisters and her resentment of her mother. But there was now a relaxation in the impenetrability of an Object that «remove the good or valuable element» (*ibid*, 96) which is part of the child's anxieties (the energetic and vigorous component within jealousy and avidity). The impenetrable Object which was incapable of containment had been projected into me, but had re-emerged after having been decontaminated through my «vision of the dream», which was a «dream of the dream», a rêverie.

SECTION THREE. THE «REPELLENT-DENUDING» OBJECT AND THE PRECURSORS OF GUILT

So far I have focused on the fundamental problem of the containment of the experience of guilt, tracing its emergence and transformation within analysis in relation to the oscillating integration of the Self. I have concentrated on the character of the Object of the relation and its different functions (as super-ego, as an agent of rêverie). In particular, I have tried to examine its appearance in transference and its transformation in relation to the process whereby the perception of guilt becomes tolerable, whereby there is a future access to responsibility.

At this point I would like to take a step backwards.

Luca had within him the image of a marble face with empty eyes that do not see, an image that gave him an unalterable sensation of non-existence, of there being something wrong in the very notion of his own existence. For her part, Rosa seemed to have an internal primary Object with the characteristics of an envious Super-ego that rejected life and the desire for life, an Object to which she was intensely and sub-missively bound.

While the appearance of this internal Object – and its mode of function – will obviously vary from patient to patient, it is these with which we have to deal sooner or later within analysis. However the Object might have developed and been remod-elled or consolidated during the course of the patient's life, its roots – with regard to the relation with guilt – go back a long way. I would, therefore, once again like to refer to the developments in psycho-analytical thought offered by Bion when he stressed how the child receives (or does not receive) more than just physical contact, support, food, pleasure and comfort from the mother. Within the mind of the mother, projective identification serves to evacuate the anxieties and primitive sensorial experience (both internal and external) which hyperstimulate the child and which he is as yet unable to deal with (the «external and internal experiences» concerned include sensations of pleasure/displeasure; the turbulence of emergent drives, the child's sensorial impact with the outside world, etc.). The mother's special psychical condition of receptivity permeated by love is what Bion calls «rêverie». She receives and accepts the projective identifications of the child «*whether they are felt by the infant to be good or bad*» (Bion 1962, 36; my italics). The maternal «alpha» function detoxifies these, restores them to the child in a psychically significant and functional form; they are transformed into emotions and feelings that can be represented and are sufficiently tolerable for the initiation of thought. I would argue that such tolerability in part also comes from the penumbral presence of an Object which returns to the child together with distinct, digested and nominated (identified) emotions. In this process, container and content co-exist in a reciprocal relation – that is, they «are dependent on each other for mutual benefit and without harm to either» (*ibid*, 91). And as this process is repeated, a specific maternal Object and its functions are gradually introjected and assimilated by the Ego, becoming part of an individual's mental structure.[5]

This is how Bion describes the characteristics of the container: «It may make by meaning clearer if I say that I am in a state of receptive observation as opposed to a state in which I pass judgement on what I observe» (*ibid*, 95).

Thus, the child acquires an internally-structured Object for which experience is to be understood and represented, not judged. I would argue that this process and this internal structure are the «base precondition» for a situation in which the sensation of

---

[5] Bion uses the term «commensal» with different nuances of meaning to describe the container/content relation in his *Learning from Experience* (1962) and *Attention and Interpretation* (1970).

guilt – even unconscious or preconscious guilt - does not destroy the mind, does not (unbeknownst to the individual) paralyse or torment life when such sensations of guilt become active at a later stage, after a certain level of integration has been achieved.

However, the relation container/content takes on a «minus» function of rejection or denudation when this exchange of comunication between mother and child breaks down. This failure can come about for a variety of reasons: the difficulty the mother encounters in receiving and «processing» what is communicated, in imagining or «dreaming» the child; the particularly high intolerance the child experiences at any frustation of its needs; the intensity and violence of the child's sensations; the prevalence of hatred and envy in those sensations; difficulties that may be intrinsic to both mother and child or else due to external factors that interfere with their relationship. It is now that occurs «the establishment internally of a projecting-identification-rejecting object [which] means that instead of an understanding object the infant has a wilfully misunderstanding object» (Bion 1967, 117). The inversion of the relation container-content and of the «K link» – that is, the misunderstanding – leads to the loss of the «commensal» reciprocity of understanding and being understood, of giving and receiving. What is lost is the striving for knowledge that is permeated with love. Bion repeatedly stresses that «the result is an object which, when installed in the patient, exercises the function of a severe and ego-destructing superego» (Bion, 1967, 107), a «superior object asserting its superiority by finding fault with everything» (Bion, 1962, 98).[6] In other words, this is an Object that neither knows nor wants to know; it only strives to judge and, through judgement, annul and annihilate. Where there is no meaning there is no existence. What remains is a sensation of nullification and death.

Would it perhaps be going too far to suggest that we are here in an area that is at least partially co-extensive with that area of psychic phenomena which Freud was talking about when discussing the rupture of the erotic bond between the Ego and the Super-ego, a rupture which makes this latter into «the pure culture of the death drive»? Can we think of it as an over-drastic (and precocious) rupture of the amorous bond between child and primary Object – a disruption which undermines the protective function of the latter and makes it into an expression of nullifying/annihilating superiority? Whether it is the mother's rêverie which is defective or the child who is incapable of putting that rêverie to use, the Doberman puppy goes mad; it no longer «knows» itself or its Object.

In the fearful chaos of impulses, sensations and overbearing emotions, a child must I think feel itself overwhelmed by an indefinable guilt (precisely because of its

---

6 Drawing upon Bion's notions with regard to the emotional relations of the infant, O'Shaughnessy suggests that, depending upon how the process develops, it can lead to a «normal Super-ego» or to a destructive «abnormal Super-ego» (1999).

chaos of feelings). It is a very primitive level of guilt: the guilt of existing, of being what he/she is, of feeling what he/she feels. In effect, it is a guilt that «has no name», and therefore cannot be the object of knowledge.[7]

Perhaps the term «guilt» is inadequate when we are referring to such a primitive and indefinable level of lived experience. What we have is a sort of «thing in itself» that precedes the more integrated levels of experience of Self and Object. Rather than guilt, this is a «precursor of guilt» an *a priori* sense of negativity, which acts as a sort of internal presence that drives the child to makes everything negative in its existence and its relations. It is a «precursor» in the sense that it forms the basis for that feeling of destruction, of what can become intolerable guilt.

I would argue that the process which Bion ascribed to the fear of death – which, if not contained and transformed, can become a «nameless dread» (Bion, 1962, 163) – might also be seen in the emergent turbulence of drives. If these inchoate impulses are not adequately contained and transformed, their intensity can become a violence which then increases exponentially to the point that it destroys Object and Self, becoming a «nameless guilt».

In these conditions, any perception of guilt or sorrow at the violence of drives and the damage they cause is completely inconceivable.

I have talked of the «base precondition» and the «precursors of guilt» because – together with the intense and profound defences that hide and distort it – guilt as such must, during the gradual integration of the Self and the Object, be perceived, suffered, elaborated and transformed repeatedly and at various levels. But the hard core of guilt – where it is most obscure and most difficult to transform – will have absorbed precisely those pre-verbal impressions which either are not mentally processed or are imperfectly processed. Where such impressions exist, they tend to result in acting-out or in models of behaviour (particularly of a self-destructive or submissive kind) rather than in stories and memories: They can also appear in dreams.

Something similar, I would argue, happened at a certain point in Rosa's analysis. But I might also cite Mrs. A, who perceived in a negative critical way even positive interpretations («she managed» was heard as «she did not manage»), or Mrs. B, who could recount good and positive things in such a way as to cast them in a rather gloomy or ambiguous critical light. This is, in fact, an area in which the inversion of sign reigns supreme.

This specific negative quality of a «denuding» Super-ego, which is assumed by the Object when it is re-introjected, has clear links with the problem of guilt and self-destructiveness. It can also, I would argue, have an important influence on analysis.

---

[7] A particular case of «guilt of existence» is recorded in Green's work on the «dead mother»: the child experiences the incomprehensible withdrawal of maternal investment as indicating his having no right to existence, thus making his own existence a source of guilt (1985).

Where, for whatever reason in his/her personal history, the patient finds him/herself in this perverse situation, we can expect it to reproduce itself in other relations. It will be reflected in the patient's transference, in the analyst's transference and counter-transference, and in the very structure of the patient's personality. Great tenacity will be required as the analyst's work will be attacked and «denuded» in a number of ways. Particular attention must be paid to observation, in order to seize and exploit the slightest signs of development within the patient. Great care must also be taken over technique so that, in neither substance nor form, do the analyst's words and interpretations convey any sense of superiority or detachment: if that were to happen, the projected Object with which the analyst is identified would be that which only sees flaws, failings and destructiveness. However, destructiveness does exist, even if one is afraid to see it, to realise that it is present within us. Still, as it can be the source of anguish and suffering, it must be faced. Another paradox.

In other words, this would seem to be the problem: Can one find an Object capable of truth that is not a matter of «home truths»?

From my point of view, an Object that «causes a sense of guilt» is already a destroyed Object (Obviously I do not mean by this that the patient should not know guilt as an emotion). It is an Object within which the capacity to know without judging has been destroyed; one that is incapable of being close to the «painful truth», of feeling the pain this causes yet also tolerating the guilt which the analyst inevitably feels because of the pain and suffering he/she has contributed to in making the patient aware of the «painful truth». But that is not all. It is also an Object that has lost its generative/creative capacity to recognise beauty, goodness, vitality and change (in the child, in the patient, in the Other); which has retained solely the ability to «see through» things, to lay them bare. If suffering, pain and guilt are to become a bearable part of lived experience, we as analysts must try to withstand these types of attack, which not only come from outside but also from within ourselves.

SUMMARY

Guilt can disintegrate and paralyze both the mind and life if it is not contained and transformed. The internal primary Object and its successive representatives, as well as Self as the primary site of perceptions, representations and affects, and their relationship are considered as the psychic places where guilt may (or may not) be contained and transformed. By looking at clinical material and the dreams of two patients, the author tries to follow the transformation of guilt in analysis, taking into consideration how this affects transference and countertransference in particular, as well as looking at certain technical issues. The author also looks at the quality of emotive exchanges in the primary mother-child relationship as a prerequisite if guilt is not to become a drive to the annihilation of the individual.

KEY WORDS: Guilt, container, transformation, L, H, K, emotional ties, denuding Super-ego, transference, countertransference.

REFERENCES

Bion W.R. (1962). *Learning from experience*. London, Heinemann.

Bion W.R. (1963). *Elements of psycho-analysis*. London, Heinemann.

Bion W.R. (1967). *Second thoughts*. London, Heinemann.

Bion W.R. (1970). *Attention and Interpretation*. London, Tavistock Publications.

Cancrini T. (2002). *Un tempo per il dolore*. Torino, Boringhieri.

Cancrini T., Corrente G. (2000). Colpa e destrutturazione della mente; come si interpreta la colpa. Read at the Conference SPI-APA, Buenos Aires, 2000, not published.

Ferro A. (2002). *Seeds of illness, seeds of recovery.* New York, Brunner-Routledge.

Freud S. (1922). *The Ego and the Id*. SE, 19, 3-66.

Freud S. (1929). *Civilization and its discontents*. SE, 32, 59-145.

Green A. (1985). The dead mother. In *Life narcissism, death narcissism*, London, Free Association, 2001.

Grinberg L. (1971). *Guilt and depression*. London, Karnac Books .

Klein M. (1935). *A contribution to the psychogenesis of manic-depressive states*. London, The Hogarth Press.

Klein M. (1940). *Mourning and its relation to manic-depressive states*. London, The Hogarth Press.

Lupinacci M. A. (1986). Le prime esperienze dolorose viste nella osservazione della relazione madre bambino. Read at the Congress of the Italian Psychoanalytic Society on «Il dolore mentale», Bologna, not published.

Lupinacci M. A. (1991). Il lavoro affettivo dell'analista ed il cambiamento in un paziente il cui stile abituale è la menzogna. In Hautmann G. e Vergine A. (Ed.), *Gli affetti nella psicoanalisi*, Roma, Borla.

O' Shaughnessy E. (1999). Relating to the superego. *Int. J. Psycho-Anal.*, 80, 861-870.

Speziale Bagliacca R. (1998). *Colpa*. Roma, Astrolabio.

Tagliacozzo R. (2005). Il sogno: progetto vitale, progetto psicoanalitico.Not published. In Bonanome N. e Tagliacozzo L. (Ed.), *Ascoltare il dolore*, Roma, Astrolabio.

Tutu D.M. (1999). *No future without forgiveness*. New York, Doubleday.

Winnicott W. (1958). *The maturational processes and the facilitating environement*. London, The Hogarth Press.

Original italian version:
Riv. Psicoanal., 2007, 4, 877-896

Maria Adelaide Lupinacci

Via Arbia, 10

00199 Roma

(Translated by Jeremy Scott)

Metaphorization between regression and withdrawal in the analysis of psychotic patients

SARANTIS THANOPULOS

First and foremost, I would like to attempt to define the relationship between the psychoanalytical work with psychotic patients and the experience that originated a devastating void of contact and reciprocity in the mother-child relationship. In the subject's experience, this void is transformed into an extremely distressing sense that *something is missing, but there is no sense of an object*, because that emptiness renders meaningless both the network of his inter-personal relationships and his psychic structure. Each time the subject finds himself in relational contexts that arouse the sense of this absence, because they arouse an excitement that is destined to remain meaningless, there is no question of the return of the repressed that can give meaning to the experience. In the analytical relationship, the actualization of the past in the transference is foreclosed and therefore the analyst tends to be divested of his metaphorical meaning.

Although for different reasons and with different emphasis, psychoanalysts today generally accept the aetiopathogenetic association of psychosis with an extended foreclosure of the capacity for the metaphorization and symbolization of subjective experience. If affective and material primary needs are not met, the child will become psychotic when the deprivation is so persistent that it stops the child from giving the experience of satisfaction a subjective meaning by metaphorizing it.

While the terms «metaphorization» and «symbolization» (of experience) may be used as synonyms in view of the clear interconnection between metaphor and symbol, it must be pointed out that in a child's psychic development, the former precedes the latter (Thanopulos, 2005). As understood in the interpretation of dreams, symbolization is a developed aspect of metaphorization that requires a sufficiently differentiated relationship between subject and object. The roots of this level lie in the transitional field (metaphor) between bodily sensation and emotion, between emotion and thought, between subject and object and between internal and external reality. In other words, the ability to metaphorize is more than just the ability to use metaphors and symbols (and their more abstract expression: signs and verbal meanings). It concerns the ability to stay in a transitional place between the undifferentiated relationship and the differentiated relationship with reality, establishing metaphorical ties between the self and the other: using the other as a representation of the self and the self as a representation of the other.[1] I believe that *primary metaphorization* has a sense of personalization, and represents the personal access to the common metaphoric patrimony, its subjective pre-signification. The use of metaphors and symbols has its own true expressive and communicative meaning only if it is rooted in the first encounter with the other, in the very moment in which the encounter of the individual with the universal (the first essence of metaphoric experience) constitutes subjectivity (Thanopulos, 2006). The foreclosure of primary metaphorization produces a de-subjectivisation («de-personalization») of experience, but not necessarily the inability to use the more developed forms of symbolic communication. The rupture of the symbolic links between desire and conscious representation of things, inevitably turns into a loss of subjective meaning in an important area of experience, but often (if the recrudescence of the tear in the psychic fabric is not emerging in an acute state) this loss is «mended» by the merely cognitive employment (imitative and alienating in nature) of the symbolic and linguistic signifiers that sews up the tear between the healthy part of the personality, able to metaphorize, and the more psychotic part, that is unable to do so.

The foreclosure of metaphorization in psychosis is a *structural fact*, the axis around which the entire psychic apparatus is structured. To be more precise, the parts that are primarily foreclosed are those of the original matrix of the metaphorization of experience, contained in the mirror function of the mother (Thanopulos, 2005). I shall come back to this later.

The lack of metaphorization, understood as the lack of subjectification and personalization, reproduces within the analytical relationship the perception of a missed encounter that is totally characteristic and this allows an experienced analyst to diagnose a psychotic condition even in the absence of any clear delusional thinking and hallucinations. This diagnosis reached through the «negative» highlights a lack of contact that varies considerably from the affective aridity that might be found in the relationships with patients who, while not psychotic, have difficulties in symbolizing their experience adequately, due to damage suffered during the development of the ability to symbolize, in a phase following the establishing of the original matrix of metaphorization.

Lack of contact in the relationship with a psychotic patient can, at times, reveal the clear presence of *different levels*, the existence (in the patient and in the analytical relationship) of two levels of truth that are destined never to meet. There is the perception of a meaning that remains wide open, incomplete, of a logic that remains open (because it lacks the connective fabric that is interwoven emotionally and not rationally), of the absence of interpenetration between primary and secondary

---

[1] The process of primary metaphorization assigns the transitional object the function of first symbol: it forms it as a means of the (symbolic) union between subject and object.

processes (or to use Matte Blanco's words, between symmetrical and asymmetrical logic). Careful introspection that was interrupted, like a broken bridge, lives side by side with the most impenetrable obtuseness and when, within the context of a relationship, past experiences could resurface, in contact with the possibility of sharing, the roads brusquely diverge. Delusion and hallucination try to correct the remarkable double vision of the psychotic view, that sees both reality and emptiness simultaneously, but inasmuch as they reduce it, they are also affected by it. The recourse to a delusional para-hallucinatory kind of thinking is always available, even during the intervals when no clear anxiety is evident, and this represents an attempt to fill the gaps left wide open in those interstitial spaces in which primary process supports, unseen, the sense of discourse.

With the help of a clinical case, I will try to show how a certain kind of support, specific to the analytical relationship, can make available to the patient a personal use of metaphorical processes. However, before presenting the clinical material, a preliminary aspect needs to be dealt with. According to a well-established line of thought in analytical tradition, to restore the ability to metaphorize his own experience, the psychotic patient would need to regress *directly* to the situation of the primary environmental deprivation, thus permitting to repair it.

I believe that this kind of regression is not possible but, at the same time, realize that the reparation of the psychotic condition in analysis is inconceivable in the total absence of any regressive movement.

THE CONCEPT OF THE «REGRESSION TO DEPENDENCY» AND THE ANALYSIS OF PSYCHOTIC PATIENTS

By introducing the concept of *regression to dependency,* Winnicott expanded the horizon of the psychoanalytical understanding of the phenomenon of regression. This kind of regression differs greatly from regression to the libidinal stages of development because: a) it is not of a defensive nature, linked to a distortion of the physiological development, but is the preliminary condition to work through the environmental failure underlying the pathology; b) it is the expression of the patient's willingness to trust the *possibility* of a positive *holding* experience, that does not have the meaning of libidinal satisfaction. «Regression to dependency» fulfils the periodic need to return to that initial phase of one's existence when, according to Winnicott's fecund intuition, the continuity of the subject's experience is entrusted to the ability of the mother to *hold* her child in the psycho-physical sense. The ability of the mother to hold her child physically and emotionally, thus inspiring a sense of security and trust, lies in her ability to internally recognize and accept the subjective modes of the child to feel and exist, without restricting her maternal function to the concrete satisfaction of his needs and the gratification of his desires.

According to my understanding of Winnicott's discourse, first and foremost regressing to a state of dependency means recovering the willingness, which was suspended earlier but not lost, to *rely on* someone else's ability to support one's own need for authentic and personal existence. When the mother holds the child «in her arms», what is happening is more than just the emotional and physical support of the child. In that moment she is also expressing her way of holding him inside and outside herself (in her desire, in her imagination, and in her thoughts) as a whole person (before the child has even reached this position and is still on his way to do so[2]). If the mother is unable to mirror the originality of his existence (or rather, she is not constant and reliable in her care for him according to his growing ability to express himself independently and to integrate the fragments of his experience) with the way in which she *holds* the child, the perception of being fed, looked after and gratified sensually does not create in the child any sense of authenticity and confirmation of his own existence. I believe it is often the case that in their work, analysts come up against maternal figures who are able to sense their child's desires and offer him libidinal gratification, even extremely intense, but are unable to do so by respecting the expressive modes of the child and the stages and vicissitudes of an autonomous process of integration and personalization of the Ego.

In clinical work with psychotic patients, it is necessary to distinguish between «regression to dependency» which is a relatively healthy manifestation of the self, and defence in terms of *withdrawal*. The latter marks the re-emergence of the psychotic component and is activated when the psychic structure is in danger of fragmentation because of the impossibility to regress into an internal place that is sufficiently stabilizing and supportive.[3] When the patient withdraws, he needs to support himself emotionally and to use his sensations and feelings to construct a form of isolation that protects him from the external threatening world. If this isolation does not go beyond a certain threshold, and does not become an impenetrable autistic shell, to a certain extent, this withdrawal space is a private one that must be respected. As long

---

[2] We owe the problematization of this type of maternal support to Lacan. Divided in its psycho-somatic experience, the child is reflected in the integrity of the maternal image to acquire an (ideal) unity that he does not yet have. The mother's attitude to regard him with the eyes of the future, as a whole, traps him in a clear risk of alienation. While I do believe that an element of alienation (of an «orthopaedic» nature to use one of Lacan's expressions) is inevitable in the ontogenetic development of every individual, I believe that with a good experience of primary holding, the mother is generally able to sense which direction the child is moving in without predetermining it. What is important is that the mother's gaze grasps the child's movement in its whole, presenting a manner of being that confers this still disorganized movement its unifying «characteristic». While the experience of the child appears fragmented on the neutral level of objective observation, this experience intrinsically (phylogenetically) tends towards a real destiny of unity that the mother must accept. The mother must not hold pieces of the child in her arms (as is unfortunately the case with some mothers who are too efficient in caring for their child bit by bit, following the guidebooks on childcare), but the whole child from the perspective of his whole existence, which she somehow has to guess but without defining it too much and thus saturating his perception with her expectations.

[3] This internal place is the product of an adequate internalization of the *relationship* with a supportive object that was sufficiently solid and reliable.

as the patient continues analysis, withdrawal may be considered a protective freezing of a potential that should not be forced. At times the analyst interprets the withdrawal as regression and thus runs the risk of attacking the patient with his empathic aspirations and reinforcing in him the experience of a hostile, persecutory environment. At other times, however, regression is erroneously regarded as withdrawal and the patient's need to be recognized and accepted in his subjective mode of being might be ignored, at the very moment when this need is becoming manifest.

In his work *Metapsychological Aspects of Regression* (1954b), in which he makes explicit reference to the psychotic patient, Winnicott underlines that «regression to dependency» requires: the internal willingness of the patient, that originates from the «true self», to regress to a situation that was previously frozen by an environmental deficit; the hope is that such a deficit might be corrected through an environmental adaptation that is more suited to his needs; the presence of a relational structure able to accept the patient's need to regress and allow this to happen in an organized manner.

The problematic aspect of this approach lies in the fact that regressing to a previous environmental deficit that was the cause of a psychotic psychic organization entails the immense fear that this fault will catastrophically be confirmed, which would then reactivate the danger of the entire psychic structure breaking down. The hope that there might be a repair of the rupture with the environment, which made an important part of the relationship with it unbearable, depriving it of meaning, belongs to a part of the self that was not *directly* involved in the breakdown which occurred within the psyche, and is therefore more or less safe from a psychotic destiny. To the same part, however, belongs the fear of an impending catastrophe, inasmuch as this part is inevitably involved, albeit *indirectly*, in the breakdown, which represents a constant threat on its very being.

No amount of trust the analyst might have earned over time will suffice in itself for the subject who has become psychotic and who, as Winnicott observed (1963), defends himself against an unrepresentable pain of the past by treating it as a future threat, because he is convinced he must put the precarious equilibrium he achieved with so much fatigue in jeopardy, and not even if he is driven to do so by the hope that he can fill the void in his existence.

Winnicott (1963) believed that the fear of breakdown could be re-experienced and resolved in the analytical relationship. I believe, however, that the fear of *breakdown*, which to a certain extent can be compared to the «nameless dread» as theorized by Bion, is not psychically containable – re-experiencing that fear means being able to bear an impending psychic death. The immediate response in terms of resolute and intense psychotic defence should be automatic.

In psychotic patients «regression to dependency» seems to be precluded unless that area is reached without the involvement of the psychotic part of their personality. Analytical work with psychotic patients in a context of regression to dependency can be a considerable help for their relatively healthy part, which is able to metaphorize the experience but by itself is unable to produce any *direct* change on the psychotic structure itself.

I do not believe that Winnicott was underestimating the fear of the psychic catastrophe that his patients harboured, and neither do I believe that he was able to dialogue only with the relatively healthy part of them, mistaking it for the psychotic part. Careful analysis of his clinical reports shows that by helping his psychotic patients to metaphorize previously meaningless experiences, he was doing the right thing. When, however, he tried to explain his work, he came up against a theoretical impasse.

I would reformulate the theoretical issue I believe Winnicott was unable to resolve, as a question: why is it sometimes possible in an analytical situation to make the foreclosed past experiences emerge without the patient once again fearing a breakdown that would force him into total psychotic defence?

The first aspect that needs clarification is the nature of the failed past experience that is to be re-lived in the analysis, so as to be able to repair it from the perspective of a change that will prove positive to its destiny. Following in Bion's footsteps, many psychoanalysts believe that what is re-experienced is an emotion that was intolerable to the child, that was not worked through and made liveable by the mother, because of some serious failure in her function of rêverie and whose meaning was therefore foreclosed,[4] although it somehow remained inscribed in the psyche (in the form of a raw, unworkable material). At first glance, this perspective would seem to diverge considerably from Winnicott's, since the latter considered the foreclosed element to be the child's spontaneous gesture rather than an experience of anxiety. In actual fact, these two notions are not incompatible with one another, as long as they are placed in two successive stages. Every time the mother is unable to relate to her child with a spontaneous gesture, mirroring it, an anxiety is created in the child and the intensity of this anxiety will depend on how long, deep and extensive the maternal «distraction» actually was.[5] The ability of the mother to accept in herself the fears that her inevitably imperfect functioning causes in the child and to work them through, so that she can return them to the child in a more tolerable form, is the second level of rêverie (the first being the mirroring of the child's spontaneous gesture). If the mother fails on this «reparatory» level of the rêverie as well, the foreclosure of the spontaneous gesture becomes final and the anxiety becomes psychically unbearable and is transformed into a «nameless dread», an indefinable and unfathomable threat of destruction of the child's internal world.

---

[4] According to Bion's beautiful expression, since there is no data available for thoughts during the waking and sleeping state.

[5] Bion associates the anxiety the maternal rêverie works on with the fear of death and I believe this corresponds to the fact that the rejection of his spontaneous gesture makes the child feel that his whole going on being is threatened.

The analyst can carry out a function of rêverie on the anxiety that has not been transformed into «nameless dread», that is, in his work with non-psychotic patients, including the work with the relatively healthy part of the psychotic patients. It is not this kind of rêverie that brings the analyst into contact with the foreclosed experience but the rêverie aimed at a *potential* spontaneous expression that survived the catastrophe. The thing that is originally foreclosed in the psychotic subject is a part of his *sensory-motor experience*, saturated in affect and desire, that collapses while it is spontaneously acquiring shape and meaning on its way to its aim. If this experience was not affected at its very roots, under favourable conditions it may remain in the psyche as a potential (following an insight by A. Racalbuto,[6] one might think of meaningless mnestic traces that are unable to give rise to a real representation) while waiting to take shape and find a possible existence.

As we can see in our clinical work, every now and then the psychotic patient tends to take an *intermediary* position between withdrawal and trust (regressive but not defensive) vis-à-vis the analyst's holding, essentially mirroring function, of experiences present in the potential state within the Self but actually never experienced and still awaiting to do so. Winnicott (1954a) establishes the condition necessary for an emerging state of withdrawal to be transformed into regression, so as to allow the repair of a failure of holding that occurred in the past:

> «I would say that *in the withdrawn state a patient is holding the self* and that if immediately the withdrawn state appears *the analyst can hold the patient,* then what would otherwise have been a withdrawal state becomes a *regression.* The advantage of a regression is that it carries with it the opportunity for correction of inadequate adaptation to needs in the past history of the patient that is to day, in the patient's infancy» (1954, 321, Winnicott's italics).

I think that in Winnicott's description, which underlines the analyst's response, needs to be added an element of *tension* and *uncertainty* which regards the patient's experience. By orienting himself towards withdrawal, what the patient is actually getting ready to support alone, is his own potential that was never expressed (because of his psychotic condition) and which, although it has never been fulfilled, plays a key role in the protection of his precarious sense of existence, in the (secret) survival of his way of being. Everything that works in his relationship with the analyst brings him to the verge of spontaneously showing himself in ways that had previously been foreclosed to the Self, but at the same time, this also poses a mortal risk so he is always on the point of retreating. If the analyst succeeds in «holding» the patient at that moment, mirroring with his own mind and emotional attitude a re-emerging

---

6 Personal communication.

subjective dimension, as if it were emerging *for the first time*, and still uncertain and hesitant in its direction, this can lead to the beginning of a new experience of being met. Should, however, this be unsuccessful, it is likely that withdrawal will take place since it is always there and ready to emerge. The analyst must bear in mind that in this area of the analytical relationship, the patient (who needs time) is proceeding step by step in terms of his efforts and the responses obtained, and he will always go through the experience of the analytic encounter within the limits imposed by his permanent tendency to withdrawal every time he comes up against a possible misunderstanding. The alternation between withdrawal and trust in the relationship (between the analyst's success and failure) is repeated over time with an uncertain outcome, before a subjective dimension that is trying to exist for the first time may take on some recognizable form and meaning.

The drive necessary to undo the protective rigidity of a psychotic compensating structure, by trying to relive in the present a past, unsuccessful holding experience in positive terms, comes from a natural and inalienable need of the patient's deformed Self. This Self tends to expand *spontaneously* to fill the meaninglessness that has cruelly conditioned his experience and overcome the deformation by taking up an adequate existential space. If this tendency is met and supported adequately, as it calls into play the threat of a definitive catastrophe, the forms of psychosis may gradually and partially give way to the possibility of coming into being of self-dimensions that had previously been foreclosed . However, these dimensions do not emerge (to the extent in which they might emerge) as precise expressive modes; rather, they arise as incompletely defined modes that fuel a new *field* of experience, which might be available from then on for conscious and unconscious thoughts and experiences.

METAPHORICAL HOLDING OF EXPERIENCE

When the analyst is in contact with the psychotic condition, he may carry out an important holding function, if he manages to *metaphorically* create on the level of a differentiated relationship, what the patient is *concretely* asking for on the level of a primary relationship. While doing so, he behaves in a similar way to the mother who, in supporting the child's sense of being a person, has to meet his potential to metaphorize experience. Satisfying the needs to metaphorize experience is an essential part of maternal holding, and its most significant moment is when the child is mirrored in the mother's face.

To a certain extent, as a mirror of the child's experience the mother's face is the dynamic composition of two expressions: what it expresses in terms of identification, and what it expresses in terms of the adult knowledge the mother has of her child. On the one hand, through direct mirroring, she feels and represents the child's experience as if it were hers, while on the other, mirroring it indirectly in its most complex way of being, she transcribes it and creates her own *corresponding* mental and emotional state. This state differs in its structural complexity as regards the child's experience but it reproduces its essential configuration. The child's relationship with the mirroring of its experience in the maternal face is its meeting with the first form (matrix) of metaphor (Thanopulos, 2005).

By means of *explicit interpretations*, when he is able to mirror the spontaneous emergence of their needs and primary desires in his complex and uninhibited discourse, the analyst can create true contact with his psychotic patients. Obviously, explicit interpretation *is neither the only nor the most important* way of mirroring the patients' experience but the *mirroring of primary experience*, which is different from *explanation* or from (re)*construction, requires a final fulfilment in the world of words* (the most differentiated and developed level of existence) *if the perspective of a long-lasting transformation is to be guaranteed.*

The analyst does not have the ability to identify with his deprived patient in the same immediate and natural way that is typical of a mother looking after a very small child. Nevertheless, he still manages to develop this capacity, to a certain extent, through his need of being in a relationship with people who are internally alive. Since psychotic subjects are not truly «alive» unless they are recognized and accepted in their most spontaneous and primary modes of existence, when dealing with the inner lifelessness in his patients, the analyst feels profound relief every time they manage to give shape and expression to their desire to live. He then becomes willing to host the patients' experiences of emerging life within himself, even when they seem to have a disorderly and destabilizing effect on his mental and emotional state. For an analyst the possibility of discovering life in death is probably the most important incentive in his work in the field of psychotic suffering.

The clinical material I shall now present has been taken from a much broader and more complex material, with a specific objective: to isolate the elements necessary to demonstrate a type of interpretative work that can carry out a holding function for the primary need of a patient, helping them to let this need sink into an area of his experience where metaphor can develop. In this context an *explicit* interpretation can display its potential to give meaning only if, at the same time, it is able to «embrace» the patient's need, «to keep in its bosom» a part of the Self, to «mirror» an experience of his as if it were mother's gaze or an expression of her face.

Anna was a single, forty-year-old woman who lived with her elderly parents. She worked as a civil servant in an office and had such extremely difficult relationships with her colleagues that she often had to change work place. Her social relationships were practically inexistent (with the exception of very rare meetings with her brother's family) because she found them so embarrassing. Three years before starting analysis she had been undergoing pharmacological treatment, basically neuroleptic drugs (she brought the prescription to the first session) as a result of acute psychological suffering which, according to her, the psychiatrist in charge had called «disassociative psy-chosis». As far as I could understand (Anna was extremely reluctant to talk about it and I avoided forcing her), this had been a delusional episode of a persecutory nature.

During the first and second year of analysis, she had to return briefly to pharmaceutical treatment twice. In both cases she had persecutory ideas concerning a conspiracy that her work colleagues had devised in order o harm her, a man and a woman (both inspired by another colleague she had met many years earlier in one of the offices where she had worked). The conspiracy consisted in the spreading of «slander» about her father (accused of having committed an indescribable deed), in the attempt to isolate her and reveal her «congenital inferiority». Jealousy of her demeanour and substantial bust had been the motive of the conspiracy. These delusional episodes had disappeared quickly but, while they persisted, there had also been an episode of food refusal, together with a bout of vomiting, which recurred periodically during her life when she was suffering from considerable relational difficulties, starting in adolescence and more precisely when she had her first timid, erotic encounters with boys. The subject of this slander remained in the background (Anna referred to it every now and then), but without any explicit link to the idea of a real conspiracy. She was convinced she had inherited a «hereditary taint» from her father, thus seriously compromising her fate as a woman. Obsessed with the idea that she was the object of mobbing, one day she brought me to read a book on the subject, written by a French therapist.

She paid close attention to the interior of my office and would notice (usually disapprovingly) the slightest change. During the sessions there were often long periods of silence, which I found endless, and at first they made me feel I had to say something, as if the patient was waiting for something I was unable to give her. At times, when she had started to describe one of her dreams, she would change her mind and stop or she would deliberately skip parts of the description. At other times, she would tell me she wanted to talk about something that was emotionally very important or a previous traumatic episode, but it ended in mutism, interrupted by moderate manifestations of anxiety that could last for two or three sessions. When my interventions seemed particularly inappropriate, she would emotionally abandon the relationship and close herself in an impenetrable state of withdrawal for varying periods of time, although these were usually not very long. On the other hand, she was very generous with me and happily accepted the attempts at reparation that followed. For a considerable length of time she would reply to my interpretations as follows: «Well, I agree with you. But *I* knew that already.» She stopped doing this when I replied: «But *I* didn't».

Around two years after therapy had started, she told me that she had been to a female analyst to tell her about an experience she had been unable to talk about with me for months. She was convinced that if I had been a woman, she would not have had this problem. Nevertheless, she had absolutely no intention of stopping her sessions with me, even though the problem continued. She knew that this had absolutely nothing to do with the quality of my work. Several months later, she told me about a dream in which she had gone into a bank and was reading the Stock Exchange quotations and was comparing them with the actual investments she had in the post office and was trying to understand the difference. In the initially promising discussion of the dream, the associative flow (that concerned the difference between the bank and the post-office and the meaning of the investments), she suddenly stopped, for no apparent reason and I found myself insisting that she should clarify the issue of the differentiation of the investments or something of the kind. There was a hint of impatience in my doing this, of which I became aware after a while. After a slight hesitation I told the patient, who was closed in perplexed silence, that I was insisting on the problem of the differentiation of things, and at that moment this did not make much sense to her. Anna remained silent a little longer and then said: «I wasn't thinking about anything complex but about simple things, how can I say … primitive things …; like eating». And, at the end of the session, she added in a tone that was both affectionate and reproachful: «You mustn't get angry when these things happen».

Around one month after this episode, Anna's mother had to undergo emergency surgery because of a malignant breast cancer that had been diagnosed just a few days earlier. The patient reacted by trying to deny she was worried and negating the impending experience of loss, saying, amongst other things, that she had been used to her mother's absence for a long time. At times she talked about a feeling of sadness, the value of which she recognized, because it made her feel more tied to life, but the origins of which, however, she could not understand.

A short while later, just before the summer holidays, Anna missed a session. I interpreted it as her attempt to face the loss by reducing the importance of the object that was about to be lost (and which, to a certain extent, had already been lost). On the other hand, I believed the meaning of the sadness, which represented her desire to preserve an internal tie with the lost objects, recognizing their value, was different.

A few days later the patient decided to tell me about an experience of loss which she had been carrying inside for months and not been able to talk to me about. It was the episode she had told the female analyst about. Her brother, who had been her main reference point for some time, had told her that he had decided to devote himself entirely to his own family and not to waste any more of his time solving the problems she came up against every day, especially at work.

During the two sessions that followed, Anna described two dreams, one in each session. In the first, a woman who lived in her block of flats (doctor by profession), gave her two earrings in the shaped of a bunch of grapes. She did not like this kind of earring and put them in two buttonholes in her jacket. Later, after she had told the woman how much experience she had with fabrics, they both went shopping together. Before she went out she put her coat on with an imperious manner (evidently, she said, the dream was set in winter). In the second part of the dream they were in a shoe shop. She was looking for high-heeled, tapering shoes, which had always been her favourites. In the end, she found a pair of shoes but the left one was just of a plain colour while the right one was tartan. She put them on and left the shop.

Anna associated the shoes with the kilt she sometimes liked to wear. Furthermore, she told me that in the gesture of putting on the coat and shoes in the dream, there had been no feeling of triumph or satisfaction, which she would normally feel in such circumstances. Finally, we both remembered that the previous winter her brother had told her he was going to distance himself.

In the second dream she was in her former office together with some of her colleagues from that period. They pointed out that she had lost her two bags. At this point, although up until that moment she had not even remembered she had them, she searched until she found them. One was a very valuable leather bag, the other made out of plastic and not well-made, an obvious imitation of a more expensive model.

Anna's comment about this dream was that what had struck her was the fact that she had not even realized she had lost the bags. If her colleagues had not told her, she would not have started looking for them. I pointed out that her colleagues' intervention seemed to be an echo of a comment I had made a short while earlier regarding the difference between reducing or recognizing the importance of lost objects. This observation of mine, which corresponded to an experience of hers, aroused her interest so she finally wanted to know the meaning of the two dreams she had, until then, regarded with a certain distance.

In the first dream there was a great deal of material regarding the phallic identifications the patient had employed to try to resolve the question of loss in the past. At this level it was possible to make meaningful interpretations, including an assessment of the patient's difficulty in creating a transitional space between the female and male elements in herself. However, it was my impression that all this was not particularly important at that moment because what I thought prevailed was that Anna was beginning to reduce her recourse to phallic solutions, the first clear attempt at giving a meaning to her feelings of sadness, as she recognized the value of things lost.

In my eyes, the discrepancy between the expensive bag and the plastic one outlined the area of a void of representability of experience in the patient's psyche, corresponding to the foreclosure of the possible transition from a mother who had clearly been too greatly idealized to be able to really make use of her, to a real worthless, actually useless mother. This also indicated the foreclosure of the possibility of working through experiences of loss.

I decided to tell the patient about my impression that with the tartan shoe she wanted to represent the possibility that a man could put himself in a woman's shoes, tolerating «wearing a skirt» (as the Scots do). I linked this view of mine to two episodes occurred earlier in her analysis: her consultation with a female analyst a couple of months previously, and later on, my misunderstanding of her experiences when I based my interpretation on her more differentiated level of functioning, whilst she was really expressing primary needs. I then formulated the idea that she expected two things from me. The first was my capacity to willingly accept,[7] in certain moments of our relationship, a female role of maternal acceptance, temporarily sacrificing the «male» interpreting work, which values the more differentiated level of experience. The second was my capacity to play such a role as a «throwaway» object (represented by the plastic bag in the second dream) which she could use without having to worry about damaging it, to express «elementary», but important needs that would otherwise have been inexpressible.

Usually very frugal with any signs of agreement or disagreement, the patient accepted my interpretation favourably, thus creating a productive climate of collaboration and exchange within the session. The concept of the «throwaway» object had proved the right thing at the right time because it made it possible to designate and identify a relational possibility, without which the internal maternal object would have remained in a state of permanent splitting into an unreachable ideal object and a real valueless object. This splitting had ended up rebounding on the patient herself, since she had always perceived herself as lacking in any female values (which she found mysterious and elusive) and not being entitled to a personal existence.

During the following session the patient was silent for a long time. She finally said: «One doesn't always need words. I was in my own company but I still felt I was in contact with you». With the patient's help, it was possible to understand that what she had found most meaningful in my interpretation was *my willingness to gather and return to her in an integrated form the whole unfolding of her discourse, which she had constructed step by step over a considerable period of time* (in other words, ever since her visit to the female analyst). Although the thought about the «throwaway» object had been formulated by me and had not existed in her mind before, that thought was a revelation for me and not for her. In the context of our relationship, she had gradually configured a set of primary needs and desires that converged on the request to use me without worrying, and she did that *by moving forward and retreating,* ready *to trust or withdraw* depending on my receptiveness. In view of the primary level of the desires she expressed, there was no point in Anna formulating a well developed concept to represent them. The important thing was *that everything left its mark on me and on the relationship and that I was able to give this mark a name, thus testifying my willingness to register it internally.* From *my* differentiated level of participation, the expression «throwaway» was what *mirrored* the primary form of *her* communication, confirming that for me this form existed and could therefore also

---

7 Without getting angry, as she had believed during the episode of the misunderstanding of her experiences. With hindsight, one could say that by asking me not to get angry, the patient was indirectly and probably not completely consciously telling me that it was only by irritating her interlocutors that she was able to «talk» about the misunderstood part of the self.

exist for her. The fundamental element was not the meaning of the expression in itself, but the fact that this expression had proved to be the most suitable to testify to us both the transformation of my emotional and mental state, which had taken place by gradually adapting to the patient's needs and relational modes.

As shown by the dreams and as is often the case with psychotics, together with the expression of primary needs, in the communication of the patient there is also a level of highly metaphorized expression. Essentially, Anna's relationship with me was on two levels. In the area of metaphorized experience, issues of sexual identity and gender, idealization of the primary object and working through of loss could clearly be seen. In an underlying area, however, the relationship was concrete and basic and often led to misunderstandings and breakdowns of the dialogue. There was no connecting thread between these two levels. The whole interpretative work on the metaphorized contents was very interesting and basically very similar to that of the analyses with non psychotic patients; but this work had absolutely no influence on the relationship developed on the level of primary communication. Every time that analysis related to the relatively healthy part of Anna and gave it priority (because the patient herself demanded it or because at that moment that was the best path to follow), the understanding between her and myself was good but I often felt that the meanings constructed in that way were without the necessary authenticity. Indeed, one part of the patient was excluded and this exclusion was two-fold: excluded from the relationship with me but also from the internal world of the patient herself who, when she was communicating on a differentiated and developed level, lost contact with the more genuine and needy part of herself.

At a primary level of her experience, the object (mother, brother, analyst) was something as basic «as ... *eating*», an object that had to be immediately available, to be used the way she wanted, without having to feel guilty. A simple object like eating, an object to eat, to use. This was evidently connected to the recurrent episodes of food refusal and bouts of vomiting. The representation «throw away» managed to capture the only point at which Anna's ability to metaphorize her experience might indirectly come into contact with her primary needs. This point was the search for integration between the female and male elements in her character, indirectly evoking the need for a quality of female acceptance and a holding maternal environment within the analysis. By abandoning the meeting place between two metaphoric languages, I had conveyed to my patient my recognition of her desire for me to be both a metaphoric and concrete substitute for her *brother*, to be able to use me as she wished, which had not been possible with him, as an available *mother*, without exposing herself to the danger of harming me with this behaviour, and thus causing the loss of me. This kind of communication, the arrival point of my silent internal work, which the patient had patiently urged, encouraged and guided (albeit unconsciously), not only gave a metaphorical gratification to her concrete need, but also allowed the part of her that was able to metaphorically express her experiences, to participate in the determination of this kind of gratification.

CONCLUSION

The two levels of psychic functioning in psychotic patients is a key aspect in the analytical approach in their therapy. In this paper I have consistently referred to the psychotic part and the relatively healthy part of the Self.[8] By psychotic part I mean all the deformations the Self suffers,[9] because of the need to contain the emptiness that has formed in the fabric of its existence. I see the psychotic subject's psychic life as a fabric that had to shrink, *to deform*, so as to contain a tear whose tendency to expand threatened the fabric with disintegration. In the area closest to the tear, the deformation is the greatest while it diminishes the further away one goes. The result is a general *compression* of the Self, which has repercussions on subjectivity and psychic structure, creating a situation within which there is a cohabitation of – *psychotic parts,* resulting from the more direct and deforming reaction to the breakdown, *archaic parts*, which are the outcome of fixations to the earliest phases of development, and the inevitable by-product of the compression which hampers development, and *relatively healthy* parts, that correspond to that part of the subject that best survived the breakdown. The articulation of these parts with one another leads to the most variable results (overdetermined by the intensity and extent of the deformation) so that the analyses of psychotic patients cannot easily fit into a particular framework, but at times, they also present deeper and more intense relational areas than certain analyses of neurotic or borderline patients.

In psychotic patients all the force of their spontaneous existence (the most original and authentic part of them that survived) drives towards the re-expansion of the compressed Self, tends to activate expressive possibilities which exist in the potential state within the Self, waiting to be fulfilled. Nevertheless, the drive of psychotics to re-expand their subjective experience also exposes them to an enormous danger - if it is not accepted, it might drag them into the void. One could say that that which nourishes their hope of a re-birth represents, at the same time, a death threat. Faced with this frequently irresolvable contradiction, which implies a permanent oscillation between a cautious sounding of the possibility of opening up and withdrawing, the analyst's work is often difficult, discontinuous and tiring.

Moments such as those I have described in this paper are «moments of grace», which might perhaps open up new clinical and theoretical perspectives, but are not

---

8 I recall the exemplary case of one of Bion's patients, in which mention is made of «black glasses». Bion formulated one interpretation by taking into consideration the psychotic part of the patient and another, more articulated and highly symbolic, addressing the part that was capable of metaphorical elaboration.

9 The «Self», anchored in my conception of the original experience of being (described by Winnicott), represents a *way of being*, that gives psychic experience its cohesion, its originality, and its ability to be self-contained.

the rule. However, I personally always keep them in mind as an essential point of reference in the therapy of all my psychotic patients, because one thing is certain. When working with psychotics, we have to communicate with the part of them that is able to metaphorize experience (including the ability to metaphorize present in delusion and hallucination) to allow a rearrangement of the psychic structure that is favourable to this part; but if we are assisted by our desire and theirs, and also with a little luck, we can help them thaw experiences that are frozen in a potential state inside, and waiting to reach a status of metaphorization and become meaningful both for the self and for others (and therefore become truly liveable). One of the practicable routes goes through the possibility that the analyst functions (with his way of feeling and thinking) as a metaphorizing mirror to the patient's unexpressed need, on its way towards the acquisition of a form of expression.

SUMMARY

During analytical work, from time to time the psychotic patient tries to remain in situations of uncertainty between withdrawal and the possibility of trusting the analyst to support his experiences that are present in a potential state but have never really been achieved before. Faced with this kind of situation the analyst can carry out a function of holding by metaphorically achieving on the level of a differentiated relationship what the patient is concretely proposing on the level of a primary relationship.

KEY WORDS: Holding, regression, metaphorization, rêverie, breakdown.

REFERENCES

BION W.R. (1967). *Second thoughts*. London, Heinemann.

THANOPULOS S. (2005). Lo spazio della cura analitica. In G. Berti Ceroni (Ed.), *Come cura la psicoanalisi*, Milano, Franco Angeli.

THANOPULOS S. (2006). L'orizzonte tragico del sogno: «dran» e isteria nella scena onirica. *Riv. di Psicoterapia Psicoanalitica*, 2, 81-97.

WINNICOTT D.W. (1954a). Regression and withdrawal. In *Through pediatrics to psycho-analysis*, London, Brunner Mazel, 1992.

WINNICOTT D.W. (1954b). Meta-psychological and clinical aspects of regression within the Psychonalytical Set up. In *Through pediatrics to psycho-analysis*, London, Brunner Mazel, 1992.

WINNICOTT D.W. (1963). Fear of breakdown. In *Psychoanalytical explorations*, London, Karnac Books, 1989.

Original italian version:
Riv. Psicoanal., 2007, 4, 897-916

Sarantis Thanopulos

Via Tasso, 628

80127 Napoli

(Translated by Tina Cawthra)

Dreams: a «transitional» area
from the body of experience to the body of thought

ELENA MOLINARI

In ancient times, the Greeks never spoke of dreaming or having a dream, but of seeing a dream, thus emphasizing the iconic form of the dream thought (Dodds, 1951). The dream can be regarded as an image, a series of images or, according to Freud, a «form», «the form into which the latent thoughts have been transmuted by the dream-work» (Freud, 1915-16, 182). As studied by Winnicott (1971), this work, which has a great deal to do with creativity and artistic processes, is able to penetrate the complexity of the transformation process that analysis supports, including the somatic aspect.

In analysis dream images may be shared by means of further transformation, a formal organization in which the moment, the context and the relationship with the analyst may take part.

There are a multitude of modes in which dreams may be described or listened to. Freud himself made a comment of this kind in his writings about dreams: «some are very short and comprise only a single image or a few, single thoughts, or even a single word, [...] There are dreams which are as clear as [waking] experience (Freud, 1915-1916, 89-90). Some are accompanied by many associations while others remain just an isolated image in the context of the session.

In correspondence to the variety of the patient's «narrative styles», today we are able to offer a similar variety of listening modes, according to the explicit or implicit theory adopted by the analyst, who thus becomes both a spectator and actor in the creative process of analysis (Petrella, 2000). Within this aesthetical multiplicity, in this paper I would like to look at one particular mode of describing and listening to a dream and the implications this might have in the study of the depth that the patient and analyst and their bodies – in all their physicality – bring to the session. I am referring to those dreams that are described with particular emphasis on the iconic elements, which one could say are drawn or painted with words. When a patient describes a dream in this manner, it generates a visualizing function in the analyst, so that both of them find themselves at the crossroads of a creative and dialogical experience that is comparable to when one is contemplating a work of art together.

In her work *The Analysis of Dreams*, Ella Sharpe already described a similar kind of relational mode between patient and analyst when she described how she had sometimes asked her patients to observe the dream as if it were a painting and to supply details and associations regarding the colours and the material the colour referred to. Following the presupposition that the dream is the product of the patient's specific creative ability, Sharpe claims that this manner of looking at the dream has confirmed her theory that «both creative imagination and artistic appreciation are firmly rooted in the earliest reality experience of taste, touch and sound» (Sharpe-Freeman, 1937, 92).

This kind of shared visualization sends both the patient and analyst back to an eidetic experience, to an aesthetic moment, an unconscious memory of an extremely primitive sensorial meeting similar to that of the child with its mother. Accordingly, as well as creating an intrapsychic transformative experience, the dream may also make it possible to take advantage of other primitive modes of relating. By primitive I do not only mean mental experiences that took place at the beginning of one's life, but also experiences that indicate a primitive functioning of the mind when particular presentation modes of the object are having difficulty developing and being worked through.

With her belief that the recovery model is generally determined by the model of maternal care, following Margaret Little's intuition (1990) it can be hypothesized that analytical treatment may revive an experience that is both traumatic and transformative at the crossroads of trans-generational experiences. Such experiences leave a twofold inscription in the body of the experience of care and the intrusion of alien aspects that might suffocate areas of existence and expressivity (Borgogno, 1999).

In this sense, some dreams constitute a sort of transitional area between elements of traumatic experience and creative re-appropriation of the aforementioned, with particular reference to the body. Through a clinical experience in which the dream narration follows the «style» described earlier, I shall try to outline the relationship between dreams and primitive bodily experiences and study the cognitive role of the dream in the field of these pre-verbal relational areas, in particular in psychosomatic patients.

THE FIRST SOMATIC AND AESTHETIC EXPERIENCES IN THE MOTHER-CHILD RELATIONSHIP

In the field of experience that the child has in its early interaction with the mother, I would like to mention two aspects that are related to the dreams I will recount from clinical practice.

1. the figuration of pre-visual sensations.
2. the role of beauty in early mental development.

1. Together with visual experience and even before this has acquired any value as a psychic organizer, the child has tactile, kinaesthetic and postural sensations that all help structure the first psychic container. This psychosensorial activity, which is particularly intense during breastfeeding, structures mental experiences that precede the beginning of fantasy prevalently linked to visual experience. In the infant's mind, before fantasy can be associated with an image, thus becoming a visual fantasy, it is experienced in the body – namely, a particular physical function is enacted and altered according to its mental significance. These «fantasies in the body», as I call them, remain usually enclosed in a primitive and exclusive body-mind-body circuit (…) in the infant's mind, «fantasies in the body» are followed by the earliest «fantasies on the body» which, unlike the first ones, are visual fantasies, and in fact represent the first mental image of the separated self (Gaddini, 1982).

Fantasies in the body need the maternal α function if the child is to integrate them into the object relationship, by linking them to the causes that produced them and the emotions they aroused. With this maternal support, the sensations and fantasies in the body can be processed by a growing α proto-function of the child that allows the creation of «memorable images» that provide the elements for the dream and the dream thought of the waking state (Vallino, 2005). Before this can take place, the proprioceptive sensations, the experiences of being nurtured, the mutual gaze with mother, being held or rocked all constitute generative proto-representations of the psychic container, and not of the fundamental unconscious psychic contents.

Experiences of contact, such as skin contact, or those involving the voluntary muscles, articular or respiratory movements constitute the bodily prototypes of a transformative mental function, a mental function that Bion calls the contact barrier.

If the perturbative elements are not excessive, the child's mental function continues to develop in response to environmental and bodily relational stimuli, and the accumulation of unprocessed elements does not interfere with the structure of the thinking apparatus.

The maternal α function starts and supports the child's mental development but also contributes its own unconscious fantasies to this process as regards relational modes, desire, the mode and possibility of being in a relationship.

With her caring gestures, the mother transmits both the good aspect of being at one with the child and problematic aspects, for example when such gestures express the difficulty of feeling distinct and separate from her child. In this second meaning some gestures that give texture to her nurturing are maternal «fantasies in the body» in the sense of the β elements conveyed through concrete gestures. The fantasies in the body of the mother and child lead to a β- β agglomerate that cannot be transformed, given the physiological immaturity of the child's apparatus for thinking thoughts.

When analytical work reactivates the transformative processes that were precociously disturbed in their development, the re-investment of the perceptive sensory traces makes it possible for the compound β elements to reappear during analysis through formal aesthetic aspects (Racalbuto, 1994; Di Benedetto, 2000). They can then be transformed into particular dream images that can serve the function of maintaining a sort of link between the passive sensory impressions received from the outside and active projective expressions, but through visualization they also mark the start of a transformational space.

In his work on the study of creative and transformative mental processes through drawing, Milner highlighted that there can be a relationship between certain formal or aesthetic characteristics of the images and those processes.

Milner writes: «I had noticed how, through staring at an outside object that one especially liked (…) staring at it in a contemplative way, (…) there had gradually emerged a feeling of change in one's whole body perception as well as a move towards a feeling of intense interest in the sheer "thusness", the separate and unique identity, of the thing I was staring at» (1987, 281).

This transformed body awareness of one's own perception of the object or vice-versa the effect that a certain kind of concentration on the object has on one's own body awareness is able to lead from a body representation to a body presentation that has no clear boundary.

This experience is similar to the meaning of the softness of the transitional object. The child's first «not me» possession, the piece of blanket or its equivalent are always soft and this is no coincidence. Being soft expresses the specific function that the transitional object represents – being a soft border between the self and the other.

Both through the experience of the softness of the transitional object and through a kind of visual experience, the subject experiences a blurred body boundary that, in a developmental sense, is linked to the nurturing of the body that the mother offers the child.

On the basis of these observations, it can be hypothesized that during analysis certain body experiences can result in dream images that make it possible to study the structuring of the me-not-me boundary. This boundary is structured through the experience of the nurturing of the body and at times, it can leave the traces of a process that disturbed its development in the patient's body. In particular, in the dream I am going to describe the formal aspect that encompasses this process is the oscillation of the image.

2. In his posthumously published article, Fornari (2005) puts forward the hypothesis that the presence of REM sleep while feeding is not just the expression of a physiological process. According to Fornari, REM sleep while feeding is related to the early outlines of dream images and therefore also to an active and creative process of the mind, able to transform the separateness of the postnatal condition into an experience of continuity with the sensations of prenatal rootedness in the maternal body. The

newly born child is therefore able to produce dream images that allow it to hallucinate the totally gratifying situation it has been uprooted from. The dream images that develop while feeding are also extremely close to pleasant interoceptive sensations linked to having eaten enough, visual sensations, and proprioceptive sensations linked to containment. According to Fornari, they could therefore blend with these body sensations and remain in the unconscious memory as proto-images in which the «goodness felt» is confused with the «goodness seen» (Fornari, 1982).

The beauty I am referring to has a different and more primitive nature than the one described by Meltzer (1973) in which the sensation of something beautiful would be the consequence of the splitting and idealization of the object and the self. The sensation of beauty I will describe has the characteristic of a beautiful-good sensation to get hold of, so as to counter a threatening situation that is ambiguously located between the outside and inside. It is something in between sensoriality and thought, a first precipitate of an α function that can cut across the distinction, primarily somatic, between the self and the not-self.

THE DREAMED BODY

Just like works of art, some dreams allow a symbolic cognitive process that sustains sound rooting in the sensory experience of the body.

Freud regarded the dream as a product of childhood wishes and in this sense, also of the body, its needs and tensions in particular, but he focussed his interest on discovering and revealing the laws that regulate the dream-thought and establish its difference from the waking state. Accordingly, Freud tends to keep the aspects of real life experiences and the experience of the body in particular in the background (Pontalis, 1974).

Later contributions (Sharpe Freeman, 1937; Bollas, 1987; Ferrari, 1998) developed Freud's insight even further, showing that the dream may be a container of original pre-verbal experiences because it is located specifically between the pole of object experience and the physicality of the experience itself. In this sense the more primitive function of the dream image may be that of a form of action rather than of cognition. Some dreams specifically stage the functioning of the body and the sensations linked to it and entrusted to a memory of the body.

This unconscious memory expresses itself in a body form, for example a particular posture or repetitive gesture and later, if transformed by the α function, into images.

Without renouncing at re-narrating in the transference the relational events of the analytical couple, some dreams can be an attempt at symbolizing very primitive experiences. They then become similar to a work of art in the sense that they are the product of the subject's specific creative ability to relive traumatic experiences, to transform them into something that can be shared (Milner, 1975; Quinodoz, 2001; Bolognini, 2000; 2005).

According to Sophje de Mijolla (1998), thinking in images is like creating a picture in words in the hope of meeting the psychic process one is immobilized in.

In the literature various authors have highlighted how dream-work can represent a critical moment of transformation for patients suffering from disorders that are concretely expressed in their bodies because they allow a re-approachment to primitive body experiences.

In particular, Mancia claims that dreams are also extremely important elements in the analysis of patients with psychosomatic disorders because they allow an understanding of the defective functioning of introjection and projection mechanisms that seem to be at the origin of psychosomatic pathologies. According to Mancia, since the experience of incorporation is at the basis of the development of the introjection and projection mechanism, it is possible that primitive aspects of what was experienced but cannot not be translated into symbolic language emerge in the dream (Mancia, 1994).

Money-Kyrle makes explicit reference to the relationship between pathological or hypochondriac manifestations of the body and a specific kind of dream he calls «dream ideograms». According to the author these dreams are an intermediary stage between a concrete representation and a conscious prevalently verbal one. He puts forward the hypothesis that there is a specific, intermediary stage between the representation of the object and the representation of the word, and that it is a different type of thought that is expressed in dreams (Money-Kyrle, 1978).

Hanna Segal also describes how a patient gave her the possibility to observe how precise body experiences can condition unconscious primitive fantasies that then «coloured and found expression in later fantasies and anxieties» (Segal, 1991, 7). This observation was possible thanks to a dream that presented itself at various moments of analysis, allowing the author to consider condensation not only according to Freud's conception, but also as a psychosomatic fantasy that can be expressed in forms that become increasingly symbolical.

More recently, Quinodoz (2001) wrote that a certain type of dream can become a selected fact, an event by which the mind could learn how to contain the primitive aspects of its experience, including the symbolic equations or rather those proto-representations in which body and unconscious phantasy seem to blend. By means of a sensitivity that has an aesthetical quality, it is possible to understand not only the content of the dream but also its form, thus enabling the analyst and the patient to start a transformative process in the direction of an improved thinkability.

I asked myself whether this kind of transformation through dreams might be of particularly profound significance in those patients who express their psychic suffering through their own bodies. After having observed several formal characteristics of what we call «dreams as holograms» (i.e. images that are changed by oscillatory movement), I was able to observe them in three patients whose bodies were an important container of mental suffering or perhaps a first experiential mode to express it.

The dream thought therefore appears to be more apt at evoking experiences that belong to the psychosomatic area and, in my opinion, in a specific manner, through an image-action (an image that contains an aspect that is close to body experience, for example movement), makes it possible to get back in touch with a defective or missing relational aspect that led to a distortion in the development process of the self. At times, suffering in the body may represent a residue of relationships that were unable to be clear and separating, and which, in the body itself then find a mute expression that is not symbolized and therefore meaningless.

In relation to the mother, during development the child finds the first possible meaning for its drawings that take form with a gesture that explores space. In adulthood there are also creative experiences that preserve the statute of encouraging a particular contact between body and mental experience. Patients who used hypochondria or psychosomatic illnesses as an attempt to cut off their traumatic experience, can symbolize it in a form that does not exclude the body, the action or a certain degree of sensorial consciousness. In this sense, «dreams like holograms» can become a sort of «transitional area» from the body of experience to the body of thought.

PAINTING THE LIVING BODY IN CLINICAL EXPERIENCE

After the birth of her first child, Maria spasmodically went in search of clinical confirmation that she had a breast cancer. During our first meeting she said that she had agreed to analysis to please her husband since nobody wanted to believe her and nobody was able to help her. She clutched to analysis tenaciously but maintained considerable ambivalence which, as she had made clear at the very beginning, was characteristic of her relying on something else.

From our very first meeting, I was struck by the particular attention she paid to the surroundings, which was translated into comments about the colours of the paintings, the objects in the room, and their arrangement. At times she would see new objects that had been in a specific place since the very first meeting. Maria's comments aroused my strong interest in seeing and led me to think of what Winnicott suggested about the fact that the development of the primitive sense of self starts with a kind of rudimental game based on mirroring.

Later it seemed that rather than mirroring, with her observations on the surroundings Maria was not so much seeing objects, but contacting aspects of herself.

Two years late her posture, which I had always been aware of, but had never found a way of putting it into words, became part of our dialogue. Maria usually adopted a contracted position on the couch, in particular with her legs tightly crossed. Taking my cue from her description of how her child never wanted to stop playing once he had started and in order to stifle his need to urinate, he would cross his legs until he had a spasm, I told her that I had observed a similar spasm in her. The idea that at that stage of life playing is more important than pleasing one's parents, made me think that perhaps in the previous session or in the structure itself of the analytical setting, Maria found my forcefulness somehow excessive and tried to oppose it, even by using her body.

«You don't always feel like putting something aside just to please the others», I said to her in a non-committal tone. In fact, it was this comment or perhaps the observation I had made earlier regarding her posture that precipitated extreme resentment between us. A curtain of impenetrable silence fell immediately. Maria only managed to tell me peremptorily that she could not talk about it and for her it was impossible to lie on the couch if she could not do so in that position.

She missed the next session and when she returned she said that it had made her happy that she had managed not to come, as if she had finally succeeded in rebelling. She went back to the subject as the hour was drawing to a close and added that after a dream she had had the night after she missed the session, she had the impression she felt better as regards anger and the desire to destroy everything.

> I am on a completely desolate snow-covered moor. In the middle of this land-scape is a beautiful house with smoke coming out and this detail tells me someone lives there. But, at the very moment when I try to go towards the house, white wolves come out of the snow – they had been lying low, completely camouflaged. I take a couple of steps back and the wolves disappear; then, when I take a step forward they reappear in 3D. I don't run away, I'm not frightened. I stay there and keep my distance because it is so beautiful.

I felt a sense of relief that the hostile mutism we had left each other in had come to an end, and also for the sense of disorientation I had felt because my observation had seemed to hurt her deeply. I thought that perhaps what I said had underlined a visual aspect that had made her lose the sensation of contact, throwing her into a state of anguish and confusion.

Now, however, the image of the dream reintroduced what had happened in a transformed form that could be shared.

I laid great emphasis on the beauty of the image and the enchantment she experienced with the luminosity of the colour white, repeating the image with words more than once so that I could share it intimately. She told me that the house reminded her of a house in the mountains where she went with her father every weekend. Her mother rarely went with them, thus expressing her resentment for years because she had been against buying it. She added that all the white in the dream had made her think of the milk in her breast which had made it impossible for the ultrasound scan to ascertain with any certainty the nature of the lumps she felt and that had caused her such anguish.

The way Maria had described the dream had aroused various visual associations in me as well.

Starting from Freud's drawing of the Wolf Man case, through several personal associations, I found myself mentally «looking at» Francis Bacon's painting of «Pope Innocent X». I said nothing about my images. Since the hour was coming to an end, I limited myself to repeating with words the image pregnant with meaning that the dream had placed between us, underlining as before how a sense of beauty and menace had appeared and how this image had been formed by the experience of having been attacked by me.

The following session another dream appeared consisting in just a single image – *In a Venice under water, the water comes to her knees and she is dragging a cart with two mattresses, shouting like the itinerant vendors of the past.*

She told me that the mattresses were light blue, like her parents. The cries of the itinerant vendor brought back the childhood memory of when, on a Sunday morning, just as she was hearing the cries of a vendor on the street, she suddenly realized how beautiful her mother's voice was, because she would sing while doing the housework. She began crying and added with great difficulty that it was hard for her to think or say anything else. She seemed to have been exhausted by some great fatigue and although no longer rigid, her body, collapsed on the couch, also seemed to have completed some intense work.

The silence was different to the hostile one at the beginning of the dream sequence. She only told me that now she felt really sad.

During the following sessions there was a change in the relational atmosphere between us and we were able to go back to discussing what appeared to have been such an important link and of the transformative work carried out by the dream as regards the body.

COMMENT

Before the dream Maria had felt the need to miss a session. Following the hypothesis that this behaviour and the somatizations might be protomental forms of «subject-object conglomerate» (Bleger, 1967; McDougall, 1989; Ogden, 1989), I thought that Maria had created a focal point around which her malaise was condensed. Through the dream she found a first creative mode to deal with both the malaise in the body and in the relationship. There is an image in Maria's first dream that can be seen as a double image. In the background is the scene represented by the warm house that evokes a relational experience of affectionate containment and another scene that is more in the foreground, represented by the appearance of the wolves that leads one to think of a more dangerous experience.

In all likelihood Maria is putting her twofold view of the relationship with me into an image in the dream. My traumatic observation modified the white purity of the field, transferred to the background with the warm, welcoming house of analysis and the appearance of the wolves that suddenly materialize and break through the actual experience with missing a session.

The same image can also be interpreted as a new photograph of her living body. In the white candour of milk is the house (body), the wolves (lumps) are identified at first only by touch, they acquire a different sensorial statute and the visual and cognitive function is no longer delegated to another. The presence or non of the lumps, the complaint about the inability of the ultrasound scanner to see them in the white sea of milk are all transformed into the image of the wolves that appear and disappear in relation to a movement that Maria herself is exploring.

The same scene is also important as regards Maria's background.

Although it was no longer customary to swaddle young children and is therefore no longer a common occurrence, the patient told me that her own mother had swaddled her legs tightly until she was six months old, in the fear they might grow crooked. She also told me that shortly after she was born, her father had a relationship with another woman, distancing himself psychically from the mother for a while.

The mother therefore introduced an additional containment in the aesthetics of looking after her little girl's body, perhaps as a concrete sign of the defence she had had to activate against her own fear of being abandoned.

In response to anxiety afflicting the maternal mind, Maria therefore experienced the sensation of not being able to move freely in her body for a long time.

I imagine that the mother had to restrain any desires of fleeing and anger and that the swaddling was a concrete way of expressing her ambivalent desire to remain, as long as she could implement her own hostile impenetrability in her relationship with her husband. The wolves were camouflaged to make room for the immaculate blanket and the inhabited house and they were meant to remain there immobile.

In all likelihood, together with the mother I had also ignored not only her posture for a long time, but also more fundamental aspects of the relationship, obstructing any possibility of them entering the field.

With an observation about the body that includes my blind spots regarding the relationship, Maria therefore returns to a traumatic experience during analysis, but in the dream manages to move the camera far enough back to be able to include what usually remains outside of the field of vision. What cannot be seen, the non-image therefore creatively becomes a double scene. The ambivalence reappears in the relationship between the scene in the foreground and the one in the background which, however, is not framed by a clear boundary that would make it into a painting within a painting, but it remains in a sort of spatial relationship that is open with the former. Maria also invents a way of keeping them together by a recourse to oscillation. She makes up a composition that allows the wolves to be both present and absent; the image against the white background but also blending with it, the wolves become a sort of picture in the picture, but with a characteristic of *tableau vivant*. The right distance seems to be a first psychic objective that allows control over the oscillation and the feeling of confusion that preceded it.

What the body did first during the session with its defensive retreat into silence and then later by missing a session finds its first complex elaboration in the dream.

The second dream seems to be a further working through of the pain, that floods her, but it also frees her from a paralyzing ambivalence, so that she comes out of the water with one's own load of personal sadness, but real separateness.

It was not until afterwards that I thought again about the image of Pope Innocent X, his open mouth to release a cry that seems to shatter the rigid pose and invaluable dignity of the portrait and I then felt I had a better understanding of what Marion Milner meant when she wrote that a drawing is the result of a convergence between thought and action (Milner, 1952, 92).

The first dream in particular belongs in a transitional area between the experienced body in the analytical space and the real one; the image of the dream both houses and participated in facts that are real and imaginary, offering itself as an interworld space – on the one hand, the extension of the space housing the picture-dream and on the other, the manifestation and exasperation of what is found in the unconscious memory of the body, the nucleus of an aggregate of unthought and unthinkable thoughts.

I believe this direction from the body to the mind, and not the other way round, which is the natural developmental direction, is an obligatory passage when the body is the main repository of suffering (Gaddini, 1982). In the dream the body Maria was exploring with her fingers as if it were a sick body in a medical relationship and also in the analytical one in someone else's power, finds a first image which allows it to be seen as a living body in relation to the other, and above all, a body that moves itself.

The dream and aesthetic experience can therefore offer the subject an experience of fusion with the object and put them back in touch with something that was never known but existentially, that is, a memory that is profoundly permeated with something that belongs to the «transformational object». In the clinical fragments the meeting first takes place with a dream image. The manner in which they are told, the emphasis on the chromatic aspects and the beauty of the dream all support a profound psycho-sensorial harmony between the analyst and patient, creating a contact point between the idiomatic aesthetics of both members of the analytical couple. At first, by favouring the visual impact over verbal communication I believe that we both invested in the maternal order with the relative exclusion of the paternal order (Bollas, 1987). In this way it was perhaps possible to share a first mental space that Florence Guignard calls «primary feminine» (Guignard, 1996).

According to Guignard it is not a matter of creating a Russian dolls system in which responsibility is naively attributed to the previous generation by using a thought of a paranoid kind. Rather it is necessary to get hold of changes in the transference and to describe to the patient his/her identifications with his/her internal objects as well as the identifications the internal objects have made with their own internal objects.

The dream appears to be an event that allows the relatively rapid birth of a part of the self, making it possible to identify an «intermediary» event that had, until then, prevented that moment from fully existing.

In this clinical sequence, the dream emerges as an event that originates as a protective membrane starting with the psychic experience of having shared a skin with the mother, but at the same time it becomes a point of arrival for a separation process.

In conclusion, there is another expression from the Greek language which I found extraordinarily suggestive. Indeed, as well as using the expressing «to see» a dream, the Greeks also wrote that a dream «visits» the dreamer but also that it «is above», thus underlining that the vision in which the dream is concretized attests its reality by leaving behind a material sign that scholars call «apport» (Dodds, 1951, 5).

SUMMARY

There are dreams that open the door to new experiences both in the real word and in analysis. The author investigates how dream-work can have a creative function in reorganizing thought, starting from a clinical case in which a dream described by the patient as «a beautiful dream» led the analytic couple to an aesthetic experience approaching that of artistic enjoyment. For both analyst and patient, looking at the dream as if it were a painting creates a meeting point in an artistic space where they experience aspects connected to the relationship with the primary object which are «known but not thought».

The dream affords access to a psychic space where the body retains remarkable power of communication, both conscious and unconscious. Receiving, sharing and describing this type of process might be an important transformational factor especially for psychosomatic patients.

KEY WORDS: Dream-work, body memory, transformational process.

REFERENCES

BLEGER J. (1967). *Simbiosis y ambigüedad, estudio psicoanalitico*. Buenos Aires, editorial Paidos.

BOLOGNINI S. (2000). Lavoro del sogno lavoro con il sogno. In *Il sogno cento anni dopo*, Torino, Bollati Boringhieri.

BOLLAS C. (1987). *The shadow of the object. Psychoanalysis of unthought known*. London, Free Assn. Books.

BOLOGNINI S. (2005). Lavoro del sogno ed elaborazione onirica.Paper read at the Congress Seminari Multipli, Bologna.

BORGOGNO F. (1999). *Psicoanalisi come percorso*. Torino, Bollati Boringhieri.

DE MIJOLLA S. (1998). *Penser la psychose. Une lecture de l'oeuvre de Piera Aulagnier.* Paris, Dunod.

DI BENEDETTO A. (2000). *Prima della parola*. Milano, Franco Angeli.

DODDS E.R. (1951). *The greeks and the irrational*. Berkeley, University of California Press.

FERRARI A. (1998). *L'alba del pensiero*. Borla, Roma.

FORNARI F. (1982). Dall'esperienza naturale di bellezza alla fondazione psicoanalitica dell'estetica. In Russo L., *Estetica e psicologia*, Bologna, Il Mulino.

FORNARI F. (2005). Il sogno durante la poppata e il transfert onirico. *Riv. Psicoanal.*, 1, 191-199.

FREUD S. (1915-1916). *Introductory lectures on Psycho-analysis*. S.E. 15.

GADDINI E. (1982). Early defensive fantasies and the psychoanalytical process. *Int. J. Psycho-Anal.*, 63, 379-388.

GUIGNARD F. (1996). *Au vif de l'infantile*. Lausanne Delachaux et Nieslè.

LITTLE M.I. (1990). *Psychotic anxieties and containment*. USA, Jason Aronson Inc.

MANCIA M. (1994). *Dall'Edipo al sogno*. Milano, Cortina.

MC DOUGALL J. (1989). *Theatres of the body*. London, Free Association Books.

MELTZER D. (1973). *The apprehension of beauty*. Perthshire, Clunie Press .

MILNER M. (1952). *On not beeing able to paint*. London, Heinemann.

MILNER M. (1975). Discussion on «In search of the Dreaming Experience». In *The suppressed madness of sane men*, London, Institute of Psychoanalysis .

MILNER M. (1987). *The suppressed madness of sane men*. London, Institute of Psychoanalysis .

MONEY-KYRLE R. (1978). *The collected papers of Roger Money-Kyrle 1927-1977*.

OGDEN T. (1989). *The primitive edge of experience*. USA, Jason Aronson Inc.

PETRELLA F. (2000). Estetica del sogno e terapia a cento anni dalla Traumdeutung. In *Il sogno cento anni dopo*, Torino, Bollati Boringhieri.

PONTALIS J. B. (1974). Dream as object. *Int. Rew. Psycho-Anal.*, 1.

QUINODOZ J. M. (2001). *Les rêves qui tournent une page*. Paris, Presses Universitaries de France.

RACALBUTO A. (1994). *Tra il fare e il dire*. Milano,Cortina.

SEGAL H. (1991). *Dream, phantasy and art*. London, Routledge/Tavistock.

SHARPE-FREEMAN E. (1937). *Dream analysis*. London, The Hogart Press.

VALLINO D., MACCIÒ M. (2005). *Essere neonati*. Roma, Borla.

WINNICOTT W.D. (1971). *Playing and reality*. London, Tavistock.

Original italian version.
Riv. Psicoanal., 2007, 3, 657-672

Elena Molinari

Viale Campari, 10/c

27100 Pavia

(Tanslated by Tina Cawthra)

Dream, transference, hallucination

ROBERTO MUSELLA

The considerations I am going to make here are motivated by my wish to work on an idea regarding basic psychic functioning. To this end, I will use the metapsychologic foundations of dream, with its hallucinatory corollary, and transference, as they seem to meet the need to find a minimum common denominator that accounts for this kind of exploration. Starting from the theory of dream, as Freud (1900) presents it in the seventh chapter of *The Interpretation of Dreams*, I aim to examine the relationship between the dreamer's psychic functioning and the concepts of transference and hallucination. Finally, by focussing on the concept of negative hallucination described by Green in *The Work of the Negative* (1993), I am going to explore the difference between dream hallucination and psychotic hallucination.

In this paper transference is considered in terms of transference on a representation or on a thinking process, such as, for example, the day's residues of dreams. Unlike some authors (see, for example, Etchegoyen, 1986), I think that there are not any real differences between the meaning of transference as we usually view it – understood as an inadequate affect for the person and the current situation upon which a transference of investment is done – and a transference on a representation.In fact, I believe that one notion encompasses intimately and metapsychologically the other. As I will analyse later, to think of a cathected transference without the mediation of a representation is quite misleading: such a transference would belong to the realm of psychosis.

Before continuing, though, I believe it is helpful to remind that for Freud:

A) the true psychic is unconscious;

B) the unconscious, under normal conditions, appears only through a transference on a preconscious representation.

To illustrate the process whereby a cathected quantity belonging to a repressed representation is transferred on an innocent representation, as it is the case of day residues, Freud (1900) makes use of two metaphors. The first, a definetely economic one, is the well-known metaphor of the capitalist and the enterpreneur: the former stands for the unconscious desire, the latter represents the former in the preconscious through transference.[1]

---

[1] Upon closer inspection, in this double personification we can already identify the agencies that many years later would become the foundations for the structural theory of the psychic apparatus.

The second metaphor, the «juridical» one, illustrates why a specific unconscious representation is not given the right of citizenship but through a transference on a preconscious representation. The example is of a skilful American dentist who, to practice in Europe, needs to turn to a figurehead, possibly an anonymous physician who, for this reason, lends himself to such transference. Thus, a capital-affect-wish-unconscious-repressed is transferred on the representation of the dentist-figurehead-enterpreneur-anonymous physician (to which we add the analyst). Clearly the substance, the true psychic, stands in the underlying unconscious psychic process – the capital – which, to show itself, invests a spokesman, a figurehead who will represent him in the psychism. The corollary of such assumptions is that psychic life has a «hard» unconscious foundation which inevitably needs the mediation of a preconscious representative representation in order to manifest itself.

From this theoretical principle results a technical principle, whereby the representation of a screen-person – the analyst – in an appropriate and ad hoc context – the setting – is literally used by the analysand as a vehicle for representing his own deep experiences.

The dream theory, illustrated by Freud through the technical device of the analytic consulting room, is consistent with the theory of psychic functioning at more than one level. Indeed, the dream model corresponds to what happens ordinarily in psychic functioning: psychic life, when everything works, is always conveyed just through transference.

My aim is to examine in greater detail how such transference takes place economically, and how its underlying processes are regulated. Let me start from the opening words in the last paragraph of chapter seven: «It will be seen on closer consideration that what the psychological discussion in the preceding section invites us to assume is not the existence of two *systems* near the motor end of the apparatus but the existence of two kinds of *processes* of *excitation* or *modes* of *its discharge*» (1900, 610).

The salient issue in this stage of Freud's work seems to be that the economic point of view, «on closer consideration», overrules the topic one. What is important, Freud says, is a discharge of excitation taking place according to two «modes» – which obviously are the primary and the secondary processes. The former works under the aegis of the pleasure principle, whereas the latter under the aegis of the reality principle; the former is peculiar to the unconscious psychic functioning, the latter to the preconscious psychic functioning; the former operates by way of perception identity, the latter by way of thought identity.

In the dream dynamic the transference on the day's residue, in its preconscious state, of some cathected quantity (transference of the energy peculiar to the unconscious wish), which is related to an unconscious representation under normal conditions, indicates a constant intrapsychic interplay between the unconscious psychic

functioning, dominated by the primary process, and the preconscious psychic func
tioning, subject to the secondary process.

This is quite an important point because, to be fair, it makes us think about the
meaning of dream as wish-fulfillment, where the ultimate wish would be to find a
representative enough representation, i.e. a way of conveying an unconscious content – otherwise not representable – by way of a preconscious representation. The
ultimate purpose is to let the dream carry out its peculiar work (*Traumarbeit*), as
Freud reminds us in the famous note added in 1925 at the end of chapter six. The
dream-work ultimately facilitates a discharge of psychic excitation from the affect to
the representation through transference.

The meaning here is that things, through the transference I have just mentioned,
have their dynamic-economic accomplishment: at bottom, this is what the dream
theory teaches us.

Usually, the primary and the secondary processes are in a dialectic relationship
with one another. To Freud, according to this dialectic, the secondary process
inhibits the primary process through a raising of its level.

Here two questions rise inevitably:

1)   What do we mean by a raising of level?
2)   What would happen if this inhibition did not occur?

Let us try to answer to the first question and we will come back to the second one
when we deal with psychosis.

The transition from an unconscious to a preconscious state does not imply a double transcription or two languages, but, as we have seen, it entails a different state of
energy: a free energy with a tendency to discharge in one case, a bound and excited
energy in the other. It is not a matter of two different places but two energy states of
the very same process. It is a state that, among other things, needs to vary its intensity
to produce the phenomenon of consciousness.

An hypercathexis at the hands of the preconscious, through what Freud calls a
raising of its level, stabilizes the system by inhibiting its free and unchecked discharge. «All that I insist upon is the idea that the activity of the *first psi*-system is
directed towards securing the *free discharge* of the quantities of excitation, while the
second system, by means of the cathexis emanating from it, succeeds in *inhibiting*
this discharge and in transforming cathexis into a quiescent one, no doubt with a
simultaneous raising of its level» (1900, 599).

The unconscious trace, in its preconscious condition, is bound by a verbal representation and it becomes excited in its thing+word state. One wonders how such conjunction can excite the apparatus. We may assume that the word, being the residue of
a sensory trace coming from without, brings through the cap of hearing – it is no
accident that Freud includes it in the structural model of the psychic apparatus

(Freud, 1923) – a surplus of energy that excites the system. Whether only the word can excite the system, by prompting a raising of level, or other perceptive modes can also act similarly remains an open question.

Clearly, the raising of level is a reinforcing step necessary to produce the phenomenon of consciousness. Already in the *Project* (Freud, 1895) the specific hallmark of consciousness is acquired by way of the link between the thing and its corresponding word.

In *The Unconscious* (1915b), Freud reasserts how the phenomenon of consciousness is produced by the link between the thing and its corresponding word. We infer that without the thing-word conjunction no intensity sufficient to awake consciousness will occur.

Consciousness, for its part, is a sense organ (Freud, 1900) that perceives psychic qualities and is potentially cathected from two different directions: from inside and from outside. The inside is defined by the pleasure-displeasure dyad and by the link between things and their word representatives; perceptions, on the other hand, come from the outside. Ideation processes, that are unbound from verbal representatives, are therefore missing the quality of consciousness; however this does not apply to perceptions. Specifically, consciousness is cathected by the excitement that attention – as a function of the preconscious – stirs in the mnestic traces and transforms their energy state. The ensuing excitement is a function of the quality of becoming conscious. The resulting equation is that this quality comes from an intensity and, ultimately, from a quantity.

In the dream the perceptive intensity peculiar to hallucination stirs the attention and thought regresses to an hallucinatory perceptive functioning.

When we sleep the excitation process, peculiar to the preconscious hypercathexis affecting consciousness, needs to be quenched. When we are lost in thought, because of the excitment of our system, we cannot sleep until our preconscious verbal thought is regressively drawn into the primary process logic.

When we sleep the censorship shifts to the supposed end of the apparatus, closing the gates to motility and consciousness. Only subsequently the dream brings the free unconscious excitment back under the domination of the preconscious, it removes the unconscious excitment, it acts as its outlet in exchange of a small amount of vigilant activity. It actually stands as a compromise in the service of both systems.

Let us track the path of the dream. We have assumed a postulate: the existence of repression and of unconscious psychic processes, in other words the true psychic. The day's residue has captured, stimulated and kept the secondary process busy during the waking life, without necessarily being aware of that. This residue has been related to an unconscious representative by way of homology or affinity and it is able to give it a meaning, to cast some light on it through transference. Without that light the unconscious trace would be invisible.

At night the system rearranges itself. The unconscious-preconscious censorship loosens and the gate to motility closes. Charges are free to circulate from the unconscious to the preconscious states, but the way leading from preconscious to consciousness is barred; therefore this progressive movement – the driving force of which is the unconscious-repressed-sexual-infantile wish – is followed by a regressive movement which assumes the conditions of figurability by stimulating the perceptive apparatus through the transformations peculiar to the dream-work (*Traumarbeit*). Consciousness is aroused and a subsequent sense of excitation directs part of the available preconscious cathexis into attention to the source of excitation. Like all perceptual experience, it needs to be organized to become consistent; it is, therefore, worked through (secondary revision) and has some arousing effect that characterizes every dream by way of preconscious cathexis and some progressive movement that goes from perception to consciousness passing through the inevitable link to the preconscious.

As Freud puts it (1900, 575): «This sensory excitation proceeds to perform what is its essential function: it directs a part of the available cathectic energy in the *Pcs.* into attention to what is causing the excitation [see 593]. It must therefore be admitted that every dream has an *arousing* effect, that it sets a part of the quiescent force of the *Pcs.* in action. The dream is then submitted by this force to the influence which we have described as secondary revision with an eye to consecutiveness and intelligibility. That is to say, the dream is treated by it just like any other perceptual content; it is met by the same anticipatory ideas, so far as its subject-matter allows [499]. In so far as this third portion of dream-process has any direction it is once again a progressive one».

From this point on, we are induced to think about an often overlooked function of the preconscious. It does not only regulate the centrifugal processes by bonding the unconscious excitement and making it representable, but it also modulates the centripetal processing by organizing the perceptions through anticipatory representations.

On the side of the dream this anticipatory function is suggested in the note already mentioned which was added in 1925 (*ibid.*, 506, note 1). Among other things, Freud says that he understands the delicate issue about the prospectic tendency of dreams – an issue raised in another note added in 1914 (*ibid.*, 579, note 3), where among the «secondary» functions of dreams, in agreement with Maeder and Adler, he includes the preliminary practice of congenital instincts and an attempt to solve conflicts. The dream would not only tend to representation but it would prospectively indicate, under certain circumstances, a direction to follow to satisfy a drive, as Freud himself proposes in the case of Dora.

Let us shift our focus from the dream to the analytic session, a dream-like apparatus (Laplanche, 1987). «[…] *Psychotherapy*», as Freud says (1900, 578), «*can pursue no other course than to bring the Ucs. under the domination of the Pcs.*». Like the dream, psychotherapy intends to favour a process whereby the preconscious binds the unconscious excitement. Psychoanalysis, as a clinical practice, succeeds when it allows to bind this psychic intensity, i.e. quantity of excitement, on the symbolic level. Freud's statement: «The catexis from the *Pcs.* which goes halfway to meet the dream after it has become perceptual, having been directed on to it by the excitation in consciousness, binds the dream's unconscious excitation and makes it powerless to act as a disturbance», could be understood in the light of the treatment apparatus which, like the dream, stands as a compromise between the two systems (1900, 578).

The day's residue, in analysis, is formed by the sum of perceptions organized by the preconscious, bound to the sensory experiences that invest the analysand and upon which the analysand projects the offshoots of his unconscious. Since some variables are considered constant and the setting is marked by some necessary immutability, the privileged sensory variable is constituted by the words of the analyst and the words of the patient, which act as preconscious verbal residues. In order for that to produce some result in the treatment, so that these residues will be cathected by the unconscious, there must be a preconscious fabric that holds the representations.

The concept of transference fits perfectly the idea of an investment of the analyst in the treatment, understood as an investment of the preconscious symbolic representation of the analyst. This emphasizes, were it necessary, the theory of the analytic setting and treatment, since it is clear that the more the analyst stands as a residue, by promoting the transference because of the very characteristics of the setting, the more the transference neurosis (an enactment, in the treatment, of the fixation of an affect on a representative representation) will find its way unbarred.

The interpretation will also be successful, because if we imagine it in the preconscious verbal form which is peculiar to it, as a catalyst of unconscious contents, it can set in motion a process that, like in the dream, activates some repressed residues by relating them to the preconscious. Also in this case, we will need to keep in mind both directions of the phenomenon which goes from the interpretation of the analyst to the repressed of the analysand and vice versa.

Analytic interpretation works according to the same model. At best, it recovers the unconscious interface of the analysand by means of the analyst's words and it meets the analysand's unconscious wish to find a preconscious representation. But mostly, it will be the patient's words that, through free associations, will find in the patient himself the unconscious cathexis in search for a representation that will then be transferred on his words. The transference on the word (Green, 1984; 2002) unfolds in two directions: toward the analyst's words and toward the analysand's words. In this perspective, I think that the preconscious verbal residue to be priviledged is the free associative flow of the «analysing», who is more capable of gradually attracting, session by session, his unconscious contents to be transferred, rather than the analyst's interventions that risk to act as a hindrance. Technically, the analyst's intervention would take the form of a discrete interpretative abstinence. This technique is applied under optimal conditions with neurotic patients who are free enough to access the symbolic level on which they would carry out this form of transference.

We could say that a typical treatment consists in allowing this transference to occur, setting the conditions so that the transference casts some light on the repressed, which then transfers its quantity on the transference. Hopefullly, once the treatment is over, the analysed will be able to continually and interminably recur to the transference on objects or thinking processes by himself.

With a normally formed psychic apparatus, the «analysing», not unlikely an ordinary person, can convey some cathected quantity by way of an interplay of preconscious-unconscious representations. Obviously, if this is supported by a continual analytic work on an almost everyday basis, it can lead to a continuity of the discourse that invests the residue to convey deep contents.

No doubt, the idea of tertiary processes, understood as the result of the interplay between primary and secondary processes, as Green says (1977; 2002), is essential in the metapsychologic field as well as in the treatment dynamics. In my view, this idea springs from Freud's notion of dream-work (*Traumarbeit*), a privileged place of exchange between the primary and secondary processes. In this in-between area, which is a cornerstone in Winnicott's theory (Winnicott, 1953), we can find how reality and fantasy are intertwined; it is a place that enables the analyst, in the neutral field of analysis, to be both a real and a fantasmatic entity, a residue and a relationship. In this in-between – the sleep-dream watchman of our mental health, as Freud says (1900) – psychic health is literally at stake. In this in-between centrifugal thrusts toward representation meet the perceptions, and the perceptions meet the anticipatory representations. Clearly, pathology originates when this in-between play area is smaller or missing (Winnicott, 1971) and subsequently the watchman is overwhelmed (Freud, 1900). Conversely, a successful treatment can lead to an expansion of this area.

To talk about hallucination in psychosis – our last and hardest effort – we still have to take a step backward and remember how, according to Freud, dream hallucination is produced. We just need to remember that one gets to the dream backwardly and we look at the fictional model of the psychic apparatus imagined by Freud (1900) in chapter seven, a model that had been preceeded, as we know, by another one illustrated in a letter to Fliess of December 6 (1896).

This apparatus has a motor end and a perceptive end, and mnestic traces are stored there. These mnestic traces are unconscious in themselves, so they are not accessible to consciousness but through a transference – let me repeat it – on a preconscious representation (Freud, 1900). During the night, the dams of the perceptive and motor ends determine the conditions whereby the apparatus is aroused backwardly, i.e. from the preconscious representations to the unconscious ones, in order to be finally learned by the conscious. The unconscious memory drags the preconscious verbal thought through a regressive mode. The process as it unfolds, instead of going toward the motor end of the apparatus, is transmitted toward its sensory end and eventually gets to the perceptible system (Freud, 1900; 1917).

The dream is allowed because of a particular psycho-physical state: the state of sleep. Only this condition, with the closure of the perceptive afferents and the preclusion of the motor efferents, allows for dream hallucination.

This is quite different from the psychotic condition, in which the psychotic hallucinates in his waking life, with an open access to motility (we just mention the baleful consequences of some incidents that may happen during hallucinatory states) and with the non-closure of the perceptive afferent. In this case, the shift of the forces at play is produced, Freud says (1900), not because of a night reduction of the energy engaged by a critical censorship, but because of its pathological weakening or a pathological strengthening of the unconscious excitements.

The psychotic does not perceive the surrounding reality but, like in a dream, he hallucinates his own psychic processes. How can this happen? How can it happen that some people, just to give an example, hallucinate a person, others have an obstinate feeling that they are seeing a person, and others dream a person. We may all have experienced the two last occurances. Sometimes, under certain conditions, when our psychic apparatus is extremely distressed, we may believe we are seeing a longed-for person, sometimes we may dream that person, following an association to a day's residue, but we hardly hallucinate that person. In the first case we assume that the unconscious thrusts have been so massive as to force our attention, through reality testing, to undergo a continual effort to adjust our perceptions; in the second case the unconscious fabric presumably takes possession of a residue to form a dream; in the third case the power of the unconscious thrusts exceeds the weak capacity of the preconscious to retain the unconscious representation that breaks into the scene and gives rise to hallucination.

These phenomena seem to be interrelated, but we do acknowledge a difference of intensity. Differences seem to be: a) of quantitative nature, and b) to what degree the apparatus can hold. A hallucination would arise because of either an eccessive excitation or the weakness of the psychic system. Thought identity and reality testing, peculiar to the secondary process, are eluded in favour of hallucinatory perception identity, peculiar to the primary process.

As I continue along the lines of this false link and the day's residue, I wonder if it is legitimate to include hallucination, with due proportions, in the above-mentioned scenario: the non-dream hallucination as a corollary to the dream theory, from which it distances itself because of quantitative issues related to the holding of the psychic apparatus.

Somnambulism and other hysterical conditions could be in-between conditions, between dream and non-dream hallucination.

On the basis of what has been said so far, I believe I need to interpret the concept of negative hallucination, as Green presents it in *The Work of the Negative* (1993).

We know that Green takes his cue from a note, which Freud (1917 [1915], 232) added in *A Metapsychological Supplement to the Theory of Dreams*, that says: «I may add by way of supplement that any attempt to explain hallucination would have to start out from *negative* rather then positive hallucination».

The note, in itself, is quite mysterious, because Freud had not spoken about negative hallucination since his hypnocatartic time, when he used to state that, among the suggestions the hypnotizer could give to his unfortunate guinea pig, there was the instruction to fail to see something that was actually there: «There is nothing in front of you, come toward me », and the unlucky person would bump against an obstacle purposely placed there to have him stumble over it.

I think that in his note Freud means that the peculiarity of hallucination consists in negativesing the perception, by placing itself above reality testing and by removing the investment of consciousness; it is not – as Green seems to suggest (1993) – an active scotoma of the perceived, a blank screen that prepares the hallucinatory projection. On the other hand, we know that Freud (1927), in dispute with Laforgue, is «allergic» to the hypothesis of scotomization, dear to Pichon, and in the case of disavowal – consistently with his point of view – he wants to emphasize that the process of defence he is thinking of refers to disownment (*Verleugnung*) and not to negative hallucination. The process of disownment, to which Freud refers, includes at the same time and on different levels the admission and disavowal of a traumatic content: castration. However, the cost of this operation, as we know, is very high and consists in a permanent splitting of the ego (Freud, 1938a).

Disavowal – as Freud himself admits – expresses an act, an energetic action to give rise and maintain the disavowal: «In the situation we are considering, on the contrary, we see that the perception has persisted, and that a very energetic action has been undertaken to maintain the disavowal» (1927 , 154). The perception, is maintained; clearly it is split, but it is not admitted (*Bejahung*) on the symbolic level (Hyppolite, 1954; Lacan, 1954; Conrotto, 2000).

We are very near to the theory of foreclosure (*Verwerfung*), a defensive process which Freud has never overtly theorized and at which he has hinted only three times in his entire work (1894; 1911; 1918). Lacan (1956; 1958) has been the one who widely explored the theory of foreclosure.

As a consequence of foreclosure, the perception, experienced but not admitted on the symbolic level and not retained by the preconscious, comes back in an hallucinated form. As we have already said, perceptions are already treated by way of a preconscious mediation. Perception, untreated by the preconscious with its anticipatory representations, would therefore fall in psychism as a bizarre element. Is it the lack of this mediation that sets the stage for hallucination? In this regard, Lacan's statement (1956, 325), «*What did not come to light in the symbolic appears in the real*», is most appropriate.

Here, I can just mention an issue with no easy solution that I intend to explore in another paper. How shall we define the difference between disavowal and foreclosure – by no means an obvious issue, as we may wrongly believe? I just notice that, upon closer inspection, Freud used both words indifferently, and the term «foreclosure» (*Verwerfung*) – with which Lacan has widely dealt starting from the case of the Wolf Man – suggests exactly the same mechanism to which the late Freud referred when he used the term «disavowal» (*Verleugnung*) several times, in particular in *Fetishism* (1927), *Splitting of the Ego in the Process of Defence* (1938a) and *An Outline of Psycho-analysis* (1938b). Clearly, this mechanism – although it is mostly referred to fetishism – is common to perversion and psychosis, as it can be inferred from what Freud himself writes in 1925 (253): «Or again, a process may set in which I should like to call a «disavowal», a process which in the mental life of children seems neither uncommon nor very dangerous but which in an adult would mean the beginning of a psychosis». In this regard, I suggest to consult the always valuable *Dictionary of Psychoanalysis* by Laplanche and Pontalis (1967) at the entries «Disavowal» and «Foreclosure».

To work with these hypotheses let us review with Freud some hallucinatory phenomena illustrated in *Further Remarks on the Neuro-Psychoses of Defence* (1896) and, following Green's suggestions (1993), in The Wolf Man (Freud, 1918).

In *Further Remarks,* Freud describes the case of a paranoid woman suffering from auditory and visual hallucinations. The interpretation work of some of these hallucinations leads the patient to recover a repressed memory: the incestuous relationship with her beloved brother. The hallucinatory experience of the patient shows the weakness of her psychic apparatus that is unable to carry out reality testing and discern the hallucinatory content of her experience. The patient hallucinates naked women in her room. The residue from which the hallucination develops, like a dream residue, concerns a recent experience. She has seen some naked women in the bathroom of a public place, which has unexpectedly elicited in her memory her old shame to be in the nude in front of her mother and sister and to feel no decency to be naked in front of her brother – a sign of her pleasure.

As regards her auditory hallucinations, she hears voices which keep on saying: «That's what the Heiteretei's cottage looked like! There's the spring and there are the bushes!». These sentences refer to the content of a book that she used to read to evoke, in a split area of her psyche, the incestuous relationship with her brother that now is voiced through the hallucination, elicited by a residue that, through a direct association, captures the sentences she read in the book. She is actually overwhelmed by this hallucination when, during a walk along a country road that she associates to the bushes described in the book, she sees a house that she associates to the cottage in the story.

Freud explains this hallucination as an «incontinent» return of the repressed (in this regard see also Freud 1892; 1915a), even though, in the light of what we have said, the repressed in question does not arise from a representation but, in its being clearly repudiated from the symbolic fabric, is «repressed originally», if you may.

Hypothetically, in a «normal» individual the day impression, through an association, would have set into action the unconscious capital that would have strengthen it, it would have remained in a preconscious state and, during the night, through the dream-work, it would have produced a dream. Thus, it seems that, ultimately, the incontinent return of the repressed is due to the inability of the apparatus to retain, by way of the things-words link, the contents that go through it in both directions.

To conclude, let us look at the hallucinatory phenomenon described by Freud in the case of the Wolf Man, which Green has widely expanded. As we shall see, I do not fully agree with the latter. Or I may rather say that I agree more with what Green seems to state in the first version of his work (Green, 1977), than with the stance he takes in his second and more comprehensive version (Green, 1993). In his last version Green says that the negative hallucination is the product of an active repudiation of perception, followed by the hallucinatory projection of the wish representation. I believe that, in the light of what I have said, the hallucination expresses an overflowing caused by an impaired holding of the psychic system, which takes the perceived into account only as a potential stimulus that can activate – by analogy with the day's residue– an unconscious quantity that floods massively into the perception and negativises it.

It is well-known that the young Russian tells Freud (1918) about an hallucination he had when he was five years-old. As he first reports it he says that he suddenly perceived his finger severed while he was carving a walnut tree.[2] The first hallucinatory version is then rectified by a second one, interpolated from the memory that the child, when he had his first hallucination, was not carving the tree. Carving is actually coming from another hallucination [3] that he had at that time: as he was carving a walnut tree he realized that the tree was bleeding.

The account of the hallucination of the severed finger is associated to an episode from the previous day (here we have the day's residue, repudiated from the symbolic order, that triggers the hallucinatory process): the boy had learned about a girl who was born with an extra finger, which had been amputated with an axe. Green, in his first version, says that the positive hallucination of the boy was preceeded by the negative hallucination of the amputated finger of the girl: «*The hallucination of the severed finger is preceded by the negative hallucination of the extra finger hidden in the hallucinatory content, the latter simply positivises, on the basis of this negative hallucination, an amputation which has already been carried out on the level of thought*» (Green, 1977, 275). It is the amputation carried out in the thought that allows us to comment that the account of the amputation, repudiated from the

---

[2] While he is reporting this fact, he adds that the tree in question is of the same kind of the tree in the famous dream. Here, we emphasize a first element of condensation and a first connection with that dream.

[3] Second condensation and second connection with the dream.

symbolic order, cannot but reappear as an hallucination. The patient had repudiated (*verwerfen*), at the level of preconscious thought, the hypothesis of castration, as if it had not existed; he had ruled it out from the symbolic level, and yet it came back to him as hallucinations: the blood gushing from the tree, his own severed finger and, I would add, the so-called dream of the wolves. Several associations evoking castration are related to the dream of the wolves: let me mention here, in open order, the story of the wolf that breaks its tail while fishing, the story of the taylor that tears off the wolf's tail and the odd issue of one wolf missing on the tree.[4]

The missing blood (the Wolf Man maintains that his severed finger did not bleed) in the first hallucinatory version of the severed finger[5] reappears in an hallucinatory mode in another version where the ill-famed and ubiquitous wallnut tree starts to bleed.

There is nothing to prevent us from thinking that there is some contemporaneous atemporality between the events (the two hallucinations and the «so-called» dream). In the dream's account the patient says, among other things: «I was three or four, at most five years-old». When he reports on the hallucination he says: «I was five years-old». The three hallucinatory episodes seem closely related and they can be treated like dreams in the same night where, by condensation and displacement, the material moves from one hallucinatory representation to another.

But then, is the dream of the Wolf Man a dream? Upon closer inspection, it is nearer to an hallucination than to a dream and, if we really had to catalogue it as a dream, we would call it a nightmare, that is to say a production incapable of holding an affect in its fabric, an affect that at any rate exceeds all capacity to hold it and leads to a traumatic and anxiety-ridden awakening.

Psychotics rarely dream and mostly have nightmares. A residue catalises an experience, but the affect that invests it is not bound by the preconscious fabric, it does not undergo any secondary working through and the resulting awakening expresses the hallucinatory aliveness that has not been captured by the preconscious fabric. The awakening is often characterized by the hallucinatory phenomenon that lasts during the waking life. In these circumstances, like with the Wolf Man, dream and hallucination show their difference as well as their continuity. We can conceive pathological hallucination as the counterpart of not being able to dream. The work of

---

[4] We know that Freud, when he interprets what the patient has told him (1918), he infers six or seven wolves from the fairy tale of *The wolf and the seven kids*. He assumes that the seventh woolf, by analogy with the tale (since in the tale the seventh kid is hidden in the pendulum clock), may not appear on the tree, which explains why the wolves can be six or seven indifferently. Nevertheless, Freud does not associate the five (not six or seven) wolves in the drawing by the Wolf Man with the two remaining fingers of the girl, and he interprets the figure five as being the supposed time when the child had seen his parents' coitus. Here we point out that the hallucination of the severed finger, because of the foreclusion of a symbolisation of the signifier of castration, triggered by the amputation of the sixth finger of the girl, is amazingly coincident with the odd issue of the missing wolf in the drawing.

[5] The severed finger literally replaces, by symbolic equation, the finger amputated with the ax (tool used to fell trees), the fruit of the disownment, on the symbolic level, of the amputation suffered by the girl.

the preconscious is missing; hallucination does not spring from a dream-thought; the unconscious discharge is not inhibited; the secondary working through is lacking.

In the psychotic (I apologize for such generalization) the function of mediation of the preconscious seems to be missing. The perceived does not coagulate the repressed unconscious representations treated within a preconscious representational fabric, instead it incessantly attracts unconscious material that breaks in on the stage of perception, bypassing the thought identity in the backward way peculiar to dream.

The hallucination in a non-psychotic person would therefore be prevented by the holding of the preconscious system, an in-between area, a mediator between the perception of the real and the unconscious content. What would it happen if the secondary process did not inhibit the primary one? We may say that the primary process would rule the psychic life by way of perception identity, that is by hallucinating the unconscious psychic processes that, uninhibited by the preconscious, characterize the lack of holding that marks psychotic thought. In hallucinatory psychosis – as the inhibition peculiar to the secondary processes with the formation of thing-word conjugates is missing – any raising of level or consequent stabilization of the psychic apparatus would not occur. Words themselves, uncaptured by the preconscious fabric, would lapse in the meaningless and bizarre state of unbound things and, since they are repudiated, they would come back to the real as hallucinations.

SUMMARY

The author's aim in this paper is to work on three psychoanalytical concepts from their metapsychological point of view: the dream, transference and hallucination. He follows the steps from Freud's *The Interpretation of dreams*, in order to describe how the dream-work, in which the transference on a representation is always at work, can be taken as the paradigm of elementary mental functioning. The transference in question is the operation in which an unconscious affective amount transfers its own charge on a preconscious representation. The author then goes on to study the relationship between reality and representation by linking the function of language and the word. This relationship is studied both from the perspective of psychic functioning and from the theory of treatment in the analytical setting. To conclude, the author looks at the difference between dream hallucination and psychotic hallucination by examining Freud's *Wolf Man* and Green's *The Work of the Negative*, concentrating on the concept of negative hallucination in particular.

KEY WORDS: Dream, transference, hallucination, representation, setting, treatment, metapsychology.

REFERENCES

CONROTTO F. (2000). *Tra il sapere e la cura*. Milano, Franco Angeli.
ETCHEGOYEN H.R. (1986). *Fundamentals of Psychoanalytic Technique*. New York, Brunner/Mazel, 1991.
FREUD S. (1892). *Draft K The Neuroses of Defence from Extracts from the Fliess Papers*. SE, 1, 220-229.

FREUD S. (1894). *The Neuro-Psychoses of Defence*. SE, 3, 41-61.

FREUD S. (1895). *Project for a Scientific Psychology*. SE, 1, 281-391.

FREUD S. (1896). Letter from Freud to Fliess, December 6, 1896. *The Complete Letters of Sigmund Freud to Wilhelm Fliess, 1887-1904*, 207-214.

FREUD S. (1896). Letter from Freud to Fliess, December 6, 1896. *The Complete Letters of Sigmund Freud to Wilhelm Fliess, 1887-1904*, 207-214.

FREUD S. (1896). *Further Remarks on the Neuro-Psychoses of Defence*. SE, 3, 157-185.

FREUD S. (1900). *The Interpretation of Dreams (Second Part)*. SE, 5, 339-626.

FREUD S. (1901). *Fragment of an Analysis of a Case of Hysteria*. SE, 7, 1-122.

FREUD S. (1911). *Psycho-Analytic Notes on an Autobiographical Account of a Case of Paranoia (Dementia Paranoides)*. SE, 12, 1-82.

FREUD S. (1915a). *Repression*. SE, 14, 141-158.

FREUD S. (1915b). *The Unconscious*. SE, 14, 159-215.

FREUD S. (1917). *A Metapsychological Supplement to the Theory of Dreams*. SE, 14, 217-235.

FREUD S. (1918). *From the History of an Infantile Neurosis*. SE,17, 1-124.

FREUD S. (1923). *The Ego and the Id*. SE, 19, 12-66.

FREUD S. (1925). *Some Psychical Consequences of the Anatomical Distinction between the Sexes*. SE, 19, 241-258.

FREUD S. (1927). *Fetishism*. SE, 21, 147-158.

FREUD S. (1938a). *Splitting of the Ego in the Process of Defence*. SE, 23, 271-278.

FREUD S. (1938b). *An Outline of Psycho-Analysis*. SE, 23, 139-208.

GREEN A. (1977). Negative Hallucination. In Green A., *The Work of the Negative*. Trans. A. Weller. London, Free Association Books, 1999.

GREEN A. (1984). Langages. Deuxièmes rencontres psychanalytiques d'Aix-en-Provence (1983). *Le langage de la psychanalyse*. Paris , Les Belles Lettres.

GREEN A. (1993). *The Work of the Negative*. Trans. A. Weller. London, Free Association Books, 1999.

GREEN A. (1995). *Propedeutique: La metapsychologie revisitée*. Editions Champ Vallon Seyssel.

GREEN A. (2002). *Key ideas for a contemporary psychoanalysis. Misrecognition and recognition of the unconscious*. London, Routledge, 2005.

HYPPOLYTE J. (1954). A Spoken commentary on Freud's «Verneinung». In Lacan J., *Ecrits (Appendix 1)*, Trans. B. Fink, New York, Norton, 2005.

LACAN J. (1954). Introduction to Jean Hyppolite's Commentary on Freud's «Verneinung». In Lacan J., *Ecrits*, Trans. B. Fink, New York, Norton, 2005.

LACAN J. (1956). Response to Jean Hyppolite's Commentary on Freud's «Verneinung». In Lacan J. *Ecrits*, Trans. B. Fink, New York, Norton, 2005.

LACAN J. (1958). On a Question Prior to Any Possible Treatment of Psychosis. In Lacan J., *Ecrits*, Trans. B. Fink, New York, Norton, 2005.

LAPLANCHE J. (1987). *Problématiques*, tome 5: Le Baquet, transcendance du transfert. Paris, Presses Universitaires De France.

LAPLANCHE J., PONTALIS J.-B. (1967). *The Language of Psycho-Analysis*. Trans. D. Nicholson-Smith. London, Hogarth Press; New York: Norton, 1973.

WINNICOTT D.W. (1953) Transitional Objects and Transitional Phenomena. In Winnicott D.W., *Playing and Reality*, London, F.R.C.P., 1971.

WINNICOTT D.W. (1971). *Playing and Reality*. London, F.R.C.P.

Original italian version:
Riv. Psicoanal., 2007, 4, 941-958

Roberto Musella

Via Manzoni, 216

80123 Napoli

(Tranlated by Isabella Negri)

Perspicuous examples

Paola Camassa and Francesco Napolitano

Perspicuous examples
Introduction

PAOLA CAMASSA AND FRANCESCO NAPOLITANO

The collection of *short contributions*, of which we here present a first instalment, calls for a few introductory words. The cases of illness which come under a psycho-analyst's observation are of course of unequal value in adding to his knowledge. There are some on which he has to bring to bear all that he knows and from which he learns nothing; and there are others which show him what he already knows in a particularly clearly marked manner and in *exceptionally revealing isolation*, so that he is indebted to them not only for a confirmation but for *an extension* of his knowledge. […] we shall choose to describe [psychical processes] as they occur in the *favourable and clear examples* [*durchsichtigen Fällen*] afforded by the latter […] the numerous *apt examples*, which […] are for the most part lost to view […]. There is therefore some advantage in the provision of a framework within which observations and examples of this kind can be published and *made generally known*.[1]

With these words in the *Internationale Zeitschrift für ärztliche Psychoanalyse* Freud introduced a set of clinical observations gathered in collaboration with Ferenczi and Tausk and intended as an initial contribution to a specific section of that journal.

Let us sum up Freud's intentions. The aim was to furnish *apt examples* assembled with a view to confirming the theory briefly and clearly, demonstrating the theory's practical value by both putting it to the test and, in particular, *proving* it. The *revealing isolation* of the examples is reminiscent of a laboratory experiment, in which *isolating* means clearly defining the experimental objects and limits in terms of the chosen intentions – and it is obvious that the Freudian laboratory par excellence is that of dreams, given that as many as eleven of Freud's thirteen *apt examples* are made up, precisely, of dreams and their interpretations. They are described as «short examples», and indeed not one of them is preceded by a statement of the *cornerstones of theory* that are here intended to be demonstrated to a greater extent than ever before in the very act of their application. They are thus like flashes of light revealing in all its clarity the *in vivo* experiment from which the theory extracted them in the guise of

---

1 Freud, S. (1913). *Observations and examples from analytic practice*. SE 13, 193 (our italics).

«samples of analysis», which, however, contain *in nuce* the seeds of possible large-scale theoretical generalizations. It is only from such examples, Freud says, that an extension of knowledge can accrue. But what kind of extension? And what did Freud expect from the participation of a bevy of analysts in the periodic compilation of collections of samples of this kind?[2]

What he expected was an exploration, at last shared, of the possibility of isomorphic or non-isomorphic extension of metapsychology. The former would comprise an increment of knowledge obtained with full retention of the network of theoretical statements, while the latter would perhaps reconsider that network, but in accordance with the well-known philosophical *principle of minimum mutilation* (or *principle of retention and exclusion*). So in the event of significant countervailing evidence, the theoretical statements are reconsidered, albeit with an adjustment of their scope so that they are sacrificed in a sequence extending strictly from those with fewer to those with more implications. In this way, respect is ensured for an economic aspect of the theory that differs little in terms of importance and rank from that specific to the psyche.

It is of course hardly necessary to point out that the present-day theoretical situation of *psychoanalysis* is no longer what it was in 1913, characterized as it is, firstly, by a huge proliferation of models which some would like to see as ecumenically coexisting in a kind of enlarged domain of *psychoanalyses*, but whose compatibility and derivability (one model from another and each from the presumed common Freudian stem) prove to be substantially unexplored; and, secondly, by the prevalence of a flexible clinical practice intended to be exempt from any theoretical commitment and directed purely and simply towards the patient's benefit.

Extrapolation of this practice to the event horizon reveals warning signs of the possible decay of what Freud saw as the only instrument of therapeutic work – namely, interpretation aimed at reducing the manifest to the latent by way of the patient's free associations. Hence the question: can we still produce and use brief, clear clinical examples along the same lines as those proposed by Freud?

The answer is yes, with two restrictions. The first is the generous and moderate application of a single background theory that is clearly deducible from the example, while relinquishing the classical canon of – in this order – a statement of intentions, a review of the literature and one or more *clinical vignettes* serving as «hairpin bends» on a road affording access to the summit represented by the hoped-for conclusion. The second restriction, which is largely synergic with the first, is that the clinical aspect should here be seen not only as the foundation of the theoretical edifice, but

---

[2] We know that Freud rejected Stekel's examples, that he accepted a few from Ferenczi and Tausk, and that he inserted many of his own examples in the 1914 and 1919 editions of *The Interpretation of Dreams* (Freud, S., 1899).

also, and in particular, as its vertex, so that it is ultimately the «hairpin bends» of the *apt example* that demonstrate the theory – the underlying theory supported by little argument but strictly understood.

Here then is an initial, introductory example presented in parallel with a classical one from Freud, in the hope that this approach may constitute a model for the future, comprising a text with two examples, a classical one already enshrined in the literature and a new one appearing for the first time. This strategy also endows the text with the flavour of an exercise, casting light across the divergent compass points of time on the stages in the life of the chosen theory and indicating its endurance, limits, decidability or otherwise, efficacy, and other aspects.

The dream of the cock-up

PAOLA CAMASSA

An example from Freud

«Here is a dream that occurred in the context of homosexual impulses: *he was going for a walk somewhere with a friend … (indistinct) … balloons*» (Freud, S., 1913, 198, my italics).

An equation's solution is the value or value system that proves the equation when applied to the unknowns. Freud's example takes the form of the solution to an equation: in the domain of the dream, «two men» (a) is a value that is now known: a couple; while «balloons» (b) is another known value – namely, the male genitals. For «going for a walk», the unknown (x), a value can be found that satisfies a and b: «going for a walk» = fulfilling a homosexual wish.

A new example: the cock-up

I shall present a dream as short as the one given by Freud, in which saying hallo to a man is *a mistake*. When I read the example he included under the new heading, I felt that it was similar in many ways to the dream and the interpretation I had chosen as my subject here. Nor did I resist the temptation to seek an analogous solution: if a man says hallo to another man and that is a mistake, then x (saying hallo to someone) stands for something illicit. Let us consider what is illicit here. It is interesting to note that in both cases the unknown is the verb – that is, the action.

The patient is a young inspector with a symptom: the fear of committing an offence. Asking to be exempted from investigations on the grounds of «incompatibility» has gradually become a fresh reason for anxiety.[3] He currently has to investigate a travel agency from which he bought tickets in the past. No one could charge him with anything, but he is afraid that this might constitute an offence – an incompatibility with his role – so he fears disciplinary proceedings. That seems enough for a meaning to be assigned to the dream:

«Last night I had a dream: I am at the office; I go in and say hallo to *someone with a moustache,* but then apologize, as I mixed him up with *a colleague* who had been subjected to *disciplinary proceedings*. I don't know who it is; he tells me I have made *a cock-up* [*impapocchio* in italian]».

---

[3] This strategy (the inhibitory manifestation) can usefully be distinguished from the symptom (anxiety about committing an offence).

The work of analysis

Associations: «I was at the office, but *it was not* actually the office. *There's anxiety* in this dream. I woke up this morning feeling anxious about the agency. I get anxious about *not knowing what to do if something like that* happens to me; I'm always afraid *that something will happen.*

What about the person with the moustache? I don't know.

There's someone I work with in the office who said *it's better to go round the back way than in front.* It was a quip in bad taste – it happened ten days ago, and *for a moment I hated him.*

Last Saturday when I was playing *with my son I thought of the scene again: my father asks* my brother to do *something*; my brother *said* no, and then my father *smashed* all his toys.

Something sort of came up: that my wife used studying to stop herself seeing that she can't control her son.

My father's face suddenly comes to mind, as I haven't seen it for a very long time – younger.

The cock-up [*impapocchio*]: Yesterday my mobile rang and I saw it was Michele calling. He wanted me to attend to a woman who had been looking for her husband for two days. I say I'll think about it. I phone the office.

I dial the number and Franco answers: *Sorry, I made a mistake.*

Michele is my friend; *I haven't seen him for a very long time.* We *always used to go for a run together.* Michele *always* used to tell me: *the family is what's inside when you bolt the door.* Franco has been promoted.

Now I'm thinking of a film – the one where a drug addict says: "*I masturbate men*" – *and then he gets buggered*».

The patient has done his analytic work, and now it's up to us.

The dream scene – I say hallo to X (the man with the moustache) and mix him up with Y (the colleague who was subjected to disciplinary proceedings) – is a substitute for something; what is it?

It is by no means arbitrary to begin with the patient's last associations, about the previous evening. The patient traces the cock-up [*impapocchio*] he is accused of in the dream back to the previous evening's episode: thinking he was dialling his office number, he actually called Franco. Now Franco is his wife's current lover. What is more, Franco is also an ex-colleague, now his superior.

The association «the drug addict who says he masturbates men and then gets buggered» is a violent projection of his present situation: I boasted of being top dog … but I've been trampled on.

Let us consider: does the deep meaning of the dream lie in these threatening latent thoughts, activated by the previous evening's slip? And what is the significance of the slip? Why does he phone Franco of all people – his wife's lover and a superior?

On the previous evening he calls Franco and apologizes. In the dream he says hallo to X, the man with the moustache, and apologizes.

Phoning Franco was the offence.

The dream is the substitute, the «attenuated» representation of his embarrassing slip – a typical displacement.

However, the displacement did not prevent the escalation of anxiety. *The man with the moustache* – the dream element to which he had no associations (*I don't know*) – is a symbolic formation. «Saying hallo to a man with a moustache» takes on a more threatening meaning than simply mixing up two people. Furthermore, in the dream Y has been subjected to disciplinary proceedings. So: if I say hallo to X, I'll be punished like Y. The dream uses the mixing up of the persons as a means of representing the element of «how».

Here, then, we have a series of derivatives: phoning and saying hallo = illicit and dangerous actions. We have learned (from the associations) that a man – in particular, a drug addict, someone who does illicit things and boasted of masturbating men – has been buggered. Are we now justified in substituting the meanings we have arrived at for the unknowns?

Any action that brings me close to X is a sexual action; «being punished» will also be a sexual action.

As we shall see, *the drug addict* is not an insignificant detail, but will take on a precise meaning.

In the morning the fear of committing «an offence» is the symptomatic representation (by augmentation of the mechanism of displacement) of the threat of having sexually approached a man – of having propositioned him sexually.[4]

Two opposing trends of thought are exerting pressure on the same unconscious content. The threatening man with the moustache does not give rise to any association, but a hateful memory immediately comes up – that of his colleague's suggestive recommendation (*it's better to go round the back way than in front*). In the session, this activates another of the day's residues: while he was with his son on the previous Saturday, he suddenly thought of the episode where his father smashed his elder brother's toys. In other words, the man with the moustache triggers the memory of the hateful comment (that it's better to go round the back way than in front), which in turn causes him to recall a nasty scene in which his father takes his revenge on his elder son, punishing him for refusing to do something. This is an infantile memory that leads back to an exemplary punishment-as-retaliation (disciplinary proceedings).

As we shall see, the scene with the father and the brother is a screen memory that masks another scene, which concerns himself and his father.

---

4 Note the sequence of psychic formations: on the previous evening a slip; in the night an anxiety dream; and in the morning the symptom. The repressed content is always the same, but the transformations undergo significant changes.

The use of tenses is interesting: first the patient uses the present («my father asks»), and then twice the past («my father said no; my father smashed his toys») – as if, in the scene with the father, what concerns the brother is to all intents and purposes a memory of the past, while what concerns the patient himself is still present.

The next association – «Something sort of came up» – has to do with the screen memory; that is to say, the thing came up, but not completely; what came up was his father's bad relationship with the brother, and his wife's bad relationship with the son, as opposed to his father's good relationship with himself and his own relationship as a father with his own son.

Note the repetition of the word «something» (if something like that happens to me; I'm afraid that something will happen; my father asks my brother something; something sort of came up).[5]

At this point, however, the *young* face of his father occurs to him – young, as he has not seen it for a long time. That is to say, in the session he recalls his father's face – but, oddly enough, it is not the angry face of the father punishing the brother, but his father's young face, which has not come into his mind for a very long time. A trace of longing lies within this vision. The session permits the expression of another component, the opposite of the feeling of hate: a vague wish to return to the arms of his father and to be clasped to his breast in his bed.

His friend Michele is someone else he hasn't seen «for a very long time»; «we always used to go for a run together»; «he always used to tell me» – comments like the one he recalled, in which violence is concealed by ancient rhetoric (the family is what's inside when you bolt the door). However, what is inside when the door is shut is in fact the «cock-up» [*impapocchio*]: the infantile wish for passive coupling with the father – a father who swung between rage and despotic violence on the one hand and all-consuming, adhesive tenderness on the other.[6] The sequence can now be considered in the following terms: the previous evening's slip – the cock-up – gives rise to a signal of anxiety in the ego (anxiety in the present), which reactivates the deep anxiety (connected with the two antagonistic trends in relation to the father). During the night the ego tries to resolve the anxiety by means of a dream, fails, and in the morning seeks an appropriate anxiety symptom.[7]

---

[5] The word «something» is semantically ambiguous: it refers to an object that does not need to be named because it is so obvious, near and known; but it is also used for an object that has to be kept hidden. Its frequent use betrays a resistance connected with the work of naming: it is a linguistic compromise formation.

[6] Caught between the two opposing impulses towards his father, the child had to reinforce that of submission in love – perhaps because he was seduced by that tenderness, or to keep the rage at bay, or to keep his hostility towards him in check (only this last is a reaction formation). However, in this case he is exposed to the threat of becoming passive, against which his masculine aspirations rebel from a certain time on (puberty).

[7] While maintaining that anxiety dreams were the category in which the dream content was the least distorted, Freud was to contend that dream anxiety, like symptomatic anxiety, was not a drive substitute but an anxiety in the service of the ego.

The scrupulous inspector could not have found a more apposite symptom: the symptom itself (anxiety about committing an offence), its secondary gain (there were not really any offences) and its inhibitory manifestation (being exempted from investigations) – all of these betray the tendency to make the offence «undone»; but the same tendency explains the «compulsion to repeat».[8]

Comparison of samples of analysis

The aim of interpretation is to recognize how a particular apparatus works on the particular meaning that generated it.

I shall now compare the first dream with others by the same patient. Significant similarities between the samples analysed – as well as significant differences – are revealed by the interpretative work.

The dream brought in the next session: The *skull-cap* [*papalina* in Italian]

«I had a skull-cap [*papalina*] on; I was walking with my *papalina*».

Associations: «In reality I use it only in my boat. I've always been a bit Tunisian – it's my Arab side, the sea, the *papalina*, fish, the bracelet, Laura, my son. The *papalina* is a bit of a habit really».

This is a wishful dream. The *papa-lina* is a compromise formation: a fortunate condensation has got the upper hand of the anxiety bound up with the deeply repressed nucleus (represented by the *im-pap-occhio* in the previous night's anxiety dream).

«Walking free and easy with the *papalina*» is an attempt to fulfil both the feminine and the masculine, heterosexual component of the wish.

Two dreams from the beginning of the analysis: *Poliziano, Momigliano* and *Tertulliano*

The first dream features Polizi*ano* and Momigli*ano* [9]; the associations reveal the link between them: the former is the [fifteenth-century] poet and the latter the critic of a short poem that exalts the «Realm of Venus» and the love of a young couple. In the second dream, Tertulli*ano* [the Italian form of Tertullian] appears as a witness «in a trial»; the associations make it clear that the figure of the Father of the Church represents two opposing battles: freedom of expression of the faith, and misogyny. By way of three linguistic formations – singular examples of a compromise between cultivated language and the language of the drives – the oscillation is turned on its head. The first dream is a wishful dream, in which the analytic couple share amorous

---

[8] Freud, S. (1925). *Inhibitions, Symptoms and Anxiety*. SE 20, 153.

[9] [Translator's note: *ano* is Italian for anus].

intentions, while the second is an anxiety dream, showing the analytic couple in antagonistic contention.[10]

Let us compare these dreams (wishful dreams and anxiety dreams) with others that belong to a different series – namely traumatic dreams.[11]

«At school an Italian exercise gets lost: the headmaster searches for it in the computer, under the name of "Quid" or "Quiz"».

«Vadigno is an amazing forward: he comes on to the field – you don't know where from – as if he didn't belong in the team; no one knows him».

Dreams like these constitute «evidence»; they are like the report of a crime, bearing witness to the absence of a *quid* [a certain element] of identity.

The absence of the mother from the analysis (and from the transference) is the sign of a real absence: the child had grown up from birth with an aunt on the third floor of the same block where his parents lived. At the age of ten, however, he was returned to the house of his father, who took him into his bed in place of the mother. There is no doubt that the only powerful structuring bond throughout his infancy was the one with his father. Given these «facts», the patient always had a passive, submissive attitude – but the traumatic dreams are the «evidence» of the secret, active presence of a different posture.[12]

If the anxiety dream (the cock-up [*impapocchio*]) were to be interpreted solely in terms of a father-related conflict, this would carry the risk of obscuring the significance of the mother's absence and its psychic consequences, as revealed by the «traumatic dreams».

Among these consequences it is possible to discern an ego activity directed towards compensating for that absence by the attribution to the father of the functions of both parents (*Mo*-migliano and *Po*-liziano) and the creation of fusional objects (the skull-cap [*papalina*]), as revealed by the «wishful dreams». On the other hand, two details of the «anxiety dreams» assume a new significance: the *drug addict* in the first dream and the *misogyny* in the dream of Tertullian.

---

10 The three linguistic formations precisely define both the time and place of their origin (the patient's time at secondary school) and the time of commencement of the transference regression.

11 Examining a variety of samples, Freud continued to classify dreams. In his final classification, he distinguished (a) wishful dreams; (b) anxiety dreams; and (c) punishment dreams. Dreams «satisfy» now one agency and now another. Traumatic dreams are the exception, although here too it seems obvious that the dream work seeks «to transform the memory traces of the traumatic event into the fulfilment of a wish» (Freud, S., 1932, Revision of dream theory, in *New Introductory Lectures on Psycho-Analysis*, SE 22, 27, 29).

12 Freud was later to investigate a particular aspect of repetition – «attempts to bring the trauma into operation once again», on the one hand, and, on the other, the different reaction of «what are called "avoidances", which may be intensified into "inhibitions" and "phobias"» (Freud, S., 1934-8), *Moses and Monotheism*, SE 23, 75f.).

All the dreams are singular representations of the various faces of a state of «loss of libidinal bearings».[13]

In Freud's example we assumed that the unknown lay in the verbal predicate, because it expresses the performance of the action. In our own examples, the work of interpretation of all the dream elements by way of the associations allows a meaning to be assigned to the verbal predicates (saying hallo to someone; going for a walk; exalting the love of women; condemning the love of women; losing the Italian exercise; coming on from off the field. The actions demonstrate the intertwining of the vicissitudes of sexual orientation and those of identity:

1. Betraying an uncertainty of sexual inclinations (the cock-up/*impapocchio*);
2. Giving a form to sexual identity (the skull-cap/*papalina*);
3. Loving the female body (*Momigliano* and *Poliziano*);
4. Hating the female body (*Tertullian*);
5. Losing one's identity (*Quid / Quiz*);
6. Asserting oneself strongly (*Vadigno*).

I have opted to concentrate on the intrapsychic aspect of the theory, observed from the classical viewpoint of the dream work. It would be extremely useful to demonstrate «clear examples» focusing on other aspects and to assess the yield of different models.

Original italian version:
Riv. Psicoanal., 2007, 3, 797-807

Paola Camassa

V.le Regina Margherita, 11/B

90138 Palermo

(Translated by Philip Slotkin MA Cantab. MITI)

---

[13] Camassa, P. Lo spaesamento libidico [The loss of libidinal bearings]. Paper presented at the Clinical Seminar Cycle held at the Palermo Psychoanalysis Centre in 1997.

DREAM	ASSOCIATIONS	THEORY
At the office, I go in and say hallo.	I was at the office, but it was not actually the office. There's anxiety in this dream. I woke up this morning feeling anxious about the agency. I get anxious about not knowing what to do if something like that happens to me; I'm always afraid that that something will happen.	Anxiety in the present: anxiety dream → symptom → inhibitory manifestation
Someone with a moustache.	What about the person with the moustache? I don't know. There's someone I work with in the office who said it's better to go round the back way than in front. It was a quip in bad taste – it happened ten days ago, and for a moment I hated him. Last Saturday when I was playing with my son I thought of the scene again: my father asks my brother to do something; my brother said no, and then my father smashed all his toys. Something sort of came up: that my wife used studying to stop herself seeing that she can't control her son. My father's face suddenly comes to mind, as I haven't seen it for a very long time – younger.	Deep anxiety: the antagonistic trends of the repressed nucleus
I apologize, as I mixed him up with a colleague who had been subjected to disciplinary proceedings. I don't know who it is; he tells me I have made a cock-up [impapocchio].	The cock-up [impapocchio]: Yesterday my mobile rang and I saw it was Michele calling. He wanted me to attend to a woman who had been looking for her husband for two days. I say I'll think about it. I phone the office. I dial the number and Franco answers: Sorry, I made a mistake. Now I'm thinking of a film – the one where a drug addict says: «I masturbate men» – and then he gets buggered.	Day's residues: the previous evening's slip

The patient as the analyst's best colleague: transformation into a dream and narrative transformations

ANTONINO FERRO

> «...the best colleague you are ever likely to have
> – besides yourself – is not an analyst or supervisor
> or parent, but the patient».[1]

I shall here apply this Bionian principle («the patient as one's best colleague») to a dream which I shall present as evidence that the α-function is constantly at work. A kind of satellite navigation system dreams in real time what takes place in the analyst's consulting room after an interpretation. This «dream» need not in my view necessarily be interpreted, but it can be used to facilitate the development of the field.

Through the example I shall give below, I also wish to share some of the salient aspects of my method of working. Whereas the concepts of the field, of unsaturated interpretation and of narrative transformation are now quite widely accepted, the notion of *transformation into a dream*, as a complement to other types of transformation, no doubt calls for some explanation. Transformation into a dream is an activity carried on constantly by the analyst's mind, which strips the patient's communication of its reality status and regards the patient's narration as a dream that assembles, transforms and constructs itself in real time in the encounter between the two minds at work. This is so because the central operation performed in analysis is deemed to be enrichment of the «dreaming ensemble» (Grotstein, 2007). In other words, development of the α-function and of the apparatus for dreaming dreams is seen as the purpose of analysis. This implies a constructivistic vision of an unconscious engaged in an ongoing process of construction and transformation – an unconscious that must at the same time be dreamed (thoughts in search of a thinker) and will expand as it is

---

[1] In Bion's second discussion at IPTAR in 1977 (Bion, 1978). A similar comment appears in the *Italian Seminars* (Bion, 1985): «... the most important assistance that a psychoanalyst is ever likely to get is not from his analyst, or supervisor, or teacher, or the books that he can read, but from his patient». Statements in the same vein can be found in the *Tavistock Seminars* (Bion, 2005).

being dreamed (*ibid.*). I must confess that, during a session, I never think about the problem of the patient's history, infancy or sexuality; I simply listen to what he[2] says, and try to contain, describe and receive his emotions, help to incorporate them into a narrative fabric, transform them into a dream, and enter into the dream of the field, while observing the functioning (or dysfunctioning) of the field as well as whatever, in the patient, is pressing to be alphabetized.

Clouds of sense data, fragments of anxieties and of split-off parts, and the rain of evacuated matter – these are the raw materials that await the operation of «analytic functions of the field» to transform the turbulence, β- and balpha-elements into visual pictograms, images, thoughts and emotions. In particular, I place my trust in the idea that, through this approach, the method and instruments for so doing will be passed on to the patient. That is to say, I expect that the patient will subliminally introject the mode of functioning of the field, even if I do not know very much about this mode of functioning. Perhaps the precipitate of all this will be narrated in a diary-type genre or in the register of infancy, but for me any other scenario would be equivalent provided that it leads to the capacity to think, feel and dream. I am more interested in memories of things that never happened (memoirs of the future, as Bion might say) than in those of the past. Again, everything that is pressing for transformation in the patient will necessarily stem from his mental functioning, which is in turn bound up with his history; hence the risk of breaking down doors that are already open if one insists on explicit reconstruction of the past – so I look more to the reconstruction, or construction for the first time, of the apparatus for dreaming dreams.

With a severely traumatized patient, I am at first not very interested in what happened to him and where and why; instead, I am concerned to «put him back together», to «sew him up», to support his vital functions, to oxygenate him and provide him with the necessary volume of fluids. My approach is to look forward rather than back; in other words, I want to make up a deficiency in the patient's dreaming function, involving the need for alphabetization, and am implicitly thinking about how to develop his capacity for «digestion and alphabetization». Given an adequately «cured» patient, the problem of «expertise» would then arise, but that is already another story.

However, let us consider these ideas on the basis of a concrete case.

Filippo (in his third year of analysis at four sessions a week; this is his Wednesday session).

(At the end of the previous session I was not satisfied with how I had worked, because it seemed to me that my comments could easily have been construed by the patient as criticisms that were out of tune with what he was saying and as premature-

---

[2] [Translator's note: For convenience, the masculine form is used here for both sexes].

ly suggesting other viewpoints. I had told myself that next day I must be more recep-
tive and accepting, and more able to grasp good things in addition to drawing atten-
tion to the negative).

Patient: I had a dream, or rather, I had the same dream twice. There were aeroplanes, explosions, a kind of bombing; and then some very long teeth appeared. They pierced through people, but didn't kill them. I managed to save my skin by hiding behind a solid wall.

Analyst *(I think this is an accurate description of his view of yesterday's session and of my having interpreted «with teeth», but prefer to avoid immediate saturation in that sense):* What does the dream suggest to you?

Patient: I don't know … it has something to do with emotions … the others were wounded, pierced through by projectiles, whereas I was able to save my skin.

Analyst *(I imagine that my interpretative excess activated explosive emotions, and that unrecognized aspects of the patient's self were wounded, but am unable to abstain from a rigid type of interpretation not based on rêverie)*: Was I perhaps a bit like a bomber who had you in his sights?

Patient: Not at all. There was a good climate in yesterday's session. Afterwards I went to my mother's for lunch, but then I had a terrible stomach ache. She/you [the Italian word *lei* can mean either] has/have no idea about hygiene when she/you make(s) something to eat. That evening I went to Milan for dinner at an ethnic restaurant and the food was indigestible. My brother was with me and said: «Where the hell have you taken me to eat? I feel like throwing up».

Analyst *(I feel the need to offer an unsaturated interpretation so as to tone down the persecution; for me, it is a transference interpretation because I «dream» the characters summoned up there, in the field)*: So, on top of your mother's indigestible food there was the African cook's? You had a double ration of indigestible food.

Patient: My mum made roulades filled with all kinds of rubbish, including old rubbish, and the cook had a saucepan full of a mixture of all sorts of stuff – an absolute mishmash.

Analyst *(I refrain from interpreting this in terms of the effect of my excessive interpretations of the previous day, followed by today's premature one, as I am wondering how to interpret in a way that won't make him «throw up» immediately).*

A brief silence follows.

Patient: And then my mother has a funny habit: she acts like that character in the TV series (a kind of witch) who cuts off the flowers from her roses, throws them away and puts just the thorny stems in the vase. Yesterday I saw a programme on TV where a boy was taken out in a boat by his mother; then he was abandoned and went to work as a chimney sweep. He was motherless but managed on his own by working. I also saw Gabriele Muccino's last film, about a father and child with no wife or mother; they live like tramps, but they somehow get by.

Analyst: All very upsetting, but hope won through in the end. *(But I can't resist adding another, superfluous comment).* I was also thinking that maybe I tended to «bite» yesterday. What I said was like sinking my teeth into you. I picked up on the thorns in what you said and emphasized only them, but threw away the flower, which is what I should have appreciated.

Patient: Why do you say that?

Analyst: Well, I criticized your way of fitting in with the law professor's wishes *(which I had seen as a paranoid trait in the patient and criticized before owning and understanding the source of the persecution)*, and above all when you mentioned the carpets and I stressed how you ought not to let yourself be trampled on *(I had wanted to interpret his way of bending to other people's wishes, but clumsily got the timing wrong)*, instead of picking up the fact that you also wanted someone to teach you how to make a carpet yourself – to weave the thread into a fabric, and to organize threads of thought.

Patient: Yes, what you said did surprise me.

Analyst: Perhaps my «biting» and then not saying anything triggered all sorts of feelings in you, from persecution to abandonment – being without a mother. You were left having to sweep all the soot from the chimney by yourself. But the main thing is that you got by even when being bombed and when you were left all alone: you managed in spite of all the difficulties.

Patient: And with his father's help, the boy in the film brought all his plans to fruition and learnt how to dream for himself.

Analyst: Let's hope the Eritrean or Sicilian cook *(the patient knows where I come from)* will not make any more indigestible food like that.

Patient *(laughs; after a short silence he goes on)*: Yesterday my dad and my girl-friend's father had an argument about how to look after a vegetable garden. Martina's dad uses a rotovator, which is very fast. My father thinks it's better to use a hoe and do it by hand, partly because it goes deeper but mostly because, though the rotovator breaks up the surface better, its pounding ends up making the soil impermeable and preventing osmosis with the deeper layers. They decided to take one piece of the veg-etable garden each, like the division into departments at the university: law on one side and economics on the other – each kept well apart.

Analyst: It sounds almost as if they need a barrier to keep the two areas separate.

Patient: Well, otherwise it ends like two cocks pecking at each other. I saw some cockfights in the Far East. They are exciting, but blood is shed and they go on peck-ing even though they are hurt. I'd rather play computer games. There is actually a cockfight game, but at least the blood isn't real.

Analyst *(I think he is drawing my attention to a risk: when I interpret too much and too automatically, this may superficially convey the feeling of a well tilled field, but can in fact make a deeper layer of the field impermeable, thus preventing even deeper levels from emerging. So I refrain from making this interpretation, which I feel would be like decoding rather than the fruit of rêverie)*: But perhaps law and eco-nomics could come to an arrangement, like the one between your father and Marti-na's.

Patient: Well, I realize that I'm also speaking about two conflicting attitudes inside myself: on the one hand experiencing emotions even if it makes me bleed because they are explosive, and on the other cowering behind a wall like at the begin-ning of the dream, or in a video game.

Analyst: But why do you think of the two attitudes in terms of «either one or the other»? There are some dishes, such as Sicilian caponata, in which salty and sweet flavours can coexist, like your mother's fiery nature and your father's excessive reserve in your own situation.

***

The style of interpretation in which I often seemed to be hunting the patient down, which also pervaded the preceding sessions – a style quite unlike my usual one – was an expression of the way the field had contracted the patient's illness, which consists in the difficulty of integrating quasi-autistic defences with a sometimes explosive passionate nature. At the same time the patient becomes *my best colleague,* who can tell me how to heal this illness of the field and work towards the integration of these aspects.

The analyst's oneiric frame of mind gives rise to α-elements and dreaming. The analyst – or rather, at this juncture, the analytic function of the field – is the guarantor of the dreaming process and of the weaving and reconnecting of narrations. This is not of course a matter of just any rêverie, dreams or narrations, but of ones that tend towards «O» or, where this is not possible, «K», and the inevitable oscillation between the two.

So my interest centres on the working of functions, instruments and apparatuses about which we do not know everything and which, as stated, we constantly enrich while working. The same applies to the unconscious, whether we see it as the depository of proto-emotions or of thoughts without a thinker (basically, what could here be described as β^1- or β^2 elements), or as what comes into being by way of, and after, dreaming.

However, what does this mean in terms of clinical work and, in particular, of technique? In my view, it means that we can look at the instruments used by the analyst differently; among the many new instruments at our disposal I should like to draw attention once more to *transformation into a dream,* mentioned earlier, which is done within the analytic field when the analyst is able to trust his own negative capability.

If all mental pathologies are due to a deficiency in the transformation of β^1 and β^2 into α (through the α-function and dreaming), healing will only be possible by boosting the functioning of the entire *apparatus for dreaming dreams.* The more successful this process, the less the mind – the patient's, the analyst's and the field's – will be falsified by the continuous action of «transformation in hallucinosis», which gives rise to evacuation, an activity that works in the opposite direction to dreaming. Only dreaming – whether in the form of the α-function, of daydreaming or of night dreams – can guarantee the recovery of mental health; that is to say, dreaming paradoxically leads to a better vision of reality and truth.

Espousal of historical reconstruction as a basic principle can actually amount to a transformation in hallucinosis of what is happening in the analytic session, which is thereby evacuated. For instance, if a patient tells how her father abused her as a child and this is simply backdated to her history and not seen also as a dream of the field in which she feels abused either by the analyst or by proto-emotional states of her own which she is unable to contain, emotions that cannot be woven into a fabric and transformed are thereby being evacuated into the history. Conversely, the fate of something that can be transformed and «dreamed» is that it can be forgotten or remembered marginally.

A possible device that both exemplifies and simplifies the process of transformation into a dream is to prefix the phrase «I dreamed that…» to every one of a patient's communications. In this connection, Paola Camassa (2007) wonders whether it is analysis as a dreaming field that produces these dreams, or whether there are patients who produce dreaming fields – i.e. who always dream, every step being a dream, so that the associations signify what is happening.

Transformation into a dream becomes the most important transformation in the analytic field, alternating with narrative transformation and the narrations accruing from the selected fact and the concatenation of such facts. Narrative transformation involves the element of additional camouflage that confers tolerability on emotions that would otherwise be inaccessible (Ferro *et al.*, 2007).

It will therefore be seen that analytic work – the analytic laboratory, or, in more homely terms, the analytic kitchen – is rich in other phenomena, other modes of functioning, obscurities, lies, fragments of «O» and «K», all of which can be used in the development of instruments. In an evolving vision of psychoanalysis (Grotstein, 2007), we have in effect moved on from a psychoanalysis of contents to one of instruments and functions for feeling emotions, thinking thoughts and dreaming dreams.

REFERENCES

BION W.R. (1978). Second discussion in New York, in: *Four Discussions with W.R. Bion*. Perthshire: Clunie Press 1978.
BION W.R. (1985). *The Italian Seminars*. Ed. F. Bion, trans. P. Slotkin. London: Karnac, 2005.
BION W.R. (2005). *The Tavistock Seminars*. Ed. F. Bion. London: Karnac.
CAMASSA P. (2007). Personal communication.
FERRO A., CIVITARESE G., COLLOVÀ M., FORESTI G., MOLINARI E., MAZZACANE F., & POLITI P. (2007). *Sognare l'analisi*. Turin: Bollati Boringhieri.
FERRO A. (2007). *Evitare le emozioni, vivere le emozioni*. Milan: Cortina.
GROTSTEIN J. (2007). *A Beam of Intense Darkness*. London: Karnac.

Original italian version:
Riv. Psicoanal., 2007, 4, 1083-1090

Antonino Ferro

Via Cardano, 77

27100 Pavia

(Translated by Philip Slotkin MA Cantab. MITI)

Stampato da "Iriprint" Città di Castello (PG)
Febbraio 2008

Selected texts from *Rivista di Psicoanalisi*
the Journal of the Italian Psychoanalytic Society

THE
ITALIAN
PSYCHOANALYTIC
ANNUAL   2007

RIVISTA DI PSICOANALISI
JOURNAL OF THE ITALIAN
PSYCHOANALYTIC SOCIETY

Freud after all

B
BORLA

CONTENTS

FRANCESCO NAPOLITANO: Transference: notes on the history of a paradox – ANTONIO ALBERTO SEMI: Transference and unconscious communication. Countertransference, theories and analyst's narcissism – FRANCESCO CONROTTO: «All dreams are wish fulfilments»: is this still a tenable thesis today? – FERNANDO RIOLO: Freud and Lichtenberg's knife – PIER LUIGI ROSSI: Travels around the Wolf Man: a diary – PATRIZIO CAMPANILE: The witch of *ha-ish-Mosheh*. Some considerations (and conjectures) on *Analysis terminable and interminable* – FAUSTO PETRELLA: The Freudian style. Terminology, metaphor and textual strategies – ENRICO MANGINI: The Schreber case: the discreet charm of the paranoic solution – DIOMIRA PETRELLI: *A case of female homosexuality.* Notes and comments on a case with no name – GIOVANNA GORETTI: A girl of intelligent and engaging looks – ALESSANDRA GINZBURG: Isomorphism. A transitional area within analysis – VALERIA EGIDI MORPURGO: Why does *Moses and Monotheism* still make us uneasy? Freud, psychoanalysis, anti-Semitism

THE ITALIAN PSYCHOANALYTIC ANNUAL is published once a year

Marketing and distribution:

In Italy: Borla Edizioni s.r.l.
00165 Roma (Italy) – Via delle Fornaci, 50
Tel.+390639376728
Fax +390639376620
www. edizioni-borla.it
e-mail: borla@edizioni-borla.it

Outside Italy: Karnac Books
118 Finchley Road, London NW3 5HT – United Kingdom
Tel: +44(0)20 7431 1075
Fax: +44(0)20 435 9076
www.karnacbooks.com
e-mail: shop@karnacbooks.com
Payment methods: Visa/Mastercard/Switch

For further information e-mail to: riv.psa@mclink.it
or write to: Rivista di Psicoanalisi – via Panama 48 – 00198 Roma (Italy)
or fax to: +390685865336

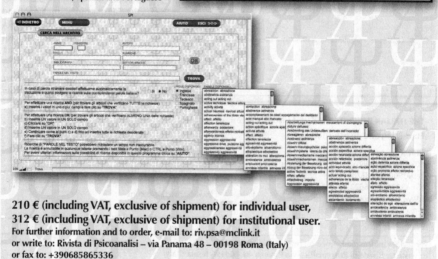